Doing Theology Today

Schubert M. Ogden

TRINITY PRESS INTERNATIONAL
Valley Forge, Pennsylvania

Trinity Press International, P.O. Box 851, Valley Forge, PA 19482-0851

Library of Congress Cataloging-in-Publication Data

Ogden, Schubert Miles, 1928–
    Doing theology today / Schubert M. Ogden.
        p.   cm.
    Includes bibliographical references and index.
    ISBN 1-56338-160-5 (pbk. : alk. paper)
    1. Theology–Methodology. 2. Theology, Doctrinal–Introductions.
3. Theology   I. Title.
BR118.042   1996
230'.01–dc20   96-16536
                                                                     CIP

Printed in the United States of America

96   97   98   99   00   01   10   9   8   7   6   5   4   3   2   1

To
VAN HARVEY
VIC FURNISH
BRIAN GERRISH
MAURICE WILES
CHRIS GAMWELL
*whose companionship along the way
has made all the difference*

Contents

Contents

Part III
THEOLOGY OF RELIGIONS

Part IV
THEOLOGY IN CONVERSATION

Preface

What does it mean to do Christian theology today, and how ought it to be done?

This is the question addressed not only by the title essay in this volume, but in one way or another by all of the other essays as well. It is addressed most explicitly — by precept as well as example — in the six essays in Part I. Here lines of thought that have long been present in my earlier writings on theological prolegomena, especially in my book *On Theology,* are further extended and, I should like to think, deepened and rendered more persuasive. If my thinking this is at all justified, much of the credit is due to the concepts and distinctions I learned to employ through my intensive study, beginning early in the 1970s, of the philosophical work of Jürgen Habermas and Karl-Otto Apel. Thanks to them, I was enabled to distinguish clearly and sharply, but without in any way separating, the two levels of living understandingly, and thus to distinguish the secondary praxis of doing theology from the primary praxis of bearing witness, which doing theology is intended to serve. The significance of this distinction for dealing with such continuingly thorny questions as the proper task of theological education and the place of theology in the university can hardly be exaggerated, as is also made clear, I trust, by the essays in this first part.

But the essays in the other parts also speak, if only implicitly or solely by example, to what it is to do theology today and how it ought to be done. Thus the essays in Part II attest in this way that, next only to achieving an adequate self-understanding, to do theology today is to be concerned above all with the fundamental questions of theology and christology — by which I mean the questions of God as the One to faith in whom we are brought through Jesus, and of Jesus as the one through whom we are brought to faith in God. These essays also confirm that to concern oneself with either of these questions today is not only to take seriously the insistence of liberation theologians and others that faith without justice is dead, but also to deal forthrightly with the problem of credibility, and thus with the demand that theological and christological assertions all be critically validated as worthy of belief by appealing, finally, to common human experience.

The essays in Part III further imply that to do theology today is to do it in a truly global context, in the presence of a perplexing plurality of ways of being human, including those represented by the non-Christian religions. This means that the theologian today must not only work at developing a formal terminology in which the real issues between the Christian way and other religious and secular ways can be fairly and understandingly formulated, but must also take up the task of working out an adequate theology of religions. More exactly, the theologian today must come to terms with "the challenge of pluralism," understanding by this not only or primarily the challenge of the plurality just referred to, but also and above all, the challenge issued by the pluralistic theology of religions that a number of Christian theologians across the globe have already put on the table. Not to respond in a critical way to their significant challenge is simply not to do theology as it must be done today.

This same point is made more generally, then, by the essays in Part IV. To do theology today is to enter into close and sustained conversation with others who either are, or have been, engaged in the same task of critical reflection. By "conversation" here I mean a procedure of not only talking to other persons, but listening to them as well, and of taking at least as many pains with critically interpreting what they say and mean as with critically validating their claims. Such a procedure seems to me to be particularly important in the case of our contemporaries and immediate predecessors who have concerned themselves with the same problems that are facing us. Only by critically appropriating what they have already done toward solving these problems are we ever likely to solve them, or to make very much progress toward solving the other problems that are peculiarly our own.

I recognize, of course, that what it is to do theology and how it ought to be done has always been a more or less controversial question in theology and that it almost certainly will remain so, regardless of the answer argued for in this book. I am also quite clear from the number of theologians to both my right and my left whom I can honestly think of only as my contemporary ancestors that one theologian's today is another's yesterday or tomorrow. But if these essays together can serve to make a reasoned case for one way of answering the question, reissuing them in this volume will have done all that I could have reasonably expected it to do.

Most of the debts I have incurred will be clear from the essays themselves as well as from the works cited at the end. But of the others who have contributed to the volume, I especially want to thank Dr. Harold W. Rast of Trinity Press International, whose collaboration in conceiving and organizing it was particularly helpful.

I would also express my gratitude to the publishers who have generously granted permission to make use of essays originally appearing in their books or journals. "Doing Theology Today" is reprinted by permission of Zondervan Publishing House from *Doing Theology in*

Today's World: Essays in Honor of Kenneth S. Kantzer, ed. John D. Woodbridge and Thomas Edward McComiskey, copyright © 1992 by the editors; "Prolegomena to Historical Theology" is reprinted by permission of the publisher from *Revisioning the Past: Prospects in Historical Theology*, ed. Mary Potter Engel and Walter E. Wyman, Jr., copyright © 1992 by Augsburg Fortress; "Theology and Biblical Interpretation" is to appear in the *Journal of Religion* 76 (1996), copyright © 1996 by The University of Chicago, and is used by permission of The University of Chicago Press; "The Service of Theology to the Servant Task of Pastoral Ministry" is reprinted by permission of the publisher from *The Pastor as Servant*, ed. Earl E. Shelp and Ronald H. Sunderland (New York: Pilgrim Press, 1986); "Christian Theology and Theological Education" is reprinted by permission of the publisher from *The Education of the Practical Theologian: Responses to Joseph Hough and John Cobb's Christian Identity and Theological Education*, ed. Don S. Browning, David Polk, and Ian E. Evison (Atlanta: Scholars Press, 1989); "Theology in the University: The Question of Integrity" is reprinted by permission of the publisher from *Theology and the University: Essays in Honor of John B. Cobb, Jr.*, ed. David Ray Griffin and Joseph C. Hough, Jr., copyright © 1991 by State University of New York Press; "Concerning Belief in God" is reprinted by permission of Chalice Press from *Faith and Creativity: Essays in Honor of Eugene H. Peters*, ed. George Nordgulen and George W. Shields (St. Louis: CBP Press, 1987); "The Metaphysics of Faith and Justice" appeared in *Process Studies* 14 (1985), copyright © 1985 by *Process Studies*, and is used by permission of the publisher; "A Priori Christology and Experience" is reprinted by permission of the publisher from *The Making and Remaking of Christian Doctrine: Essays in Honour of Maurice Wiles*, ed. Sarah Coakley and David A. Pailin (Oxford: Clarendon Press, 1993); " 'For Freedom Christ Has Set Us Free': The Christian Understanding of Ultimate Transformation" appeared in *Buddhist-Christian Studies* 7 (1987), copyright © 1987 by University of Hawaii Press, and is used by permission of the publisher; "Problems in the Case for a Pluralistic Theology of Religions" appeared in the *Journal of Religion* 68 (1988), copyright © 1988 by The University of Chicago, and is used by permission of The University of Chicago Press; "Is There Only One True Religion or Are There Many?" appeared in German translation as "Gibt es nur eine wahre Religion oder mehrere?" in *Zeitschrift für Theologie und Kirche* 88 (1991) and is used by permission of J. C. B. Mohr (Paul Siebeck); "The Experience of God: Critical Reflections on Charles Hartshorne's Theory of Analogy" is reprinted by permission of The University of Chicago Press from *Existence and Actuality: Conversations with Charles Hartshorne*, ed. John B. Cobb, Jr. and Franklin I. Gamwell, copyright © 1984 by The University of Chicago; "Rudolf Bultmann and the Future of Revisionary Christology" is reprinted by permission of the publisher from *Rudolf Bultmanns Werk und Wirkung,* ed. Bernd Jaspert (Darmstadt: Wissenschaftliche Buchgesellschaft, 1984); and "*Fundamentum Fidei:* Critical Reflections on Willi Marxsen's Contribution to Systematic Theology" appeared in *Modern Theology* 6 (1989) and is used by permission of Blackwell Publishers.

Rollinsville, Colorado   S.M.O.
October 1995

No man...will ever be much use to his generation, who does not apply himself mainly to the questions which are occupying those who belong to it.... But there are...questions which we have not inherited — questions which belong more expressly to us than they did to our immediate predecessors. These...we must humbly study for ourselves, though the difference will be very great to us, whether we invent a way of investigation for ourselves, or try to walk in a path in which better men who have been before us have with great labour cleared of its rubbish, and by footmarks and sign-posts have made known to us.

— FREDERICK DENISON MAURICE

Part I

Theology of Theology

– *I* –

Doing Theology Today

I. The Question

What is it to do Christian systematic theology today?

This is the more precise formulation of the question to be addressed in this essay. We are not to inquire about doing theology in general, but about doing *Christian* theology in particular; moreover, the doing of Christian theology that is the object of our inquiry is not the doing of it in any or all of the ways in which it might be done, but in that specific way that is properly distinguished as *systematic* theology. But if this makes it clear how the term "theology" and its cognates are henceforth to be understood in the absence of explicit indication to the contrary, just how we are to understand our question is still far from obvious and in need of further clarification.

We should note, first of all, that while we could well ask the question from the standpoint of a number of different inquiries, we are to ask it here from the standpoint of theology, and thus as itself a properly theological question. Clearly, doing theology is one of the many things that human beings do, and so it might very well be asked about in one way or another by any of the special sciences concerned with human praxis, as well as by history and philosophy, which in their somewhat different ways share this same concern. Our way of asking about it, however, is theological; and this has some implications that we need to keep in mind. It implies, for one thing, that just what it means to ask the question can be made clear only by answering it. But it also implies that we can answer the question only by doing the very thing it asks about doing. We have to do theology ourselves if we are to ask theologically what it is to do theology today.

More precisely, we have to do systematic theology, since the second thing to note is that this is not only a question *about* systematic theology, but also a question *of* it. We are asking what it is to do systematic theology today as itself a properly systematic theological question. Here again, just what it means to say this can be made clear only by answering the question. For the present, suffice it to say that systematic theology is a properly systematic inquiry, and that systematic inquiries in general are distinguished from properly historical inquiries, on the one hand, and properly practical inquiries, on the other. Whereas his-

3

torical inquiries have to do with what human beings have thought, said, and done in any situation already past; and practical inquiries have to do with what human beings are to think, say, and do in some situation still future; systematic inquiries have to do with what human beings would be justified in thinking, saying, and doing in this or any other situation now present, whatever may have happened in the past or ought to happen in the future. To say that this question is a systematic theological question, then, is to distinguish it both from a historical question such as might well be asked by historical theology and from a practical question of the sort that practical theology might very well want to ask.

Of course, the question is not just about theology, but about doing it, and doing it today; and it is only reasonable to expect that this essay should serve in its way to advance the actual praxis of theology in today's world. But as true and important as this is, our inquiry is nonetheless a systematic, rather than a practical, theological inquiry. Although we are indeed concerned with what it is to do theology today, ours is not the properly practical question about what still ought to be thought, said, and done about theology in the upcoming future, but rather the properly systematic question about what it would be right to think, say, and do about theology in this or any other present in which such thinking, saying, and doing might be required.

The difference between our inquiry and that proper to historical theology can be made clear by distinguishing two ways of construing our question, What is it to do theology today? Construed in one way, this question asks for a *description* of what in fact is being done in doing theology today. And this is how historical theology would ask and answer it in describing one or more of the approaches currently being made to the doing of theology. But it can also be construed as asking for a *prescription* of what by right ought to be done today in order to do theology. And this is how we are construing the question here in asking it as a systematic theological question.

To be sure, any approach to doing theology, including the approach being made in this essay, is itself thoroughly historical, even as systematic theology. Like everything else that we think, say, and do as human beings, theology is historically conditioned and situationally located relative to some particular society and culture with their distinctive links to the past and their peculiar possibilities for the future. This means, among other things, that any approach to doing theology has to be made within the limits and by means of the resources of its particular situation. But it also means that each such approach is only one among many others, past and present, with some of which it is more closely, with yet others of which it is more distantly, related. Even so, it is the task of historical theology, rather than the systematic theology that we are concerned with here, to undertake the description of any of the various approaches to the doing of theology. And this is so even when the approach described happens to be one's own or one with which one's own is closely related. Because the question we are seeking to answer is a systematic theological one, I need not describe any approach to the doing of systematic theology, not even my own, but may go ahead and do it by prescribing as simply as possible what it is to do so.

So much by way of clarifying the question. We may now proceed to answer it by considering in turn two more specific questions having to do respectively with the *what* and the *how* of doing theology today. In conclusion, then, we may reflect briefly on the validity of the answer.

2. What Is There to Do?

Literally defined, "theology" means *logos* about *theos,* or, as we may translate, thought and speech about God. This seems to indicate that to do theology today, just as in any other day, is to think and speak about God. But while this may well serve as an initial answer to our question, there are certain points at which it must be developed if it is to be an adequate answer.

In the first place, we need to recall that speech is one thing, while using language to say something is another. Although our various speech acts are typically performed by uttering certain words and thus by saying something, we can also speak quite eloquently without saying anything at all; hence the familiar adage, "Actions speak louder than words." This means that the speech proper to theology may very well comprise *doing* along with *saying,* and that theology must accordingly be understood not only as what is thought and said about God, but as what is done about God as well.

This leads to another point where the initial answer is in need of development. Granted that theology is thinking, saying, and doing about God, there is more than one way in which God can be the object of what is thought, said, and done. This is so because there is more than one kind of question about God that human beings may be concerned to ask and answer by what they think, say, and do. Of course, any way of asking about God is a way of asking about something real beyond ourselves and the other persons and things that make up the world around us. In fact, in radically monotheistic religions such as Judaism, Christianity, and Islam, the term "God" refers to the strictly ultimate reality that is the necessary condition of the possibility not only of ourselves and the world, but of anything whatever that is so much as conceivable. But characteristic of these religions precisely as religions is that they ask about this strictly ultimate reality not merely abstractly, in its structure in itself, but rather concretely, in its meaning for us. In other words, in asserting that God is the strictly ultimate reality, these religions not only answer the question of who God is, but at the same time also address the question of who we ourselves are supposed to be in relation to this strictly ultimate reality. By contrast, metaphysics asks about God, insofar as it does so, in pursuit of its rather different, if by no means unrelated, kind of question. While it, too, asks about the strictly ultimate reality that theistic religions understand as God, it does so non-existentially, by abstracting from the meaning of this reality for us so as to inquire simply into its structure in itself. In this respect, metaphysics is much more like science than religion, although the reality about whose structure it inquires abstractly is the same reality about which religion asks concretely — namely, the ultimate reality of our own existence in relation to others and the strictly ultimate.

Because their questions are of different kinds, what religion and metaphysics respectively have to think, say, and do about God are also different. And this naturally raises a question about theology, itself understood as thinking, saying, and doing about God. Does theology ask and answer yet a third kind of question, or does its question belong to one of the other two kinds? Pending a more nuanced answer that can be given in due course, let us say simply that the question of theology is existential in kind and therefore is more like the concrete question of religion than like the abstract question of metaphysics. This means that what theology thinks, says, and does about God all has to do with the meaning of God for us, not merely with the structure of God in itself. In the nature of the case, however, theology and metaphysics are closely related; for while theology goes beyond metaphysics as the concrete exceeds the abstract, it nonetheless includes or implies metaphysics as an abstract aspect of itself.

But even with this much development, the initial answer to our question is still wanting at a crucial point. We noted at the outset that the theology about the doing of which we are inquiring is not theology in general but Christian theology in particular. Up to now, however, nothing said in developing the initial answer accounts for theology's having this particular scope. That its question about God is existential rather than merely metaphysical, and that it includes what is done about God as well as what is thought and said, still does not explain what makes it *Christian* theology. To explain this, we must take account of what alone makes anything properly Christian — namely, that particular experience of Jesus as of decisive significance for human existence which somehow comes to expression in all that Christians think, say, and do. To be a Christian is to have experienced Jesus as thus significant; for it is decisively through him that one's own existential question about the meaning of ultimate reality for us receives its answer. If what it is to do theology, then, is to think and speak about God, by what one does as well as by what one says, so as to address this same existential question, what it is to do Christian theology in particular is to do exactly this as a Christian — out of one's own Christian experience and in such a way as to be appropriate to Jesus as Christians experience him.

The question now, however, is whether even this developed understanding of what it is to do theology allows us to see what there is to do. Is all there is to do already done simply by whatever one thinks, says, and does about God existentially on the basis of one's Christian experience? I do not believe so. And in point of fact, I question whether what we have so far understood theology to be ought still to be called theology at all in the proper sense of the word.

One reason for questioning this is that the word "theology" has long since come to be used by both Christians in general and Christian theologians in particular in a much stricter sense. Far from referring to *all* that Christians think, say, and do about God, "theology" is commonly taken to refer to only *some* of it — namely, to such as is involved in reflecting more or less critically on the validity of all of it. Thus, on this common use of the word, what it is to do theology properly so-called is not done at all unless and until one engages in just such critical reflection. It is not at all surprising, then, that Christians today typically disclaim doing theology simply by what they think, say, and do about God in expressing their Christian experience.

The other and deeper reason for my question is what finally lies behind this typical disclaimer and the much stricter sense of "theology" that it reflects. I refer to the fact that in all that Christians think, say, and do about God on the basis of their experience of Jesus, they necessarily make or imply certain distinctive claims to validity. Specifically, they express or imply two claims: first, that what they think, say, and do is adequate to its content; and, second, that their thinking, saying, and doing it is fitting to its situation. Actually, they make or imply three claims, since the claim to be adequate itself involves two further claims: first, that what is thought, said, and done is appropriate to Jesus as Christians experience him; and, second, that it is credible to human existence as any woman or man experiences it. In most cases, no doubt, these claims to validity are not made explicitly but are merely implied. Even so, there is no alternative to at least implying them, insofar as they are necessarily involved in anything that Christians think, say, and do about God in expressing their Christian experience. The sufficient proof of this is that no Christian ever intends to think, say, or do anything that is either inadequate to its content, because inappropriate to Jesus or incredible to human existence, or else not fitting to its situation.

But what Christians intend to do is one question, and what they succeed in doing, another. And by the same token, it is one thing to make or imply claims to validity, but another and clearly different thing to validate such claims critically. Because of this difference, there are the best of reasons why the term "theology" should have come to have the much stricter sense in which it is now commonly used. Instead of referring to all that Christians think, say, and do about God on the basis of their experience of Jesus, the term is quite reasonably used to refer to either the process or the product of a certain kind of critical reflection — namely, the kind that is required to validate the claims to validity that Christians either make or imply in expressing their experience.

Recognizing this, I take the stricter sense of "theology" to be its proper sense, and it is in this sense alone that I will henceforth use the word. For what is called theology in the broader sense of all that Christians think, say, and do about God, I prefer and will use the term "witness." Thus, in my terms, what it is to do theology proper is adequately understood, not simply as bearing witness, but only as critically reflecting on witness with a view to validating its claims to validity.

What there is for theology to do, then, is just such critical reflection. And it is clear enough that there must always be plenty for theology to do. In the nature of the case, the claims made or implied in bearing witness either are or become more or less problematic. The claims of any witness can be invalid insofar as it fails in some way to be either adequate to its content or fitting to its situation. Moreover, the claims of any one witness to be valid must be immediately called into question by every other witness that is sufficiently different that the claims of both witnesses logically cannot be valid claims. But a plurality of witnesses, obviously, is just the condition in which Christians have typically found themselves from the earliest days of their history as a community. There has never been simply one Christian witness; there have always been only many Christian witnesses. And as often as not, the differences between them have been such that their claims to validity could not all be equally valid. There is no question, then, that Christian witness itself makes critical reflection on its validity not only possible, but also necessary, and in many cases, urgent.

But if this kind of critical reflection is what there is for theology as such to do, what is there for specifically *systematic* theology to do? My answer is that the specific task of systematic theology is to reflect critically on the claim of Christian witness to be adequate to its content. Remember that on the analysis offered above this is one of two claims that are expressed or implied in bearing Christian witness, the other being that witness is fitting to its situation. In my view, the difference between these two claims allows for the self-differentiation of theology as such into the two ways of doing it that I distinguish respectively as systematic and practical theology. Thus, while the specific task of practical theology is to validate the claim of witness to be fitting to the situation in and for which it is borne, the object of systematic theology's reflection is the other claim of witness to be adequate to its own content as Christian witness.

To validate this claim, systematic theology must validate the two further claims that, as we have seen, it involves. There is, first of all, the claim that witness is appropriate to Jesus Christ, in the sense that what is thought, said, and done in bearing witness suitably expresses the experience of Jesus that is properly Christian. Secondly, then, there is the claim that witness is credible to human existence, in the sense that what Christians think, say, and do in bearing it is worthy of belief, practically as well as theoretically, by any woman or man simply as a human being. Of course, for any Christian, to validate the first claim is tantamount to validating the second, this being the very meaning of the assertion that constitutes Christian witness explicitly as such — namely, the christological assertion that Jesus is of decisive significance for human existence. If this assertion is true, any witness that is appropriate could not fail to be credible as well. But although this explains why both claims must be valid if Christian witness is to be adequate to its content, it in no way allows for a confusion of the two claims or for the reduction of either claim to the other. On the contrary, the claims are so related that they are logically independent and mutually irreducible. Thus, notwithstanding the christological assertion, which might, after all, be false, a witness that is appropriate to Jesus Christ need not, for all that, also be credible to human existence, and vice versa.

Because this is so, the specific task of systematic theology is really always two tasks — namely, critically validating both of these claims, neither of which can be validated merely by validating the other. This has been recognized to some extent by the traditional division of systematic theology into dogmatics, on the one hand, and apologetics, on the other — the first serving to validate the claim of witness to be appropriate; the second, its claim to be credible. My own preference is simply to distinguish the two tasks, dogmatic and apologetic, as both being included in the one task of systematic theology to reflect critically on the claim of witness to be adequate to its content. But however we take account of it, what there is for systematic theology to do is not only one thing but two, and that simply because the one claim it has to validate critically comprises two other distinct claims.

There is a final point to be made before proceeding to ask how systematic theology is to accomplish its tasks. I said earlier that the question theology asks and answers is existential in kind and therefore more like the concrete question of religion than like the abstract question of metaphysics. Meanwhile, we have seen good reason to distinguish clearly between the witness that may be called theology only in a broad, improper sense of the word, and the critical reflection on witness to which "theology" strictly and properly refers. Given this distinction, however, it becomes clear that there must also be a difference between the way in which the existential question is asked and answered by witness and the way in which theology proper asks and answers it. Whereas witness addresses the question on the primary level of self-understanding and life-praxis, theology addresses it on the secondary level of critical reflection and proper theory, which is the only place where the claims to validity that are expressed or implied on the primary level can be critically validated. Thus, while the question of theology is indeed the same in kind as the existential question of religion, theology's way of addressing this question is indirect as compared with the direct way of witness.

To understand this, however, is to realize something very important about what there is for theology to do. What there is to do, I have argued, is to reflect critically on the claims to validity that witness itself makes or implies so as to validate them critically. But to do this is obviously to be of real service both to bearing witness itself and to anyone who asks the existential question that witness addresses. On the other hand, because to do theology is not to bear witness but to reflect critically on its validity, the only service that theology is ever in a position to perform for either witness or existence is the *indirect* service of just such critical reflection.

3. How Is It to Be Done?

If we now have some idea of what there is for theology to do, our next question is how, exactly, to do it. To approach an answer to this question — so far, at least, as we can hope to answer it here — I want to start with a point that could have been made perhaps equally well at the end of the preceding section as at the beginning of this one.

As I understand it, to do theology is not simply to bear witness, but to reflect critically on the claims to validity that bearing witness expresses or implies. But this understanding of theology as being in essence critical reflection may seem to suggest that the only way to do it is retrospectively, in the sense of passing critical judgment on particular witnesses that have already been borne. In point of fact, however, the critical reflection of theology can also be done prospectively, in the sense of making a constructive statement of what must be thought, said, and done in order to still bear a witness that is adequate as well as fitting and, therefore, both appropriate and credible. At first glance, perhaps, making such a constructive statement may seem to be indistinguishable from actually bearing witness, especially in the form of Christian teaching; and this impression may be reinforced by the observation that the constructive statements of theology, once made, have usually been integrated into the later witness of Christians and the doctrines of the church. But upon more careful consideration, it is clear that the difference remains between even a constructive theological statement of what a valid witness would need to be and the act or process of actually bearing a witness that claims to be valid. In fact, this difference remains even when the concepts and terms in which theology and witness are formulated are not different but the same.

The first thing to say, then, about how theology is to be done is that it is to be done constructively as well as critically, with a prospective view to bearing witness as well as a retrospective view of witness borne.

To say this, however, scarcely goes beyond saying in different words what there is for theology to do. We do not speak of the real question about the *how* of doing theology until we address the question of theological method — of the way or procedure that theology has to follow to accomplish its tasks, whether it does so prospectively or merely retrospectively. As we have seen, these tasks are, first, the dogmatic task of critically validating the claim of witness to be appropriate to Jesus Christ, and then, second, the apologetic task of validating witness's claim to be credible to human existence. The question of theological method, then, is just how theology is to perform these successive validations.

For our purposes here, I propose to answer this question by distinguishing three phases in the single process of theological reflection. These phases can be clearly distinguished because each of them involves theology's primarily following a specifically different kind of method. Thus in my view, the method of theology is in the nature of the case complex, being in effect a method-encompassing method. Moreover, none of the different methods it encompasses is peculiarly "theological," because each is followed in human reflection generally in one or more of the so-called secular fields or disciplines. What makes any of theology's different methods theological, insofar as it is so, is the encompassing method of theological reflection of which it is a part and, in particular, the distinctive claims to validity that following it somehow contributes toward critically validating. Naturally, each of the methods specific to one or the other of the three phases may itself be complex, in that it may encompass, in turn, other still more specific methods. Thus historical method, for instance, is commonly reckoned to include, among others, the more specific methods of text criticism, source criticism, form criticism, and tradition criticism. But to pursue our question down to this level of detail is not necessary for our purposes; therefore, I will speak simply of the three methods specific to the three phases of theological reflection without going into the complexity that each of them may itself involve.

The first phase of theology is its *historical* phase; and the method specific to it is historical method. In this phase, the objective of theological reflection is to meet the first of the two conditions that are necessary to validating the claim of witness to be appropriate to Jesus Christ. To validate this claim, theology must first determine both in principle and in fact what is to count as formally normative witness. By "normative witness" I mean any witness that, being itself appropriate, may properly function as a norm for critically validating the appropriateness of some or all other witnesses. If it properly functions to validate *some* other witnesses, I distinguish it as "*substantially* normative," because it thereby agrees in substance with all other appropriate witnesses. If, on the other hand, it properly functions to validate the appropriateness of *all* other witnesses, I speak of it as "*formally* normative," because it is the witness with which any other has to agree in substance in order to be appropriate. Theology's first objective, then, is to identify what properly functions in this sense as formally normative witness in fact as well as in principle. Theology can do this only by determining the conditions that any witness must satisfy to function properly as formally normative, and by then identifying the particular witness that satisfies these conditions.

The method it must follow to do this can only be historical method. For what is to count as formally normative witness both in principle and in fact is what witness itself asserts or implies to be so; and this, like witness, is given only through particular historical experience and can be determined, therefore, only by following a properly historical method of reflection. This explains why in its first phase, in which it has to follow such a method, systematic theology properly relies not only on its sister theological discipline, historical theology, including biblical theology, but also on the secular field of history.

The specific task of historical theology, in performing which it is continuous at every point with secular history, is to identify and understand the whole history of witness, beginning with the earliest traditions lying behind, and now accessible only through, the writings of the New Testament. In performing this task, historical theology naturally comes to understand, among other things, what has in fact counted as formally normative witness in all the situations now past in which one witness or another has been borne. But it is just this that systematic theology evidently has to know in order to perform its specific tasks by first determining what is to count as formally normative witness. There is every reason, therefore, why the systematic theologian should learn as much as possible from all who do historical theology, including biblical theologians as well as secular historians. This does not mean, of course, that any of these fellow inquirers can be expected to do the systematic theologian's job or that she or he is obliged to accept the results of their inquiries without criticism. Although what witness is to count as formally normative can be determined only by historical inquiry, determining it is no part of any historical theologian's job, much less that of a secular historian. This remains the inalienable responsibility of the systematic theologian; and in discharging it, she or he may by all means be critical of the results achieved by historical theologians and historians, provided only that the grounds for any criticism are themselves the results of historical inquiry.

But if how theology is to proceed in this first phase is clear enough, how it is actually to be done is anything but easy, especially today. This is because there has never been complete consensus in witness and theology about what is to count as formally normative, either in principle or in fact. To be sure, from at least the second century there has been widespread agreement about the basic principle: the witness that is to count as formally normative is *apostolic* witness, in the strict sense of being the original and originating, and therefore constitutive, witness of the church. But aside from the fact evidenced by the history of the canon that there has always been disagreement about just what witness or witnesses can be validated as apostolic, exactly what apostolicity itself is to mean has been profoundly controversial. Thus, while Protestants, Roman Catholics, and Orthodox have all traditionally accepted the same apostolic principle, they have understood it in sharply different ways — Protestants appealing to "scripture alone" as apostolic, Roman Catholics and Orthodox invoking alternative understandings of "scripture and tradition" as the real meaning of apostolicity. And as if this were not enough, the revisionary forms of witness and theology that have emerged in the course of modern Christian history have challenged the very principle of apostolicity, replacing it with an appeal to "the historical Jesus" as the real principle of formally normative witness.

There is little question, then, that any determination a theologian today can make of what is to count as formally normative witness will be even more controversial than ever before. The range of options has never been as great; and none of them is so free from objections as to make it the only reasonable choice. This does not imply, in my judgment, that no option is sufficiently better than all of the others to be at least relatively preferable. But it certainly does mean that validating the appropriateness of witness today can never be easy and that doing theology responsibly requires one to reckon with its difficulties.

Much the same can be said about the second phase of theology, the *hermeneutical* phase, where it follows a specifically hermeneutical method. Here there are two objectives of theological reflection, even though both are accomplished by doing one and the same thing. The one objective is to meet the second of the two conditions that are necessary to validating the claim of witness to be adequate to its content because it is appropriate to Jesus Christ. To validate this claim, theology not only has to determine what witness is in fact to count as formally normative, but also must understand and therefore interpret this witness so that it can actually perform its proper function as formal norm. But the interpretation of the norm that is thus required to validate the appropriateness of witness is exactly what is also required to accomplish the other objective of theological reflection in its second phase — namely, to meet the first of the two conditions that are necessary to validate the claim of witness to be adequate to its content because it is credible to human existence. Before the credibility of witness can be validated by the truth about human existence, what it does and does not assert or imply concerning such truth has to be understood; and this too requires interpretation of formally normative witness.

The method that such interpretation calls for is what I mean by "hermeneutical method," although it could perhaps also be called "exegetical method." By either name, it is the procedure one has to follow in order to understand and interpret formally normative witness in relation to the kind of human question to which it is addressed as an answer. Assuming, as I have argued, that the question addressed by witness (and, therefore, formally normative witness also) is the existential question about the meaning of ultimate reality for us, we may say that the proper hermeneutical method for theology is existentialist interpretation. But whether we call it this or not, if witness is addressed to the existential question, it must be understood and interpreted accordingly; and this means that it must be critically interpreted in concepts and terms in which this question today can be rightly asked and answered, and human existence itself rightly thought and spoken about. This is the reason that in this second hermeneutical phase, in which systematic theology must work out just such an interpretation, it properly looks for help not only to historical theology and secular history, but also to the secular field of philosophy and to its discipline of philosophical theology in particular.

That systematic theology should rely here too on historical theology and, indirectly, on secular history will be obvious. As understanding of the whole history of witness, historical theology, and biblical theology in particular, includes understanding of formally normative witness as well. But because understanding witness also requires interpreting it, historical theology itself is already dependent on philosophy and philosophical theology. This is so because to interpret what is thought and spoken in one set of concepts and terms always requires another set in which to interpret it. And it is precisely the business of philosophy — and, in the case of the existential question addressed by witness, of philosophical theology — to provide the requisite concepts and terms. Consequently, systematic theologians have every reason to learn whatever they can, not only from historical theologians and secular historians, but also from all who do secular philosophy in general and philosophical theology in particular. Again, this does not imply that the systematic theologian can ever abdicate her or his own responsibility either to historians or to philosophers, or that she or he must accept uncritically whatever they happen to say. Interpretation of the witness that is to count as formally normative as being precisely that, ever remains the systematic theologian's responsibility. And this means that she or he is also responsible for criticizing the work of philosophers as well as historians, provided only that the method followed in doing so is the same hermeneutical method that they in their ways must play a role in developing.

But as I have already indicated, how theology is actually to be done in this second phase is also problematic, especially for anyone doing it today. In this phase, the source of the difficulties is the extensive plurality of both theologies and philosophies, a plurality that has only continued to grow with the passage of time. I remarked earlier that there has never been simply one witness, but always only many witnesses, through which Christians have expressed their experience of the decisive significance of Jesus. This plurality at the primary level of self-understanding and life-praxis, however, is scarcely reduced even at the secondary level of critical reflection and proper theory, where there has never been simply one critical interpretation of formally normative witness but always only many. A principal reason for this, of course, is that there have also always been many philosophies, in the sense of secular interpretations of human culture and religion generally. Depending, then, on which of these many philosophies have provided their concepts and terms, there have also been many theologies. This means that the new philosophies that have continued to be developed have allowed for yet other theological interpretations beyond those already represented by traditional theologies.

The upshot of this is that no interpretation of formally normative witness today can expect to surmount this ever-growing plurality of other theologies and philosophies. At best, it will be but one interpretation among many; and if this need not preclude its being at least relatively more appropriate than other interpretations, the odds against its actually being so have never been greater.

This brings us to the third and last phase of theology, which is its *philosophical* phase, the method specific to which is philosophical method. In this phase, the objective of reflection is to meet the second condition that is necessary for critically validating the claim of witness to be credible to human existence. To validate this claim, theology must not only interpret the witness that is to count as formally normative, but also determine both in principle and in fact what is to count as the truth about human existence. Here again I am assuming that the human question to which witness is addressed is the existential question about the meaning of ultimate reality for us. If this is correct, the claim to credibility that witness makes or implies is a claim to existential credibility. It claims to be worthy of belief because it expresses existential truth. But then to validate its claim, theology has to determine what is to count as such truth, and that in fact as well as in principle. It can do this only by determining the criteria that any assertion must satisfy to be existentially true and then formulating an understanding of ultimate reality that satisfies these criteria.

The method required to do this has to be philosophical method. For what is to count as existential truth both in principle and in fact is what human existence itself discloses to be so; and this, like existence, is given only through common human experience and can be determined, therefore, only by following a properly philosophical method of reflection. Because this is so, theology in its third phase, in which it must follow such a method, also properly relies on the assistance of the secular field of philosophy and of its particular discipline, philosophical theology.

I have already indicated that in my sense of the word, philosophy is the secular interpretation of human culture and religion in general. This is the reason, indeed, that theology properly looks for philosophy's help, and especially for philosophical theology's help, in working out its own interpretation of witness in particular. But if philosophy too has a hermeneutical phase, the objective in its final phase — or, at any rate, in the final phase of philosophical theology — is a reflective understanding of the truth about human existence, and thus of the criteria proper for validating all formulations of this truth. Just such an understanding, however, is what theology clearly has to have in order to carry out its specific tasks by finally determining what is to count as existential truth. Therefore, in this phase also, theologians have the best of reasons for learning everything they can from secular philosophers and philosophical theologians. Once again, this in no way implies either that they can leave their job to these others or that they must accept without question anything that the others have to say. They remain fully responsible for validating the credibility of witness; and in exercising this responsibility, they not only may, but also must, ask questions about the others' claims to existential truth, provided only that their reasons for doing so arise out of their own pursuit of a philosophical method of reflection.

In this phase too, however, how theology is actually to be done involves serious difficulties, especially for anyone attempting it today. The reason for this, of course, is the ever-growing plurality of theologies and philosophies as well as of religions and cultures already referred to. Not only have human beings always had many different and often conflicting understandings of existential truth, but they have also never been able to agree on the criteria proper for adjudicating their differences. In fact, some of the bitterest and most intractable human conflicts have arisen from irresolvable differences over just these criteria. Nor has the extent of such plurality at the primary level of self-understanding and life-praxis ever been significantly reduced at the secondary level of critical reflection and proper theory. There also the one truth about existence has been present only in the many claims to truth, not all of which can be valid.

But if this has always been more or less the case in any situation in which theology could have been done, it is still more strikingly the case in our situation today. With the emergence of a single, truly global human community, the plurality of claims to truth with which theology somehow has to reckon has become practically limitless. It now comprises not only all the traditional expressions of world cultures and religions but also all the more or less radical revisions of these expressions, including the modern secularistic humanisms, both evolutionary and revolutionary. And of particular importance for theology are the significant challenges to all traditional understandings of truth that are now coming from groups and individuals hitherto marginalized and unheard from for reasons of class, race, gender, or culture. These several challenges converge in insisting that the truth about existence is not only to be believed, but also to be done, and that therefore any claims to tell it must be credible practically as well as theoretically.

The import of all this is that theology today has an all but impossible job in determining what is to count as the truth about human existence. My own belief is that the job can still be done — or reasonably attempted, at any rate — insofar as some understandings of the truth are at least relatively more credible than others. But if there ever was a time when theologians could have been excused for looking to some one theology or philosophy to provide such an understanding, it has long since passed. We today are without excuse for all of our traditional provincialisms, and we must scrupulously avoid even a hint of dogmatism in our attempts to formulate existential truth.

This, then, is my answer to the question of theological method, and thus of how theology is to be done today. Admittedly, there are certain dangers in distinguishing, as I have done, between its three different phases, insofar as they may be falsely separated or the order of priority between them may be too simply construed. Even so, the phases, like their methods, are as distinct as they are inseparable; and their order is preserved even though it is evident upon careful reflection that the first in a way presupposes the second, just as the second in a way presupposes the third.

4. The Answer

Having now answered the question of what it is to do theology today, I want to add a few concluding reflections on the validity of my answer. We noted at the outset that the question itself is a properly theological —

more exactly, systematic theological — question; and this implies that
any answer to it must be validated as a properly systematic theological
answer. But just how is such an answer to be validated?

It is evident that the criteria proper for validating it must be the same
criteria by which the adequacy of witness itself has to be validated. Thus
an answer to the question is valid if, and only if, it is at its own level adequate to its content and therefore both appropriate to Jesus Christ and
credible to human existence. The question, then, is whether the answer
for which I have argued can be validated in this way.

That this is certainly not an academic question is evident from the
very different understanding of theology that continues to be widely represented by theologians even today. According to this understanding, the
apologetic task of validating witness as credible either is not acknowledged at all as a proper theological task or else is held to be reducible,
in effect, to the properly dogmatic task of validating witness as appropriate. Thus, even though theology is understood to be critical reflection
on witness, it is regarded as involving only the first and second of the
three phases into which I have distinguished it. Consistent with this,
then, the credibility of at least formally normative witness is assumed
to be already accepted by the theologian as a necessary condition of the
possibility of her or his doing theology at all.

Clearly, the differences between this common understanding of theology and my own are sufficiently great to render the validity of my
answer problematic. Nevertheless, the reasons that can be given for it
seem to me to be weighty enough that it cannot be easily dismissed as
invalid.

This strikes me as particularly obvious in the matter of its appropriateness. The test of this, it will be recalled, is agreement in substance
with formally normative witness. But there seems little question that this
test can be met, since the understanding of theology as including critical
reflection on the claim of witness to be credible exactly corresponds to
the logical structure of witness as such and therefore to any and all witnesses, including formally normative witness. Any witness at all makes
or implies the claim to be adequate, and hence makes or implies the further claims to be credible as well as appropriate. But then any witness
simply as such makes critical reflection on both claims alike not only
possible, but necessary — as soon, at least, as they are sufficiently problematic. Consequently, to understand theology as I have presented it, as
just such critical reflection, is only to take witness at its word and to
make fully explicit the understanding of theology that any witness itself
already necessarily implies.

As for the credibility of this understanding, the case for it also appears to me to be strong, even if any case in this matter is bound to be
more controversial. The test here is whether the understanding of the-

ology is validated as credible by the truth about human existence. The problem, of course, is that there is nothing like a consensus about what is to count as such truth. But precisely in a pluralistic situation all but overwhelmed by a plurality of understandings of the truth, no claims to truth are likely to be regarded as exempt from the requirement of critical validation. By the same token, no theology is likely to be accepted as critical reflection in the full and proper sense of the words that excludes critically validating the credibility of the witness on which it reflects. On the contrary, any understanding of theology that insists on its including such validation is bound to seem more credible than any understanding that precludes it.

So far as I can see, then, the answer for which I have argued can be theologically validated — in the sense that it can claim at least the relative adequacy that is also the most that any theology today can responsibly claim.

- 2 -

Prolegomena to
Historical Theology

I

Human beings obviously differ both in their aptitude for self-reflection and in their exercise of it. But perhaps most persons seriously engaged in doing anything find themselves reflecting sooner or later on just what it means to do it and on how it ought to be done. As and when they do so, they may naturally look for help from any who bear professional responsibility for asking and answering this kind of self-reflective questions.

In the case of those who do Christian theology, it is from the systematic theologians among them that they may especially expect to receive such help. Here too, of course, differences in aptitude for self-reflection and in its exercise will be reflected in the help that individual theologians are in a position to provide. But to be a systematic theologian at all is to be responsible for reflecting on theology itself — on just what it means to do it and on how it ought to be done. This explains why among the perennial questions of systematic theology are those commonly designated "prolegomena," which is not a bad term for them, provided one construes it with Karl Barth to mean not the things that are said *before* one does theology, but rather the things that are said *first*, as soon as one begins to do it.

Like other such perennial questions, however, those included in prolegomena arise in rather different ways in different situations. They acquire their particular shape and urgency from changes in the larger context of theology in the church and in the world, changes that bear on the self-understanding of theologians both as such and as working in one or the other of its particular disciplines. Thus it is generally recognized that throughout the modern period, systematic theologians have been forced to pay particular attention to the most fundamental questions of prolegomena. Faced with the transition to secular culture effected by modern science and technology and a growing historical consciousness, they have had to ask with unprecedented seriousness whether there can even be such a thing as theology as a legitimate form of critical reflection. Moreover, it is widely supposed that they have become in-

20

creasingly caught in an impossible situation in their attempts to answer this question: if they understand theology so that it is subject to the same standards applying to all other fields and disciplines now institutionalized in the university, they can no longer understand it in accordance with its own constitution as specifically Christian theology.

Happily, there are growing signs that this supposed dilemma is not inescapable. More and more theologians are calling for a "paradigm change in theology," which includes at its center such a change in theology's traditional self-understanding as allows it to be nothing other or less than specifically Christian theology even while rightly claiming a place in the university alongside the other fields or disciplines (see, e.g., Griffin and Hough 1991; Küng and Tracy 1989; Wood 1985; 1994). But there are, unfortunately, other signs as well that the modern struggle for a more adequate understanding and practice of theology is anything but over. This is the deeper significance of such a well-known case as that of *Charles E. Curran v. The Catholic University of America*. For while important features of this case are peculiarly Roman Catholic, the basic issues it raises are thoroughly ecumenical. As theology is still widely understood and practiced in all of the churches, and even by a large number of academic theologians, it simply cannot be a field of study on a par with other fields and disciplines. Consequently, the fundamental question of prolegomena, of how theology as such is to be understood and practiced, remains even now a pressing question (see below, pp. 80–91).

Other questions pertaining to the particular disciplines of theology have also become more or less urgent as a result of ongoing changes in the larger theological context. Thus, for example, throughout the nineteenth century right up to the present, Protestant theology has commonly been organized into the four distinct disciplines of biblical, historical, systematic, and practical theology. But among the consequences of consistently following historical-critical methods of study in theology has been the complete breakdown of the distinction between scripture and tradition that lay behind thus distinguishing between biblical and historical theology. Therefore, there is good reason to ask whether biblical theology ought not now to be regarded simply as a special case of historical theology, with the result that the field as a whole should be organized into three rather than four distinct disciplines (see Ogden 1992c, 8ff., 96; Wood 1985, 43f.).

Yet another and more fundamental question has also continued to arise about historical theology itself as a distinct theological discipline. If its being properly historical in the now generally accepted sense of the term has required clearly distinguishing it from the other theological disciplines, its also being properly theology has appeared to blur any such clear distinction. Thus it is not surprising that historical theologians sometimes have difficulty acquiring and maintaining a clear self-understanding. Also understandable is that systematic theologians attempting to understand historical theology have at least appeared to be caught in yet another impossible situation: if they understand it so that it is subject to the same standards applying to all other studies now generally judged to be historical, they can no longer understand it in accordance with its own constitution as a discipline of Christian theology.

Here too, however, I am convinced that the apparent dilemma is merely that, and that historical theology can be so understood as to escape from it. In fact, I am convinced that there is an exact analogy between so understanding historical theology as a discipline and adequately understanding theology as a field. My purpose in what follows, then, is to develop this analogy so as to justify these convictions. If in this way I shall offer little more than a sketch of the prolegomena promised by my title, one advantage of the procedure seems clear: it should serve to situate a regional prolegomena to historical theology within its only proper context — that is, within a fundamental prolegomena to theology as such.

2

The key to a fundamental prolegomena is rightly distinguishing theology from Christian faith and witness. This distinction, however, is a special case of a much more general one, with which it is helpful to begin in trying to understand it. I refer to the fundamental distinction between what I call "critical reflection and proper theory," on the one hand, and "self-understanding and life-praxis," on the other (cf. Habermas 1973, 382–393).

To be human is not only to live, but also to understand one's life and, within limits, to be free to lead it and responsible for doing so. Of course, in understanding one's life, one understands indefinitely more than oneself — not only all the others, human and nonhuman, without which one could not live at all, but also the encompassing whole of reality of which both oneself and all others are parts. But thus to live understandingly, and so also freely and responsibly, is precisely to lead one's life according to certain norms or principles of validity, whether authenticity and sincerity, or truth, goodness, and beauty. This means that one's very life as a human being involves asking certain questions — whether the existential question about the authentic understanding of oneself and others in relation to the whole, or other hardly less vital questions about the true, the good, and the beautiful. It also means, however, that the whole of one's life-praxis, and so whatever one thinks, says, or does, in effect answers these same questions, thereby making or implying certain corresponding claims to validity.

Thus, to say or imply that so-and-so is the case is to answer the question about the true and at least to imply a claim to truth in doing so. But if thus implying or making a truth claim is a typical exercise of our essentially human capacity to live understandingly, it is by no means the only such exercise. Not only do we just as typically make or imply all sorts of other claims — to authenticity and rightness as well as to goodness and beauty — but we also ask, at least under certain circumstances, about the validity of our several claims. We ask, for example, whether what is *said* to be the case is *really* the case, and, in this sense, whether the claim to truth expressed or implied by the saying is a valid claim. This example suffices to show that our capacity to live understandingly is typically exercised not merely on one level, but on two. On the primary level of self-understanding and life-praxis, it is exercised by asking and answering the question of truth and all of our other vital questions and by making or implying claims to validity in answering them. On the secondary level of critical reflection and proper theory, it is exercised by critically interpreting our answers in relation to our questions and by critically validating the claims to validity that the answers make or imply.

Distinct as they are, these two levels of living understandingly are also inseparable, each in its way also involving the other. This becomes evident as soon as one reflects that living so is always done by individual women and men in community with other human beings living in the same understanding way. Thus, to make or imply a claim to validity on the primary level of self-understanding and life-praxis is in effect to issue a promise to all other members of this human community — the promise, namely, to submit one's claim to critical validation as and when it becomes problematic and needs to be critically validated. In this way, living on the primary level of living understandingly already anticipates living on the secondary level, which it makes both possible and, under certain circumstances, necessary. On the other hand, to critically validate a claim to validity on the secondary level of critical reflection and proper theory is neither possible nor necessary unless some such claim has already been made or implied on the primary level. Critical reflection requires something to reflect on and a reason for doing so; thus it necessarily presupposes the self-understanding and life-praxis out of which it arises and which it is constituted to serve.

But if the two levels of human living cannot be rightly separated, neither can they be rightly identified. Being as different as they are united, they can only be rightly distinguished, by which I mean, so distinguished as to be seen in their unity as well as their difference, and in their difference as well as their unity. This is done, I believe, by stressing both the difference and the unity between making or implying claims to validity, on the one hand, and critically validating these claims, on the other.

The bearing that this distinction has on the understanding of theology may be brought out by briefly considering the meaning of the phrase "Christian faith and witness." Construed in a purely formal sense, this phrase refers to human self-understanding and life-praxis insofar as they are mediated — immediately or mediately — through experience of Jesus Christ. This assumes that the Christian *proprium,* in the sense of what alone makes anything properly Christian, is the experience of Jesus as the Christ, or, as we might say today, the experience of Jesus as of decisive significance for human existence. One experiences Jesus to be thus significant insofar as it is decisively through him that one's own existential question about authentic self-understanding is directly and explicitly answered. But the faith that is of a piece with such experience and through which this answer is received is, in purely formal terms, an explicit self-understanding — an understanding of oneself and others in relation to the whole, decisively re-presented through Jesus as the all-encompassing love of God.

In the same way, the witness through which this faith then comes and must come to manifold expression is correctly understood purely formally as the life-praxis that necessarily follows from just such a self-understanding. Insofar as one understands oneself through Jesus, one exists in unreserved trust in God's love and in unqualified loyalty to it, which means loyalty both to God and to all — others as well as oneself — to whom God is loyal. This existence in trust and loyalty, then, naturally comes to expression either explicitly or implicitly in action — in the whole of one's life-praxis, and so in everything that one thinks, says, and does. It comes to explicit expression as praxis of the Christian religion, which, like all religion, functions as the primary form of culture that explicitly mediates authentic self-understanding and the life-praxis that follows from it. But existence in faith is also expressed implicitly through all of the other so-called secular forms of praxis and culture, both primary and secondary. Whatever one thinks, says, or does somehow expresses one's faith as a Christian and therefore cannot fail to be at least implicit Christian witness.

Implicit or explicit, however, all Christian witness, like any other life-praxis, makes or implies certain claims to validity. Different as these claims clearly are materially, because of the *proprium* of Christian witness, they are nonetheless similar formally to those made or implied by other cases of life-praxis both religious and secular. Thus not only the Christian religion, but any religion lays claim to decisive existential authority because it also claims to be the true religion — in the sense that it makes explicit the true answer to the existential question and properly functions, therefore, as the formal norm for determining all other religious truth. So, too, with implicit Christian witness, which is in no way different formally from the implicit witness of any other faith in also claiming to mediate, in its way, authentic self-understanding.

There is another important respect in which the claims to validity made or implied by Christian witness are formally the same as those of any other witness of faith. This becomes evident as soon as one reflects on the systematic ambiguity of the term "witness," which can mean both the *that* of witness, in the sense of the act of witnessing, and the *what* of witness, in the sense of its expression of its content, either explicitly or by implication. Thus, like any other witness of faith, any instance of Christian witness, whether explicit or implicit, makes or implies a twofold claim to validity corresponding to its twofold structure as witness: insofar as it is an act of witnessing, it claims at least implicitly to be fitting to its situation; and insofar as it is an explication or implication of the content of witness, it makes or implies the claim to be adequate to this content.

What is distinctive about any instance of Christian witness, of course, is its content, which is determined by its *proprium* in the experience of Jesus as of decisive existential significance. But even here there is a formal similarity to other witnesses of faith, or to the other specific religions through which such witnesses become explicit. Not only the Christian religion, but any religion is constituted as such by some explicit primal source through which its particular self-understanding is decisively re-presented. At the same time, any religion, as we have seen, lays claim to decisive existential authority because it also claims that its particular self-understanding is true and hence of universal significance. So, in claiming as it does to be adequate to its content as well as fitting to its situation, any instance of witness claims in effect to be both authorized by its explicit primal source and worthy of belief by any woman or man simply as a human being. In the case of Christian witness, this becomes the distinctive twofold claim to be both appropriate to Jesus Christ, or to Jesus as Christians experience him, and credible to human existence.

But if these are the claims to validity that are made or implied by any instance of Christian witness, then to bear this witness on the primary level of self-understanding and life-praxis is already to anticipate critically validating these claims on the secondary level of critical reflection and proper theory. This is so, at any rate, on the assumption that to make or imply these claims is also in effect to issue a promise to all other members of the human community — the same promise, namely, to allow the claims to be critically validated whenever they become sufficiently problematic to be in need of such validation. In this way, simply bearing Christian witness necessarily involves doing theology. For what is properly meant by "theology" in the specific sense of "Christian the-

ology" is simply the form of critical reflection constituted as such by
asking whether the validity claims made or implied by any instance of
Christian witness are, in fact, valid claims. Is the witness in question
both fitting to its situation and adequate to its content, in that it is appropriate to Jesus Christ and credible to human existence? Or, to put
the same question in the more constructive way in which it may also be
asked: What witness would be both fitting to its situation and adequate
to its content, because it is authorized by Jesus Christ and worthy of
being believed by anyone encountering it? (cf. Wood 1985, 40).

This question makes it clear that the unity between Christian witness and theology runs the other way as well. The theology that the
question constitutes would be neither possible nor necessary but for the
prior existence of the Christian witness with its claims to be fitting and
adequate, and so appropriate and credible. In fact, the theology arises
out of this witness and is constituted to serve it by critically validating
its claims. But if the question thus confirms the unity between theology
and witness, it also reveals their difference. It makes clear that bearing
witness and doing theology properly take place on two distinct levels —
witness being borne on the primary level of self-understanding and life-
praxis, theology being done on the secondary level of critical reflection
and proper theory. Thus, while bearing Christian witness is a matter
of answering our vital questions — specifically, our existential question
about authentically understanding ourselves and others as parts of the
whole — doing theology is a matter of critically interpreting this answer
and of critically validating the claims to validity that giving it at least
implies.

As clear as this distinction is, however, there are reasons why it is not
always easy to draw in particular cases. One such reason is that many of
the concepts and terms in which theological reflection is done are naturally the same as those in which Christian witness is borne. Thus if one
considers only language, and ignores the different functions that even
the identical language may perform, one may very well confuse a case
of doing theology with a case of bearing witness. Another closely related reason for confusion is that even the novel products of theological
reflection, once they have been produced, are commonly taken up into
Christian witness as its own forms of thought and speech. Here again,
the distinction may not be easy to make unless one looks beneath the
obvious similarity in the formulations to the underlying difference in the
purposes for using them. But perhaps the most fundamental reason why
bearing Christian witness and doing theology may be hard to distinguish
is that bearing witness itself can be done in two different ways, one of
which is easily mistaken for doing theology.

I refer to the difference between the direct witness of Christian proclamation and the indirect witness of Christian teaching. This difference is

particularly obvious in the paradigm cases, or representative forms, of both ways of bearing witness. These forms are, with respect to the first way of proclamation, preaching the word and administering the sacraments and, with respect to the second way of teaching, the instruction in Christian faith and in Christian belief and action that is generally understood to be yet a third official function of the representative minister.

In the cases of both preaching the word and administering the sacraments, witness directly offers the possibility of an explicit self-understanding and demands that it be actualized through the free personal decision of the hearer or receiver. This explains why proclamation in either case is typically cast in the form of imperatives, or of indicatives having a clear imperative meaning — as, for example, "Be reconciled to God!" (2Co 5:20), or "The body (blood) of Christ, given for you." In the case of teaching, by contrast, sentences are typically cast in the indicative mood. This is true, indeed, even of the instruction in Christian action that is one important part of such teaching. This instruction does not directly call for doing things, but rather elucidates *agenda,* things to be done, given the self-understanding of Christian faith. Likewise, the instruction in Christian belief that is another important part of the same teaching does not directly call for believing things, but rather expounds *credenda,* things to be believed, insofar as one has a Christian self-understanding. The explanation of this is that Christian teaching in all of its parts is precisely not Christian proclamation. It does not directly offer the possibility of Christian faith and demand that the learner actualize it, but does this only indirectly, by clarifying the meaning of this possibility itself, both as such and in its necessary implications for belief and action.

Because of this indirectness, however, Christian teaching, in contrast to Christian proclamation, may not seem to be all that different from doing theology. And this is the more likely because doing theology is, in fact, necessary to Christian teaching, even as it is to the direct way of bearing Christian witness. Nevertheless, Christian teaching is not the same as doing theology, but is a way of bearing Christian witness; and it therefore takes place on the primary level of self-understanding and life-praxis. This means that, for all of the indirectness with which it does so, Christian teaching still intends to answer the existential question to which bearing Christian witness in either of its ways is addressed. Doing theology, by contrast, takes place on the secondary level of critical reflection and proper theory. This means not only that it is related indirectly even to Christian teaching, but also that it has another and quite different intention: not to answer the existential question, but to interpret the answer given to it by bearing Christian witness and to validate the claims to validity that this witness makes or implies.

To understand this difference is to realize why any attempt to subject doing theology to the teaching office of the church must be profoundly misguided. As much as bearing Christian witness — including Christian teaching — may be quite properly subjected to such control, this is emphatically not the case with doing theology. On the contrary, doing theology cannot possibly perform the service for bearing witness that it is constituted to provide unless it is free to validate all instances of Christian witness, including not least those comprising the official teaching of the church. As a matter of fact, it is precisely the church's official teaching that is, above all, subject to, and in need of, the critical control of theology. For one of the defining characteristics of such teaching, as distinct from all unofficial teaching and proclamation, is that it does not merely imply claims to be fitting and adequate, and so appropriate and credible, but makes these claims explicitly and even formally. Consequently, the promise it in effect issues to other members of the human community is correspondingly obvious and all the more clearly in need of the redemption that doing theology alone is able to provide.

But if doing theology cannot be controlled by the church's teaching office without forfeiting its proper service to bearing Christian witness, there is no good reason why theology may not rightly claim a place in the university alongside the other fields or disciplines. On the contrary, it is only when theology is understood to be subject to the same standards applying to any legitimate field or discipline that it can be reasonably expected to validate the validity claims that are made or implied in bearing Christian witness.

This is not to ignore the specific difference between doing theology and pursuing any other form of critical reflection. Nor is it to imply that theology has to be among the fields or disciplines rightly represented in any university simply as such. The inseparable unity of theology with Christian witness uniquely distinguishes it from all other forms of critical reflection, and hence from all other fields and disciplines represented in the university. And this same unity entails that theology's right to a place in the university is not absolute but relative — deriving not from the constitution of any university simply as such, but from that of a university (for example, an explicitly Christian university) that privileges critically interpreting and validating the claims to validity that the specifically Christian witness of faith makes or implies (see Ogden 1992c, 128–133). But none of this alters the fact that theology is a form of reflection that can and must be as critical as any other and may therefore very well be a field of study on a par with all the other fields and disciplines. Indeed, only if it is, can it perform the service of critical interpretation and validation that theology as such, as specifically Christian theology, is constituted to provide.

I conclude, therefore, that the supposed dilemma of a fundamental prolegomena is merely that. It arises not from theology itself, given the institutionalization of critical reflection in the modern university, but only from what theology is supposed to be insofar as its difference from Christian witness is missed or misunderstood. To take account of this difference and to understand it as I have done here, however, is in no way to deny the unity between Christian witness and theology. It is only rightly to distinguish them.

3

The question now is how, within this understanding of theology as a field, historical theology as a discipline is to be understood. I have already stated my conviction that there should be an exact analogy between the two understandings. But if this conviction is right, it would seem that the key to a regional prolegomena to historical theology must be — as in the case of distinguishing theology from Christian faith and witness — rightly distinguishing things that cannot be rightly separated any more than they can be rightly identified. In this case, the key would be rightly distinguishing historical theology from theology, although here too this would presumably mean so distinguishing them as to see them in their unity as well as their difference, and in their difference as well as their unity. The fact, however, that "theology" appears on both sides of the distinction clearly indicates their unity, while also indicating that there can be at most an analogy between distinguishing them and distinguishing theology from Christian faith and witness. Historical theology is itself theology, and this means that it too is done on the secondary level of critical reflection and proper theory, not on the primary level of self-understanding and life-praxis on which Christian witness is borne. But then how does it really differ from theology otherwise? And how can its difference be really analogous to that between theology and Christian witness?

To answer these questions, we need to recall what has already been said about the scope of critical reflection, both in general and in the specific form of theology. On the foregoing analysis, critical reflection generally is constituted by asking about the claims to validity that are made or implied in answering our various vital questions. But if such reflection thus necessarily includes what I have referred to as "critical validation," this is not all that it includes. No less necessary is what I have distinguished as "critical interpretation"; for whether the answer to a vital question is valid in whatever ways it makes or implies a claim to be so cannot be determined until the answer itself has been rightly understood. This is so, too, in the case of theology, which is constituted as specifically Christian theology by asking whether the answer to our existential question given by Christian witness is valid in the several ways in which it at least implicitly claims to be so. Before this question can be answered, Christian witness first has to be understood as an answer to the existential question. Therefore, the scope of theology, as constituted by its own constitutive question, is greater than this question, simply on the face of it, might seem to indicate. Precisely as critical reflection on Christian witness, theology includes critical interpretation of this witness as the necessary condition of critically validating its claims to validity.

To the first question, then, of how historical theology really differs, the answer would seem to be this: historical theology differs from theology otherwise as the critical interpretation necessarily included in theology differs from the critical validation that it also includes. In other words, what is properly meant by "historical theology" is simply such critical interpretation of Christian witness as is required to answer the constitutive question of theology as such — whether the validity claims made or implied by any instance of such witness are, in fact, valid claims.

But what critical interpretation of Christian witness is thus required? From what has been said, it should be clear that at least the particular instance of Christian witness whose validity is in question has to be critically interpreted. To attempt to validate its claims without first rightly understanding it would run the risk of not validating its claims at all, but only what are misunderstood to be its claims. It is also the case, however, that this cannot be all the critical interpretation that is necessary.

Part of the twofold claim made or implied by any instance of Christian witness is the claim to be adequate to its content. But as we have seen, this claim itself is twofold, in that it is the claim both to be appropriate to Jesus Christ and to be credible to human existence. In the nature of the case, there are two, and only two, conditions under which the first part of this claim could be valid: either the particular instance of witness is itself the constitutive and therefore formally normative instance of Christian witness by which the appropriateness of all other instances has to be determined; or else it is one of these other instances that so agrees with the formally normative instance that it too is appropriate and therefore substantially normative for determining the appropriateness of other such instances. Consequently, to validate the appropriateness of any instance of Christian witness is to show that one or the other of these conditions is satisfied. But to show that either of them is satisfied requires critically interpreting the constitutive and therefore formally normative instance of Christian witness.

That this is so if one is to show that the second condition is satisfied is obvious enough, since no instance of witness can be determined to be in substantial agreement with another unless both instances are rightly understood. But it is no less so even if one is to show that the first condition is satisfied; for whether an instance of witness is itself constitutive and therefore formally normative, in turn depends upon its satisfying certain necessary conditions. Specifically, it has to make or imply the claim to be appropriate to Jesus Christ by asserting or implying that Jesus is of decisive significance for human existence; and it has to be not just *an* instance of asserting or implying this, but *the* instance of doing so, in the sense of the original and originating and, therefore, constitutive such instance. But, once again, whether an instance of Christian witness satisfies these conditions and thus is the constitutive instance can be determined only by first rightly understanding it.

The critical interpretation that theology requires, then, is of nothing less than all instances of Christian witness whose claims to be appropriate as well as credible and fitting need to be critically validated. Since the claims of any instance of witness may, under certain circumstances, need to be validated, any instance of witness may also need to be interpreted. This means that the scope of historical theology coincides, in principle, with the whole history of Christian witness, beginning with the earliest instances lying behind, and now accessible only through, the writings of the New Testament, and continuing right up to the latest instances comprising contemporary Christian life-praxis. If one recalls the many forms and kinds of such witness — explicit and implicit, direct and indirect, official and unofficial, and so on — the scope of historical theology will seem vast indeed.

Having recognized this, however, I want to return to what seemed to be its difference from theology otherwise and especially to the other question raised above, whether this difference can really be analogous to that between theology and Christian witness. Historical theology is different, it seemed, because the critical interpretation that theology includes is different from the critical validation that it also includes. While historical theology is concerned with rightly understanding Christian witness, theology otherwise, through its other two disciplines of systematic and practical theology, is concerned with determining whether Christian witness itself is right, in the sense of validly claiming to be both adequate to its content and fitting to its situation. Notwithstanding this difference, however, we have just seen that historical theology is also united with theology otherwise, and thus with its sister disciplines. The critical validation that they are constituted to perform requires, and hence necessarily presupposes, its critical interpretation. To this extent, we have already observed a certain analogy with the difference and the unity between Christian witness and theology.

To be sure, the analogy is reversed, in that it is theology that presupposes historical theology, rather than the other way around. But given the difference that analogy must allow for, it is entirely consistent to allow for this reversal. And there is the more reason to do so because the unity between historical theology and theology likewise runs both ways. In other words, while doing theology presupposes doing historical theology, doing historical theology anticipates doing theology — just as bearing Christian witness anticipates doing theology, while doing theology presupposes bearing Christian witness.

This becomes evident as soon as one reflects that, in general, we seek to understand what others think, say, and do in order to answer our own vital questions. Thus the critical interpretation of the past provided by historical reflection generally is of a piece with, and is naturally directed toward, the critical validation to be performed by systematic and practical reflection. It is no different in the specific case of theological reflection: the critical interpretation of the past provided by historical theology is never simply an end in itself, but also always the means, even if the indispensable means, to the ulterior end of critical validation that systematic and practical theology are constituted to perform. In this sense, doing historical theology, from its end, anticipates the work of its sister disciplines, even as they, for their part, necessarily presuppose its work.

But if the analogy seems clear with respect to the unity between the disciplines, it is equally clear with respect to their difference. Corresponding to the difference between somehow explicating or implying the content of Christian witness and the act of witnessing, and hence between Christian witness's claim to be adequate to its content and its claim to be fitting to its situation, is the difference between systematic and practical theology respectively. Although they are united in both having to do with critical validation, they are also different in each having to validate only one of these two claims. But just as Christian witness in both of its aspects is one thing, while theology is something else, so theology in both of these disciplines involves one type of critical reflection, while historical theology involves the other. Whereas systematic and practical theology are both a matter of critically validating the claims of Christian witness to be adequate and fitting, historical theology is a matter of critically interpreting this witness so that its claims can be thus validated. This difference is admittedly not as great as the difference in levels of living understandingly that obtains between bearing Christian witness and doing theology. And yet it is a difference in types of reflecting critically and, therefore, is certainly great enough to be analogous.

Here too, however, there are reasons why a distinction that is clear in itself may not always seem so. One such reason is that systematic theology itself perforce has a historical aspect or phase. Because its first task, indeed, is the "dogmatic" task of critically validating the claim of Christian witness to be appropriate to Jesus Christ, its first main objective, for reasons already explained, is to identify what is to count both in principle and in fact as the formally normative instance of Christian witness. It lies in the nature of the case, however, that systematic theology can attain this objective only by pursuing properly historical methods of study and by learning from historical theology as well as historical studies generally. Thus it may not seem to be really distinct from historical theology, and the term "historical theology" may even be used to designate its own historical aspect or phase (see Wood 1985, 41–45). But another and perhaps more important reason why historical theology may not be clearly distinguished from the other theological disciplines is that its own proper task is described as *critical* interpretation of Christian witness.

Of course, the point in so describing it is to bring out that, while there is indeed a difference in types between the critical interpretation of historical theology and the critical validation of systematic and practical theology, the first as much as the second is precisely a matter of *critical* reflection. But from what has already been said it should be clear that the critical interpretation provided by historical theology is like that of any other form of historical reflection in interpreting what has been thought, said, and done in the past in its meaning for the present. This implies that historical theology critically interprets particular instances of Christian witness in relation to the existential question to which they are properly addressed. Only by thus interpreting them as answers to a vital human question can it rightly understand what they mean for us, or even what they meant for those for whom they were originally intended. But this kind of critical interpretation allows for and, under certain circumstances, requires an immanent criticism of what has been thought, said, and done in Christian witness by reference to its own basic intention. Thus if an instance of witness shows signs of having confused addressing its own properly existential question with speaking to some other logically different question, historical theology precisely as critical interpretation includes criticizing the witness accordingly. And the same is true insofar as the witness is otherwise self-inconsistent or the concepts and terms in which it is cast are in principle inappropriate for formulating any answer to the existential question.

Because historical theology allows for such immanent criticism, however, it may itself seem to be a matter of critically validating Christian witness rather than, or as well as, critically interpreting it. This is the more probable insofar as immanent criticism is, in fact, critical validation of certain validity claims that Christian witness, like any other life-praxis, makes or implies. Still, historical theology is not the same as systematic and practical theology, even if it too may include a certain kind of criticism of Christian witness. An immanent criticism is one thing, a transcendent criticism, something different; and as much as historical theology may indeed include the first, it cannot possibly include the second except by ceasing to be itself. What makes it or any other historical study properly historical is precisely its "methodical abstraction" from any kind of critical validation requiring transcendent norms, in the sense of norms that go beyond what is thought, said, and done in the objects of its study themselves (see Apel 1973, 2:112–120). Thus, while it may indeed validate the claim to be self-consistent that any instance of Christian witness necessarily implies, it may not validate any of the other claims of witness to be fitting and adequate, and so appropriate and credible. Practical and systematic theology, by contrast, are constituted for the precise purpose of critically validating these other claims, and thus of effecting the transcendent criticism that historical theology as such necessarily precludes.

Once this difference is understood, however, it is obvious why any attempt to subject historical theological study to systematic and practical theological control is completely out of line. However much the findings of historical theology do indeed need to be thus controlled before they can be accepted as normative for Christian faith and witness, this is emphatically not the case with historical theology itself (cf. Marxsen 1969, 198–213; 1985; 1986). On the contrary, it cannot possibly perform the service for its sister disciplines that it is constituted to provide unless it is free to interpret all instances of Christian witness as they need to be interpreted if they are to be rightly understood. This includes not least all instances of witness that have hitherto been accepted as normative, both formally and substantially. That an instance of witness has been accepted as normative in no way implies that it deserves to be so accepted. But to determine its right to be accepted requires critically validating its claim to be appropriate; and there is no way to validate this or any of its other claims to validity without first critically interpreting it in entire independence of systematic and practical theological control.

But if historical theology cannot perform its proper service unless it is done thus independently, there is no good reason for it not to be subject to the same standards applying to all other studies now generally judged to be properly historical. On the contrary, it is only when historical theology is understood to be subject to these very standards that it can be reasonably expected to interpret Christian witness so as to rightly understand it, and thus satisfy the necessary condition of critically validating its claims to be valid.

Of course, historical theology is specifically different from every other historical study; and its right to be reckoned among such studies generally is exactly as relative as the right of theology as a field to a place alongside all the other fields and disciplines institutionalized in the university. But this in no way implies that historical theology is not also continuous at every point with historical studies in general and therefore subject to identically the same standards.

I conclude, then, that the analogy is exact between a regional prolegomena to historical theology as a discipline and a fundamental prolegomena to theology as a field. This means that the apparent dilemma of such a regional prolegomena is exactly that. It arises not from what historical theology really is, given the now generally accepted sense of what is properly historical, but only from what historical theology appears to be insofar as its difference from theology otherwise is missed or misunderstood. To recognize this difference, however, and to understand it as I have argued one should is in no way to question that historical theology is constituted as a discipline of Christian theology. It is only to contend that it is also eminently historical.

– 3 –

Theology and
Biblical Interpretation

I

Is there at present a way to construe the Bible that is authentically theological and yet respects the integrity of critical biblical scholarship?

This is the question I propose to address in this essay by arguing for an affirmative answer. I shall develop my argument in three main parts, each devoted to clarifying a basic normative concept — specifically, the two generative concepts indicated by my title, "theology" and "biblical interpretation," and the derivative concept, "theological interpretation of the Bible." My contention is that to understand these concepts as an adequate theology now requires is to have all the reason one needs to answer the question affirmatively.

The question is genuine and even urgent, of course, because of a widespread perception that it should be answered negatively — or, in the case of some perceivers, perhaps that one should have serious misgivings about answering it affirmatively. Given what is seen to be the growing estrangement over the last two centuries between theology, on the one hand, and biblical scholarship, on the other, many at present judge it to be difficult, if not impossible, to point to an interpretation of the Bible that is authentically theological and yet respects the integrity of critical biblical scholarship by also being critical, not in some different sense, but in the same sense in which biblical interpretation otherwise may be said to be so. I have considerable sympathy with this judgment and no intention whatever of simply rejecting it. In fact, I would be forced to make it myself if the traditional understanding of theology, and thus of what is authentically theological, were the only or the most adequate understanding presently available to us.

Nor do I have any illusions about the extent to which this traditional understanding continues to dominate the theory as well as the praxis of theology right up to today. I note, rather, that even in discussions of this very question that are self-consciously methodological and both informed and informing about the developments in biblical scholarship giving rise to it, theology continues to be understood in such a way as to make impossible an answer to it that is at once affirmative and coher-

36

ent. Thus, in the in many ways helpful book written by Robert Morgan with John Barton, *Biblical Interpretation* (1988), the understanding of theology from which the authors argue leads them to represent as "a classic case" of "interpreting the Bible theologically" what is patently a case of allegorical, and so clearly uncritical, interpretation — namely, that recorded in Acts 8:30–35, where Philip teaches the Ethiopian eunuch to read Isaiah through "the Christian master code" (Morgan with Barton 1988, 274; cf. 296).

Even so, convinced as I am that this traditional understanding of theology no longer remains unchallenged, but is now relativized by another, theologically more adequate understanding, I see real prospects of overcoming the perceived estrangement between theology and biblical scholarship. My purpose here, however, is not to argue *for* this alternative way of understanding theology, but rather to argue *from* it — as well as from what I am prepared to defend as a comparably adequate understanding of biblical interpretation. Since I take both understandings to be properly theological, I acknowledge the need to validate their adequacy in the same way in which that of any other theological understanding would need to be validated. But I shall not attempt such validation here; rather, simply assuming their adequacy, I shall seek to show that the understanding of theological interpretation of the Bible derived from them is sufficient reason for giving an affirmative answer to our question.

Recognizing this limitation of my argument, the reader is certainly free to think of it as at best conditional or hypothetical, pending theological validation of the understandings it assumes but does not argue for. But I trust there is also no uncertainty that it is precisely theological validation that is logically required to validate them and that the understandings necessary to any other answer to the question would need to be validated at least philosophically, if not also theologically. I take it to be clear, in other words, that just because the question is properly methodological, in that it calls for a normative rather than a descriptive understanding of what it is to interpret the Bible theologically, only theology — more exactly, systematic theology — and philosophy are logically positioned to answer it.

This is not to say, of course, that relevant discussion of the question is limited to specialists in systematic theology and philosophy. It is not only possible, but also likely, that others also, including specialists in biblical scholarship and in historical studies generally, will have thought about it sufficiently to be well qualified to discuss it. But if they are, it will not be as and because they are specialists in such other fields or disciplines, but only because they also have a nonspecialized, or possibly, in some cases, a specialized, competence as systematic theologians or philosophers.

As for my formulation of the question, I have reasons for wanting to ask about construing or interpreting "the Bible" rather than "scripture." Although for most purposes the two terms may very well be used interchangeably, the second usually not only refers, like the first, to a specific collection of books or writings, but also suggests their status or function, severally as well as collectively, as uniquely authoritative. Indeed, in traditional theological usage, to speak of "scripture" is to speak of the *norma normans, sed non normata* — that which is not merely substantially, but also formally, normative for all Christian witness and theology. In my view, however, one of the most important consequences of critical biblical scholarship over the last two hundred years is its having sharply posed the question of whether this traditional understanding of the status or function of the biblical writings as formally normative can any longer be upheld (cf. Ogden 1992c, 45–68). Therefore, I am concerned to recognize this important question for the genuinely disputed question it has now become, and I do not want it to be begged simply by the way in which the question before us here is formulated. It is arguable, I realize, that I do not, in fact, have this option, because the Bible's status or function as scripture, or its lack thereof, is "hermeneutically relevant," in that it bears in some way on how the Bible is to be interpreted (see Wood 1994, 55–70, esp. 57). But such arguments to this effect as I have examined have not convinced me, and so I shall proceed on the assumption that one can very well understand what it is to interpret the Bible theologically without first having to decide whether it is, or is not, rightly regarded as formally normative.

2

It will have already become apparent that I am using the word "theology" in this discussion in the specific sense of "Christian theology." In asking, then, as I shall now do, about the normative concept meant by this word, I shall be asking, in effect, how specifically Christian theology is to be normatively conceived. I propose to approach an answer to this question, however, by first considering what I distinguish as the generic sense of the word "theology."

Not uncommonly, theology in this generic sense is taken to mean a secondary form of praxis and culture consisting in more or less critical reflection on a particular religion. Thus Michael Oakeshot, for example, observes that, "[l]ike anything else, a religion may evoke a reflective consideration of its postulates and a theology may emerge from this engagement; but, although a faith is an understanding, a theoretical understanding of a faith is not itself a faith" (Oakeshot 1975, 81). Oakeshot's caution, in my view, is very much to the point. But his analysis of a theology as a reflective consideration of the postulates of a religion, while right in what it includes, is too narrow. Although the understand-

ing — or, as I should say, self-understanding — that is a faith is indeed
expressed explicitly through some religion and its postulates, it must
also find expression, if only implicitly, through all of the other, so-called
secular forms of praxis and culture. Recognizing this, I take it to be more
accurate to say that "theology" in the generic sense means critical reflection on, or the proper theory of, the self-understanding and life-praxis
explicitly mediated by a religion.

It follows that "theology" in the specific sense of "Christian theology" means critical reflection on the self-understanding and life-praxis
explicitly mediated by the Christian religion. As such, theology very definitely includes critical reflection on the Christian religion, insofar as
religious praxis is among the several forms of praxis that the Christian
religion mediates. But it also includes critical reflection on everything
else that human beings may think, say, and do insofar as it too is explicitly mediated by the Christian religion. Considering, then, the traditional
terms for self-understanding and life-praxis insofar as they are explicitly
mediated by the Christian religion, one may also say, as I usually do,
that "theology" in the specific sense in which we are using the word
here means critical reflection on Christian faith and witness — or, since
it is only through Christian witness that Christian faith is actually given
for reflection, simply, critical reflection on Christian witness.

A possible objection to this analysis is that it fails to distinguish theology from other forms of critical reflection that may also have Christian
witness as their object, such as religious studies or philosophy. This objection can be met by distinguishing between the object of a form of
reflection and its *constitutive* object, meaning by the second, the object reflection on which is constitutive of the form of reflection as such.
Given this distinction, there is little question that, while other forms of
critical reflection may indeed reflect on Christian witness as their object,
they do not have it as their constitutive object. On the other hand, theology is constituted as such, as the distinct form of critical reflection it
is, by having the Christian witness as the object of its reflection.

Analysis confirms, however, that something else is involved in Christian witness's being the constitutive object of theology as a form of
critical reflection. As a general rule, a form of critical reflection is constituted as such not only or primarily by *what* it reflects on, but also and
first of all by *how* it does so, in the sense of the question or questions it
asks and seeks to answer just as and because it is that form of reflection.
For this reason, a form of critical reflection is always constituted, in the
first place, by some theoretical question or questions; and its constitutive
object is never simply what it reflects on but always what it reflects on
as asked about by its constitutive question or questions.

Theology, in my view, is no exception to this general rule, but an illus-
tration of it. It too is constituted by a certain theoretical question; and

while the constitutive object of its reflection is indeed Christian witness, it is Christian witness only as it appears within the horizon opened up by asking *this* theoretical question.

If we ask now what the constitutive question of theology is, the answer, I hold, is that it is the theoretical question that Christian witness itself, just as and because it is borne, makes not only possible but necessary — and, under certain conditions, urgent. I refer to the twofold question about the validity of the claims made or implied in bearing Christian witness, and hence about the meaning of this witness; and I speak of it as a theoretical question in order to distinguish it from the vital question — specifically, the existential question — to which bearing Christian witness itself is addressed.

In addressing this or any other vital question, one makes or implies certain claims to validity, thereby in effect promising one's companions to validate one's claims critically whenever it becomes necessary to do so in order to remain in communication with them. In this sense, to make or imply any claims to validity is to anticipate both the theoretical question of whether they are, in fact, valid claims and the form of critical reflection constituted by this question. Generally, however, one can ask theoretically about the validity of what is said or done only if one first answers the other, equally theoretical question about its meaning. Consequently, in anticipating the theoretical question of validity, one generally anticipates the twofold theoretical question of validity *and* meaning — or, as we may better say in order to respect the logical priority just indicated, meaning and validity.

Here again, I maintain, theology is adequately understood only as a special case under general rules. Its constitutive question about the meaning of Christian witness and the validity of the claims made or implied in bearing it is simply the twofold theoretical question always already anticipated in bearing Christian witness itself. In this sense, one may say that bearing Christian witness anticipates doing theology as a form of critical reflection, even as doing theology presupposes bearing Christian witness as the constitutive object on which it reflects.

As for the claims to validity that bearing Christian witness makes or implies, and that theology as such is constituted to validate critically, suffice it to say that there are two or three such claims, depending upon how closely one analyzes them. Corresponding to the systematic ambiguity of the word "witness," which refers both to the *what* of witness, in the sense of its expression of its content, either explicitly or by implication, and to the *that* of witness, in the sense of the act of witnessing, the claims made or implied in bearing Christian witness are mainly two: that, as an explication or implication of the content of witness, it is adequate to its content; and that, as an act of witnessing, it is fitting to its situation. Analyzed more closely, however, the first claim, that witness is adequate to its content, proves to comprise two further claims: that it is appropriate to Jesus Christ, or to Jesus as Christians experience him; and that it is credible to human existence as any woman or man experiences it.

Insofar, then, as theology is constituted as such, as a distinct form of critical reflection, by the theoretical question concerning the validity of the claims made or implied in bearing Christian witness, it is constituted to ask: first, about the meaning of Christian witness; second, about the adequacy of Christian witness to its content, and thus about both its appropriateness to Jesus Christ and its credibility to human existence; and third, about the fittingness of Christian witness to the situation in and for which it is borne. In this way the constitution of theology as a single field of critical reflection is *eo ipso* the constitution of the three theological disciplines of historical, systematic, and practical theology respectively — the first being constituted by the theoretical question about the meaning of Christian witness; the second and third, by the theoretical question about its validity, the second asking about its adequacy, the third, about its fittingness. And here too the distinction made earlier between anticipating and presupposing is relevant. Just as, in general, one may say that critical interpretation anticipates critical validation, even as critical validation presupposes critical interpretation, so one may say that in the special case of the theological disciplines, historical theology anticipates systematic and practical theology, even as they, for their part, each presuppose it.

Obviously, much more could be said to clarify the normative concept of theology as I understand it. But I must limit myself to drawing the implications of two distinctions that should already be clear from the foregoing analysis, but that are of particular importance in delimiting my understanding from what I have called "the traditional understanding of theology." I may add that when I speak of "distinction" here, I intend to refer not only to difference, but also to unity, since the terms of the distinction in each case, although definitely not identical, are nonetheless inseparable.

The first such distinction is that between Christian witness, on the one hand, and theology, on the other. The first, as we have seen, is the special case in which human life-praxis, like the self-understanding guiding it, is explicitly mediated by the Christian religion, while the second is the special case in which critical reflection is constituted by the theoretical question about the validity and therefore also the meaning of such life-praxis. Logically, then, doing theology is related to bearing Christian witness as a special case of means being related to end — as a secondary praxis of critical reflection that is intended to serve the primary praxis of leading one's life according to a certain self-understanding. But this implies, in turn, that theology's service to Christian witness, indispens-

able as it is, is always only the *indirect* service that critical reflection and
proper theory are in a position to perform for self-understanding and
life-praxis. Therefore, any attempt to make doing theology serve Christian witness directly, by subjecting it to controls that may be properly
applied to bearing Christian witness but not to it, subverts its proper
service and does away with it as critical reflection, by affirming only its
essential unity with Christian witness, in effect denying their essential
difference.

The other distinction that is particularly important for an adequate
understanding of theology is closely analogous — namely, the distinction between historical theology, on the one hand, and systematic and
practical theology, on the other (see above, pp. 20–35). The first, we
have learned, is the special case in which the critical interpretation presupposed by critical validation is constituted by the theoretical question
about the meaning of Christian witness; while the second are the special
cases in which the critical validation anticipated by critical interpretation is constituted respectively by the theoretical questions about the
adequacy, and so the appropriateness and the credibility of Christian
witness, and by the theoretical question about its fittingness. Logically,
then, doing historical theology is related to doing systematic and practical theology as yet another special case of means being related to end —
as the secondary praxis of critical interpretation that is supposed to serve
the other secondary praxis of critically validating certain claims to validity. But this further implies that historical theology's service to systematic
and practical theology, however indispensable, is also always only the
indirect service that critical interpretation is positioned to perform for
critical validation. Therefore, any attempt to make doing historical theology serve its sister disciplines directly, by subjecting it to controls that
may be properly applied to doing them but not to it, destroys its proper
service and abolishes it as critical interpretation, by affirming only its
essential unity with its sister disciplines, in effect denying its essential
difference from them.

If we ask now, in concluding this first part of the argument, what
conditions a way of construing the Bible would need to meet in order to
be authentically theological, there would appear to be at least two such
necessary conditions. First of all, since theology, although inseparable
from Christian witness, is nonetheless distinct from it in being critical
reflection on it, a way of construing the Bible could be authentically
theological only by being a special case of such critical reflection, as distinct from the life-praxis of bearing Christian witness on which theology
reflects. Then, secondly, since construing the Bible is presumably only
verbally different from interpreting it, a way of construing it could be
authentically theological only by being a special case of interpretation,
which, being also theological, could only be critical interpretation, as

distinct from the critical validation of Christian witness that theology is also constituted to perform. In other words, an authentically theological way of construing the Bible could only be a special case of historical theology, as distinct from both systematic and practical theology — namely, the special case in which the Christian witness whose meaning is to be critically interpreted is the Christian witness of the Bible.

3

This brings us to the second main part of the argument in which my concern is to clarify the other normative concept expressed by my title, "biblical interpretation." The ulterior purpose of this clarification, just as of the preceding clarification of "theology," is to achieve a clear understanding of the third concept, "theological interpretation of the Bible." Moreover, I have emphasized that the understanding of all three concepts that is required to answer our question is theological — more exactly, systematic theological — or, at least, philosophical. But our immediate purpose in this part of the argument is to achieve such an understanding, not of theological interpretation of the Bible specifically as such, but of biblical interpretation in general, and thus of the other more general concept from which "theological interpretation of the Bible" is also derived as a special case.

By the phrase, "biblical interpretation," I mean simply what could just as well be called "interpretation of the Bible," construing the second phrase as an objective genitive referring to the process of understanding, and possibly also explicating, what the Bible means. It is true, of course, that the phrase may also be construed as a subjective genitive, since the Bible, or, at any rate, the writings collected in it, are not only the objects of interpretation, but the subjects of interpretation as well. The New Testament writings, for example, are themselves quite properly understood as interpretations — ways of understanding and explicating the meaning, proximately, of the earlier traditions of Christian witness, oral and/or written, that source and tradition criticism disclose as lying behind them; and remotely, of the event of decisive existential significance of which all of the earlier traditions themselves are already interpretations. In fact, it is precisely because the New Testament writings — and, I take it, the biblical writings generally — are in these or analogous ways subjects of interpretation in their own right, that they have become, in turn, objects of interpretation in the sense in which I understand "biblical interpretation."

To speak simply of "biblical interpretation" in the singular, however, is evidently to speak at a high level of abstraction. This is confirmed by reflecting on what is right and what is wrong in the familiar statement frequently made by theologians as well as other biblical interpreters that the biblical writings should be interpreted in the same way in which we interpret any other writings. What is usually meant by this statement, presumably, is that such status or function as the biblical writings may have as Christian scripture is of no relevance to interpreting their meaning correctly; and with this, as I have said, I, at least, have no reason to argue. But the fact remains that the statement is at best misleading insofar as there is not one way of interpreting writings, including the biblical writings, but only many ways.

One reason for this is that not only different writings, but even the same writing, may be addressed to different questions and may therefore require to be interpreted in different ways oriented by these different questions if they are to be interpreted in accordance with their own intentions as indicated by their grammatical meaning. But another no less important reason is that interpreters of writings, for their part, may be interested in asking any of a number of different questions that may very well orient their interpretations, whatever the questions to which the writings themselves are addressed. What is thus true of interpreting writings generally, however, is equally true of interpreting the biblical writings. Consequently, all that can possibly be meant by "biblical interpretation" is not any single way of interpreting the biblical writings, but only a plurality of such ways, only some of which either are or need to be oriented by the question or questions to which the biblical writings themselves intend to give answer.

Thus, for example, the New Testament writings, being themselves interpretations (of interpretations) of a particular historical event, may be quite properly interpreted as sources for reconstructing this event and other events connected with it. And this is so, even though the prospects of such an interpretation may not be particularly bright because the empirical-historical question orienting it is very different from the existential-historical question to which these writings themselves are addressed in bearing witness to the event. Or again, the interest, and hence the question, orienting an interpretation of the New Testament writings, along with other writings of the early Christian movement, may be those orienting one or the other of the modern social sciences — sociology, say, or anthropology, or even such "critical social sciences" as psychoanalysis and critique of ideology (see Apel 1979). Here too the results of such an interpretation may be more or less limited by the fact that the writings themselves are quite innocent of any such interest and are addressed to a very different question. But the interpretation is still a proper way of interpreting the New Testament writings, even though it is no more the only such way than any number of others, all also proper interpretations.

The same is true, needless to say, of any interpretation of the New Testament writings oriented by the same vital question that they themselves directly address. Being writings that, like the other biblical writings, are rightly taken to be properly religious, they are explicitly addressed to the most vital of our vital questions, which I speak of, following Rudolf Bultmann and others, as "the existential question." By this I mean the question that we human beings seem universally interested in somehow asking and answering, about the meaning of our own existence in its ultimate setting as part of the encompassing whole. Because the New Testament writings, like religious writings generally, are, above all, interested in explicitly answering this existential question, they are quite properly made the objects of existentialist interpretation, which is to say, the way of interpreting writings that is oriented by this same existential question and therefore asks about the possibility of self-understanding, or the understanding of existence, that the writings make explicit as our authentic possibility (see Bultmann 1952a, 211–235; 1952b, 191–195; cf. 1984b, 69–93, 105–110). As a matter of fact, such an existentialist interpretation of the New Testament writings may well be said to be the most appropriate way of interpreting them precisely because it is thus oriented by the same existential question that they themselves intend to answer.

But if the first thing to be said about the concept "biblical interpretation" is that it is, in effect, an abstract variable that has or can have a number of different values, the second thing to be said about it is comparably important. Many and different as they are, interpretations of the biblical writings, as of writings generally, may be conceived as taking place on either or both of the levels of living understandingly that I have already had occasion to distinguish — namely, the primary level of self-understanding and life-praxis; and the secondary level of critical reflection and proper theory.

Any interpretation of the biblical writings on the primary level is already constituted simply by the same vital question that orients it — in the way, for instance, in which existentialist interpretation of the writings on that level is already constituted as well as oriented by the existential question about the meaning of our existence. By contrast, any interpretation of the biblical writings on the secondary level, although also oriented by some vital question, is constituted only by what I have previously referred to as the theoretical question about their meaning — not simply as such, of course, but in one or the other of the many different ways of asking it, depending upon the different vital interests and questions that may move us to do so. Thus, to stay with the same example, existentialist interpretation of the biblical writings on the secondary level, although oriented by the same existential question orienting it on the primary level, is constituted only by the theoretical question about the existential meaning of the writings. It is constituted, in other words, by asking what the biblical writings *really* mean existentially, as distinct from what they may be *said* to mean existentially on the primary level of interpreting them.

Our main interest here, obviously, is in biblical interpretation on the secondary level, since it alone is properly critical and may therefore be presumed to be appropriate to critical biblical scholarship. Our task narrows, then, to asking about the normative concept of *critical* biblical interpretation, keeping in mind that it too can only be an abstract variable, having as its values, not one, but many ways of interpreting the biblical writings critically.

Beyond what has already been said, I want to make two points by way of answering this question. The first is that any critical interpretation of the biblical writings, whatever its way of asking theoretically about their meaning, is like every other in having to follow essentially the same methods of historical- and literary-critical research in determining what the writings say. Regardless of the question that a biblical writing itself addresses, or that different interpreters, for their part, may be interested in putting to it, it is given as such, as a writing, only as something that, in different respects, is both historical and literary. Consequently, what it really means, however one asks about its meaning, cannot be critically determined at all until one first determines critically what it really says by following the appropriate historical- and literary-critical methods for determining this. My first point, then, is substantially Bultmann's, when he insists that among the things that any "scientific," or properly critical, exegesis of the biblical writings necessarily presupposes is not only "a particular way of asking questions" arising out of the interpreter's life-relation to, and preunderstanding of, their subject matter, but also "the method of historical-critical research," or what he elsewhere speaks of as "the old hermeneutical rules of grammatical interpretation, formal analysis [*sc.*, of structure and style], and explanation in terms of contemporary conditions" (Bultmann 1960a, 143–150; 1952a, 231, 212ff.; cf. 1984b, 146–153, 86, 70f.).

The second point can be made by recalling my earlier statement that any way of interpreting the biblical writings critically is constituted as such only by some way of asking the theoretical question about their meaning. The point of this statement in context was to insist that a critical way of interpreting the biblical writings, although oriented by some vital question, is not constituted by it, but only by some way of asking the *theoretical* question of meaning. But the statement may also be read, with only a slight change of emphasis, as making the other no less important point that it is some way of asking the theoretical question of *meaning*, and of meaning alone, that constitutes a way of interpreting the biblical writings as properly critical. In other words, what is ruled out on this reading of the statement is that some way of interpreting the biblical writings critically could possibly require answering on some level the closely related, but logically distinct, question about their *validity*, in the sense of the validity of the claims that they make or imply in addressing the question that they themselves intend to answer.

This insistence that no way of interpreting the biblical writings can be critical without abstracting completely from validating their own claims to validity means that its results must be free from control by anything and anyone other than what is said and meant by the writings themselves. Thus any interpretation of the meaning of a biblical writing whose results are controlled externally by what the interpreter or someone else either believes to be valid or critically validates as being so, cannot be a critical interpretation. Bultmann puts this by saying that, while no exegesis is possible without presuppositions, the one thing that no "scientific," or properly critical, exegesis can presuppose is its results — in the way in which it belongs to an allegorical interpretation, for example, to do (Bultmann 1960a, 142f., 114f.; 1952b, 191; cf. 1984b, 145f., 138, 106). And I could say substantially the same thing in terms previously employed here by saying that as much as a critical interpretation of the biblical writings may indeed anticipate the theoretical *question* about their validity, it cannot anticipate and it may not presuppose any *answer* to this question, any more than it may allow its results to be controlled by what anyone believes to be true or right.

Considering, then, all that has been said to clarify the normative concept of biblical interpretation, we may conclude this second part of the argument also, by recalling the terms of our question and asking, What conditions would a way of construing the Bible have to meet in order to respect the integrity of critical biblical scholarship? Assuming that what it would mean for a way of interpreting the biblical writings to show such respect would be for it to be critical, not in some different sense, but in the same sense in which biblical interpretations otherwise are properly said to be so, we need no longer be in doubt about the answer. The necessary conditions of any interpretation's being critical in this sense are simply the conditions that we have now seen to be implied by the normative concept of critical biblical interpretation.

4

Given now the preceding clarifications of "theology" and "biblical interpretation," the task of this third and final part of my argument is to clarify the derivative concept, "theological interpretation of the Bible." I speak of this concept as derivative because it is derived logically as a special case from the other two concepts, in that to understand both of them is also to understand it. But this means that the understanding of this concept that I shall now set forth, on the assumption that it also is theologically adequate, is likewise derivative, insofar as it is derived

from the understandings already developed of the two more general
concepts that together generate it.

Whatever, exactly, may be meant by the phrase "theological interpretation of the Bible," also construed as an objective genitive, it evidently
refers to a way of understanding, and presumably also explicating, the
meaning of the biblical writings that is, in the terms of our question,
"authentically theological." If we recall, then, the conclusion reached at
the end of the first part of the argument, we may say that theological
interpretation of the Bible is a special case of interpreting the biblical
writings that at the same time is also a special case not only of theology
in general, in the sense of critical reflection on Christian witness, but
also of historical theology in particular, understood as critical interpretation of the meaning of Christian witness, as distinct from the critical
validation of its claims to validity that is the proper business, in their
different ways, of systematic and practical theology. Specifically, it is the
case of such critical interpretation in which the *interpretanda,* the meaning of whose Christian witness is to be understood and explicated, are
the biblical writings. But just what does it mean to say this?

It means, first of all, that theological interpretation of the biblical
writings is a way of understanding and explicating their meaning that
is oriented by the same existential question to which they themselves intend to give answer. I said earlier that theology is constituted, both as a
single field of critical reflection and in its three disciplines, by the theoretical question about the meaning and validity of Christian witness. But
while theology is indeed constituted by this theoretical question, it is so
only by the particular way of asking the question that depends, in turn,
upon the vital question by which it, like the constitutive object of its reflection, is oriented — namely, the existential question. Because this is the
question to which Christian witness itself intends, above all, to give answer, theology as critical reflection on its claims to validity, and therefore
also on its meaning, must be oriented by the same question and is constituted only by the way of asking about its validity and meaning that this
question moves one to ask. But this means, then, that theological interpretation of the biblical writings can only be existentialist interpretation
of them — more exactly, the existentialist interpretation of them constituted respectively by the constitutive questions of theology as a field and
of historical theology as the first of its three disciplines.

However, because the constitutive questions of theology and of historical theology are not merely vital questions, but theoretical questions,
theological interpretation of the biblical writings is existentialist interpretation of them, not just on the primary level of self-understanding
and life-praxis, but on the secondary level of critical reflection and
proper theory. In other words, it is *critical* existentialist interpretation
of them — more exactly, the critical existentialist interpretation of them

constituted by the constitutive questions of theology and of historical theology respectively. This means that while it too is oriented by the same existential question that the biblical writings themselves primarily intend to answer, it is constituted by the theoretical question about what they *really* mean existentially, as distinct from what they may be *said* to mean existentially on the primary level of understanding and explicating their meaning.

Obviously, I can hardly expect my statement that theological interpretation of the biblical writings is such critical existentialist interpretation of them to go unchallenged. But I can try to forestall irrelevant objections, especially any that may arise from too narrow an understanding of what is properly meant by "the existential question" and hence by "existentialist interpretation."

As I explained earlier, I understand the existential question to be the question we all ask as human beings about the meaning of our own existence in its ultimate setting. As such, it has two distinct but inseparable aspects: a metaphysical aspect, in which it asks about the reality of our existence as part of the encompassing whole; and a moral aspect, in which it asks about how we are to understand ourselves realistically in accordance with this reality, and, in this sense, authentically. Therefore, while the existential question is neither the properly metaphysical question nor the properly moral question, it is nevertheless logically related to both questions, and any answer to it implies certain answers to them, even as, conversely, any answer to either of them also implies some answer to it. This means, among other things, that any existentialist interpretation of the biblical writings, oriented, as it must be, by the existential question, not only must allow for, but even requires, both properly metaphysical and properly moral ways of interpreting them.

Nor are these the only ways of interpreting the biblical writings that an existentialist interpretation of them allows for or requires. I have myself sought to show elsewhere that it not only requires a properly moral interpretation of them, but also allows for a specifically political interpretation, notwithstanding that the biblical writings themselves have little, if anything, to say that is directly and explicitly "political" in the sense in which we use the word today (see Ogden 1992b, 95f., 148–168; 1992c, 134–150). There is also the consideration that Bultmann characteristically stresses, that while "genuine interpretation" of the biblical writings is an existentialist interpretation of them oriented by the same existential question to which they themselves are addressed, "other ways of asking questions . . . have a legitimate place in the service of genuine understanding." This is true, for example, of the historical — or, perhaps better, historicist — interpretation of the biblical writings as "sources" for reconstructing a picture of their own age; "[f]or any interpretation necessarily moves in a circle: on the one hand, the individual phenomenon is understandable only in terms of its time and place; on the other hand, it itself first makes its time and place understandable." But Bultmann says much the same also for literary ways of interpreting the biblical writings, such as "formal analysis . . . undertaken from the aesthetic standpoint:" although "to carry out such analysis is not to achieve real understanding," still "it can be prepared for by such analysis" (Bultmann 1952a, 222ff.; cf. 1984b, 78ff.).

By these and other considerations, it can be shown, I believe, that both the existential question and existentialist interpretation can and should be understood rather differently from the way in which they are frequently understood. In any event, if they are understood as I understand them, I am prepared to stand by my statement that theological interpretation of the biblical writings is the critical existentialist interpretation of them constituted remotely by the constitutive question of theology, and proximately by the constitutive question of historical theology.

The crucial point, however, is that this one difference, that theological interpretation of the biblical writings is constituted by the theoretical questions of theology and of historical theology respectively, is its *only* difference from any other critical existentialist interpretation of the biblical writings, however otherwise constituted. In other words, it is in every respect critical existentialist interpretation, not in some different sense of "critical," but in identically the same sense in which any other interpretation of the biblical writings, existentialist or otherwise, is properly said to be so.

Because theology and historical theology are both in their respective ways critical in precisely this sense, since otherwise they neither would nor could be theology at all, as distinct from the Christian witness on which they are the reflection, the existentialist interpretation of the biblical writings that they respectively constitute could not fail to meet the necessary conditions of any interpretation's being properly critical. Thus not only must it be constituted by a properly theoretical, as distinct from a merely vital, question, but it must also rely on the same historical- and literary-critical methods that any other critical interpretation has to rely on in determining what the biblical writings say. But most importantly, it too must abstract completely from validating the claims to validity that the biblical writings make or imply in bearing their Christian witness; and this means that the only control on its results, also, must be what is said and meant by these writings themselves when they are interpreted as answering their own existential question.

Indeed, it is clear that if the critical existentialist interpretation of the biblical writings that is constituted respectively by theology and historical theology were not to meet these conditions, it could no more be said to be "authentically theological" than it could be said to be "critical" in the relevant sense of the word. Only because it is critical in the same sense in which any other critical interpretation may be said to be so, can it perform its proper service as theological interpretation: to understand and explicate correctly the existential meaning of the biblical writings, as the means necessary to the end both of theologically validating their own claims to validity and of making the right use of them in theologically validating the claims of all other Christian witness.

Consequently, I see reason enough to conclude that if theological interpretation of the biblical writings is adequately understood to be just such a critical existentialist interpretation of them, then the only correct answer to our question is affirmative. Because there is at present this way of understanding the normative meaning of "theological interpretation of the Bible," there is also at present a way of construing the Bible that is authentically theological and yet respects the integrity of critical biblical scholarship.

It remains to be determined, of course, whether the understandings of the other concepts from which this understanding has been derived can be critically validated as adequate, theologically as well as philosophically. But if they can, as I, for one, am convinced they can, then the affirmative answer to our question can be not merely conditional or hypothetical, but categorical. In any event, there can be no doubt about the import of the answer, for praxis as well as for theory. Although the answer as such must in the nature of the case be theoretical, it nonetheless has everything to do with praxis: not only the secondary praxis of doing theology and interpreting the Bible theologically, but also the primary praxis that this secondary praxis is intended to serve — namely, bearing Christian witness and interpreting the Bible in bearing it, through the indirect witness of Christian teaching as well as the direct witness of Christian proclamation.

– 4 –

The Service of Theology to the Servant Task of Pastoral Ministry

The general topic of this essay is the pastoral ministry of the church and, more specifically, the servant task of pastoral ministry. But its special topic is the service of theology to the servant task of the church's ministry. Although there is widespread agreement that theology performs an essential service to pastoral ministry, there has long been, and continues to be, considerable disagreement as to just how this service is to be understood and performed. Assuming, then, that the service of theology is also essential to pastoral ministry's servant task, one cannot understand this task itself without understanding how theology properly serves it.

The understanding that is needed, however, calls for a discussion in systematic theology rather than in historical or practical theology. Since one of the things that will have to be done in the course of the essay is to clarify just what it is that distinguishes such discussion, there is no need to go into that here. Suffice it to say that one of the questions that systematic theology has the task of answering is the question about the nature and task of theology itself. Of course, both historical and practical theology have contributions to make toward answering this as much as any other theological question. But to ask, as I propose to do, how theology properly serves the servant task of pastoral ministry, is to ask the kind of question that systematic theology is required to answer.

I. The Scope of the Question

My first task is to clarify the scope of the question, given what I have said is the general topic of the discussion. Such clarification is necessary because both of the terms in which this topic is formulated are ambiguous in that each can be reasonably taken in more than one sense.

Consider, first, "the pastoral ministry of the church," which is doubly ambiguous taken simply in itself. It is ambiguous in one way because it can mean either (1) the general ministry that is constitutive of the visible church and to which, therefore, all Christians are called; or (2) the special ministry that, being constituted by the visible church rather than constitutive of it, is representative of it and to which, therefore, only some Christians are called. But the term is ambiguous in yet another way in that it can mean either (1) the special ministry of the visible church in all of its forms; or (2) one particular form of the special ministry. Thus even when it is taken alone, "the pastoral ministry of the church" has at least three senses that can and should be distinguished — namely, those in which it can mean either (1) the general ministry of the visible church; (2) the special ministry of the visible church in all its forms; or (3) one particular form of special ministry, which I shall refer to hereafter as a specialized ministry.

The other term, "the servant task of pastoral ministry," involves still more ambiguity because of the different things that can also be understood by "the servant task." What lies behind this term, obviously, is the well-known christological distinction according to which the work of Jesus Christ is interpreted in terms of the Old Testament offices of "prophet," "priest," and "king." Depending upon how one construes these terms, one can take them or their cognate adjectives either as designating three tasks of Christ's work or as three metaphors for understanding its one and only task. Applied to the visible church, then, talk of Christ's work as king becomes talk of the church's work as servant, while still allowing for both of these interpretations. Thus "the servant task of pastoral ministry" can mean either (1) one of its tasks among others, properly spoken of as its "servant" task, as distinct from its "priestly" and "prophetic" tasks; or (2) its one and only task understood in terms of the metaphor of "servant" rather than the other biblical metaphors of "priest" and "prophet."

Taking all of these ambiguities into account, we may say that "the servant task of pastoral ministry" has at least six senses, in which it can mean either (1) the one task of the general ministry of the visible church; (2) one among other tasks of the general ministry; (3) the one task of the special ministry of the visible church; (4) one among other tasks of the special ministry; (5) the one task of a specialized ministry of the visible church; or (6) one among other tasks of this specialized ministry. To ask, then, about the service of theology to the servant task of pastoral ministry is to ask a question whose scope covers at least six questions, ranging all the way from the first and most general sense of the terms in which it is formulated to the last and most specific sense of these terms. It will be well to keep this in mind throughout the discussion, since I shall not pursue the question in all the different senses in which it might be pursued. And this is true even though, as I now hope to show, the different senses of the terms can all be seen to be deeply united once the key term "ministry" is understood to have the meaning that properly belongs to it.

2. Ministry as Witness

My proposal for understanding the term "ministry" is that it be interpreted in terms of "witness" and, more exactly, "the act of witnessing."
In making this proposal, I am following up two lines of reflection that
together seem naturally to lead to it.

The first originates in the exegesis of Paul's statement about ministry in 2 Corinthians 5:18f., that God "gave us [*sc.*, each and every
Christian] the ministry of reconciliation." What is striking about this
statement is that it is closely related to, indeed coordinate with, two
other statements that Paul makes in these same verses — namely, that
God "has reconciled us to himself through Christ" and "has established among us the word of reconciliation" (Furnish 1984, 306; see also
Furnish 1977; 1981). Clearly, the two phrases, "the *ministry* of reconciliation" and "the *word* of reconciliation," are to be interpreted in terms
of each other as both referring to the means instituted by God whereby
through Christians the event of reconciliation is again and again made
present or re-presented. Insofar, then, as they are not simply two ways
of saying the same thing, they serve to bring out two distinguishable
moments of the one process of re-presenting this event.

At this point the other line of reflection converges with the first.
It begins with the realization that the term "witness" is systematically
ambiguous in much the same way as the term "tradition" and may
therefore be clarified by a parallel analysis. Just as *traditio* has been
understood to mean both *actus tradendi,* or "the act of traditioning,"
and one or the other of the many *traditiones,* or "traditions," through
which the *traditum trandendum,* or "the tradition being traditioned,"
has been handed on, so "witness" can be understood to mean both the
that of witness, in the sense of the act of witnessing, and the *what* of witness, in the sense of its expression of its content, either explicitly or by
implication (Ebeling 1964, 115–117; Outler 1957, 105–142; cf. above,
pp. 25, 40f.). In the light of this analysis, the thought naturally suggests
itself that it is precisely these two moments of witness that are brought
out by Paul's distinction between "the ministry" and "the word" of reconciliation. In that case, to be guided in one's understanding of ministry
by his statement about it is to interpret it as the act of witnessing, as distinct from expression of the content of witness, which he distinguishes
by speaking of "the word."

Of course, in proposing that we so interpret it, I am as concerned
as Paul that we recognize the interdependence of these two moments
even as we distinguish between them. Just as, in his view, the ministry of
reconciliation both depends on and is in turn depended on by the word
of reconciliation, so, in my view, the same is true of the act of witnessing
and expression of its content. Indeed, one of the gains in interpreting

Paul's statement by the single term "witness" is that the interdependence of these two moments becomes all the more evident.

But there is another thing about the term "witness" that is of the utmost importance to my proposal to use it. It not only allows for, but also requires, the distinction between *explicit* and *implicit* witness. Obviously, the sense of "witness" in this entire discussion is the sense it has as a shorthand expression for "the Christian witness of faith." So understood, it refers simply to the expression of Christian faith through words and deeds that are at once from faith and for faith, in that they both arise out of the self-understanding that is faith and are directed toward evoking the same self-understanding. But just as self-understanding in general necessarily finds expression through the whole of human life-praxis and culture, so the self-understanding of Christian faith cannot but be expressed somehow through all that a Christian thinks, says, and does, secular as well as religious. Even so, there is a difference between the religious and the secular insofar as religion explicitly expresses the self-understanding of faith that everything secular expresses only implicitly. Because of this difference, Christian faith also must always find expression not only explicitly through the Christian religion, but also implicitly through all of the secular forms of life-praxis and culture. This explains why the "witness" in terms of which ministry is to be interpreted can and must be understood as both explicit and implicit witness.

Given this understanding, however, one is in a position to interpret all of the different senses of the terms in which the question is formulated as well as to recognize the profound unity between them. If the one task of ministry in any of its senses is properly understood as the task of witnessing, then by "the servant task of pastoral ministry" in the first, third, and fifth senses previously clarified, is meant just this task of witnessing both explicitly and implicitly as general, special, and specialized ministry respectively. This assumes, of course, that such a task is appropriately understood in terms of the biblical metaphor of "servant." But this assumption is surely warranted if explicit and implicit witness together exhaust the ways of serving God by serving those of whom God has always already become the servant. On the other hand, explicit and implicit witness are different; and there are good reasons for understanding the task of witnessing explicitly in terms of the other metaphors of "priest" and "prophet," leaving "servant" to interpret the task of witnessing implicitly only. In that case, "the servant task of pastoral ministry" would need to be taken in either the second, fourth, or sixth sense of the term and interpreted to mean the task of witnessing implicitly only as either general, special, or specialized ministry.

On this interpretation, "the servant task of pastoral ministry" ranges in meaning between two different but deeply united tasks of witnessing. In its first and most general sense, it means the task of witnessing both explicitly and implicitly that belongs to the general ministry of the church and is therefore the responsibility of each and every Christian. In my view, this is also its foundational sense; for not only does it include both explicit and implicit witness, but it also refers to the most basic level of such witness, which alone is constitutive of the visible church. By contrast, in its sixth and most specific sense, it means the task of witnessing implicitly that belongs only to the special ministry of the church in one of its particular forms, and is therefore the responsibility solely of the relatively few Christians called to such specialized ministry. This, I take it, is the sense illustrated by the specialized ministry usually called "pastoral counseling." In my view, at any rate, such a ministry is specialized not only by being concerned with the particular needs of individual persons, but also by being addressed to such of these needs as cannot be met except by implicit witness.

3. Theology as Critical Reflection on Witness

This brings us to the central task of understanding the other main term in which the question is formulated — namely, "theology." In my judgment, the easiest way to achieve such understanding is to look more closely at the act of witnessing meant by "ministry" in the several senses of the term.

From the standpoint of contemporary philosophical analysis, the act of witnessing is one among a large number of acts that human beings typically perform that are generically described as "speech acts" (see Brümmer 1982, 9–33). Thus it is in important respects like such other more or less different acts as making statements, issuing commands, and making promises. One such respect is the characteristic double structure it involves, of which we already took notice when we distinguished between the act of witnessing and the expression of its content with which it is interdependent (see Habermas 1976, 224f.). Another respect in which it is like other speech acts is that it too may be performed and yet need not be performed by performing a language act, which is to say, an act of uttering certain words. As true as it is that having language enables one to perform the act of witnessing with greater ease and clarity about one's intention than would otherwise be possible, one may nevertheless perform it without uttering any words at all, just as one can issue a command to close the door by waving one's arm, or promise to be faithful to one's spouse by giving a kiss (see Wolterstorff 1969, 11).

Above all, the act of witnessing is like other speech acts in that it expresses or implies certain claims to validity. For our purposes here, it is sufficient to focus on the two validity claims that are specific to witnessing as such.

By virtue of the characteristic double structure it involves, any act of witnessing is both an explication or implication of the content of witness and a performance of the act itself in some particular situation. Correspondingly, any such act expresses or implies the claim to be both adequate to its content and fitting to its situation. For the most part, these two claims to validity are made only implicitly simply by the act of witnessing itself. But in certain special cases, such as the formal definition of what is to count as normative witness, the claims to be adequate to the content of witness as well as fitting to the situation may be made quite explicitly. In either case, the making of the two claims is entirely of a piece with the act of witnessing, since it cannot be performed except by somehow making them.

The difficulty, however, is that both claims may be invalid insofar as any act of witnessing may always fail to be either adequate or fitting. Furthermore, both claims can be rendered problematic in a given case as soon as there is any other act of witnessing either already performed or in prospect that is sufficiently different from the first that the claims of both logically cannot be valid claims. But this, obviously, is just the situation that at least appears to develop, given a plurality of acts of witnessing. On the face of it, then, the validity claims expressed or implied by one such act are rendered problematic by the corresponding claims of another contrary one.

This is particularly clear in the case of the claim that an act of witnessing is adequate to its content. The content of witness that is explicitly formulated in some terms or other is what I call "the constitutive christological assertion," which is classically formulated by confessing that "Jesus is the Christ," and can be formulated today by saying that Jesus is the decisive re-presentation of the meaning of ultimate reality for us (Ogden 1992b, 20–40). In the nature of the case, the claim of any act of witnessing to be adequate to its content is itself a twofold claim: it is the claim, first of all, that the act in question is appropriate to the christological assertion because it either is or agrees with normative Christian witness; and it is the claim, secondly, that the act in question is credible to human existence because it is in agreement with common human experience. But obviously both of these claims are and must be problematic, given the actual plurality of acts of witnessing and the still greater plurality of alternative, non-Christian answers to the existential question about the meaning of ultimate reality for us.

Not only are there contrary acts of witnessing, not all of which can be appropriate to their content, but there is also no agreement among Christians about what is to count as normative witness. While Protestants have traditionally appealed to "scripture alone" against the classic Roman Catholic principle of "scripture and tradition," revisionary believers and theologians in both communions have increasingly looked to the so-called historical Jesus as the real Christian norm. But if this means that no claim to appropriateness can be anything but more or less problematic, the same is even more obviously true of any claim to credibility. Once we recognize, as we must, that Christian witness in all its forms represents but one among a number of different and even contrary faiths and ideologies whereby human beings have sought to bear witness to the meaning of their existence, we cannot deny that the claim of any act of witnessing to be credible is extremely hard to validate. It could not be otherwise, considering that there certainly is no agreement among human beings generally about the criteria of meaning and truth that are given implicitly in common human experience.

There is one further respect in which the act of witnessing is like other speech acts. Once the claims to validity that it necessarily involves have been rendered sufficiently problematic, there is nothing to be done if it is still to be performed except to validate its claims by way of critical reflection. The reason for this is that one cannot express or imply such claims in good faith except by assuming the obligation to validate them as and when they are seriously questioned (see Habermas 1976, 249–255). Consequently, to perform the act of witnessing obligates one to give reasons for its claims to be both adequate to its content, and so credible as well as appropriate, and fitting to its situation. My contention is that what is properly meant by "theology" is either the process or the product of giving such reasons. In this sense, I define "theology" in the context of this discussion as critical reflection on the witness that, in turn, is the meaning of ministry.

Of course, this is not the only sense in which the term "theology" may be understood. If one is guided simply by the literal meaning of the word, "theology" is *logos* about *theos,* and so thought and speech about God. But if "theology" is taken so broadly as to mean *all* thought and speech about God, it is simply another word for what I have been calling "witness," or, more exactly, "expression of the content of witness," as distinct from "the act of witnessing." I readily allow that there is clear precedent in tradition for using "theology" in such a broad sense, and I have no objection to its still being so used. Even so, there is also clear precedent for using the term more strictly, in something like the sense that I have been trying to distinguish. So used, it no longer means all thought and speech about God, but only such as are involved in either the process or the product of critically reflecting on such thought and speech, including the deeds as well as the words through which faith finds expression. In any event, the critical point is the difference in principle between *making* validity claims, as one does in performing the act of witnessing, and *critically reflecting* on such claims, as one does in engaging in what I, at least, take "theology" properly to mean. However this difference may be expressed, it is what has to be understood if what I mean by "the service of theology to the servant task of pastoral ministry" is to make sense. That service, quite simply, is the service of reflecting sufficiently on the validity claims expressed or implied in carrying out this servant task to be able to validate these claims.

Before inquiring further as to the precise character of this service, I want to develop briefly the understanding of theology that I have proposed by making two comments: first, on how it allows for the division of theology into the three main disciplines of historical, systematic, and practical theology; and second, on the account it requires of the relation of theology to the other so-called secular forms of critical reflection.

It will be clear from what has been said that an act of witnessing is constituted as such only by somehow expressing the content of witness on which it depends. Except for its being a particular expression of this content, the act neither would nor could be an act of bearing the Christian witness of faith that I have throughout supposed the term "witness" to mean. This implies, among other things, that no question about the validity of the claim of witness to be fitting to its situation would even arise but for its other claim to be adequate to its content and therefore both appropriate and credible. Accordingly, the one question theology has to ask about witness is the question about the validity of this other claim to adequacy, and hence to appropriateness and credibility. Once this question is asked, the process of theological reflection is under way. On the contrary, until this question is asked, theological reflection has not begun.

At the same time, the question about the validity of the claim of witness to be adequate to its content, and hence appropriate and credible, is not the only question theology must ask. Aside from the fact that any act of witnessing also makes the claim to be fitting to its situation, thereby anticipating the question about the validity of this claim, the claim of witness to be appropriate cannot be validated except by asking yet another theological question. If this claim means, as we have seen, that the witness in question is in agreement with normative Christian witness, it can be established as valid only by first determining what is really meant by normative witness. But since normative witness must be just as much a matter of history as any other Christian witness, what it really means can be determined only by asking a properly historical kind of question.

So it is that the understanding of theology for which I have argued allows for its asking not only the one question about the validity of the claim of witness to be adequate to its content, but also the two further questions about the validity of its claim to be fitting to its situation and about what is really meant by the normative witness by which its claim to be appropriate can alone be validated. But this means, I submit, that this understanding of theology allows for its division into the three main

disciplines of systematic, practical, and historical theology, which have
the responsibilities, respectively, of asking these three questions.

This leads to the second comment about the account this understanding requires of theology's relation to the other secular forms of critical
reflection. The essential point here is that although theology is critical reflection on witness and therefore irreducibly different from every
other form of reflection, it is nonetheless related to these other forms
and dependent on them. Thus historical theology necessarily depends
on historical reflection generally as well as on philosophy and the various special sciences, natural and human, on which history, in turn, is
itself dependent. Likewise, practical theology is essentially dependent on
all the secular forms of reflection on praxis for critically understanding
the particular situation of witness, its possibilities and limitations. So
too, systematic theology necessarily depends on philosophical theology
and philosophy in general in order to validate the claim of witness to be
credible, because it is in agreement with the common human experience
that it is the proper business of philosophy to understand.

In sum: theology can perform its own distinctive service only by depending on the service of these other secular forms of critical reflection.
Moreover, the whole value of their service turns on their being precisely
secular forms of reflection that as such are independent of theology.

4. The Service of Theology as Indirect Service

The point I now wish to make is that there must be an analogous relation in turn between theology, on the one hand, and the servant task
of pastoral ministry, on the other. If theology is properly understood as
critical reflection on witness, it must be, in its own way, independent of
the witness on which it reflects. For this reason, the service of theology
about which we are asking cannot be direct, but only indirect, service.

This contention may scarcely seem controversial as long as "theology" is understood in the excessively narrow sense in which we often
take it. Given the specialization of roles and functions long since institutionalized in modern society and culture, it may seem only natural to
think and speak of theology simply as academic theology, which is to
say, the process of critically reflecting on witness carried on by certain
academic specialists whose expertise at once requires and makes possible
a correspondingly specialized form of higher education. Because academic theology, in this sense, is indeed only indirectly related to the task
of witnessing as it, for its part, is normally institutionalized in our society and culture, the claim that theology's service to this task is indirect
only may seem too obvious to be worth making.

But this is not the sense — at any rate, not the only sense — that I
have allowed to the term "theology." On the contrary, I have proposed

that it be understood essentially simply as the process of critical reflection required to validate the claims of witness to be both adequate to its content and fitting to its situation. Therefore, while I readily agree that this process can and should be carried out at a professional level and in an academic form, I should no more think to restrict it to this form than I should suppose that the specialized form of the special ministry of the church is the only form of pastoral ministry. Indeed, the most basic level of theology, exactly like the most basic level of ministry, is lay rather than professional. It belongs not only to some Christians, but to all Christians to reflect critically on the claims to validity that are expressed or implied by the act of witnessing.

My point, however, is that even at this most basic lay level, the service of theology can only be indirect. Precisely because it is just such critical reflection, not because it happens to be carried on by professionals or academics, it differs in principle from the witness on which it reflects and therefore can serve this witness only indirectly.

But this, clearly, is far from being a noncontroversial point. In fact, today, even as throughout most of Christian history, theology is generally understood and performed as direct service to the task of witnessing. This is evident from the fact that even academic theologians are all but universally expected to be Christian believers and to carry on their reflection within the limits set by normative Christian witness.

To be sure, these expectations do not come to exactly the same thing in the different contexts in which theology may be carried on because, as I noted earlier, there is no agreement among Christians about what is to count as normative witness. If in a traditional Roman Catholic context, it is scripture and tradition, in a traditional Protestant context, it is scripture alone. Correspondingly, the Catholic theologian is typically expected to believe and reflect within the one institutional church whose magisterium alone has the authority to interpret the scriptural witness normatively, while the Protestant theologian is typically expected to believe and reflect within the one visible church that is always more or less visible in all the institutional churches but is never to be identified with any of them. Notwithstanding this important difference, however, theologians in both contexts are evidently expected to perform the same kind of direct service to the task of witnessing.

Nor is it otherwise with theologians who carry on their reflection, not in a traditional, but in a revisionary context, in which the norm of Christian witness is neither scripture and tradition nor scripture alone, but the historical Jesus. However Jesus may be understood in such a context, whether as the moral and religious teacher of an earlier liberal theology or as the more radical figure of contemporary political theology and theology of liberation, theology is understood to be possible at all only on the basis of a prior commitment to Jesus' cause.

There are reasons, naturally, why this way of understanding and performing theology should be so long established and widely shared. No
doubt most academic theologians are, in some sense, Christian believers,
if only because anyone who was not would hardly be motivated sufficiently to assume the task. Moreover, whether or not one has to be a
Christian to do theology, one evidently has to do theology to be a Christian. This is so, at any rate, if every Christian is called to the general
ministry of witnessing and therefore to bearing a witness that is valid
according to its own, at least implicit, claims to validity. For clearly the
only way to validate these claims is by the process of critical reflection
that is properly called theology. Furthermore, it lies in the nature of the
decision of faith to accept the truth of Christian witness and therefore
to believe that any witness that is appropriate because it is in agreement with what is normatively Christian must by that very fact also be
credible because it is in agreement with what is commonly experienced.
Consequently, from the standpoint of Christian believers, there is a certain logic in expecting theologians to carry on their reflection within the
limits set by normative witness. Finally, one ought not to forget the ambiguity of the term "theology," which in one of its senses, as we have
seen, is equivalent simply to "witness." Considering, then, that witness
indeed ought to be performed on the basis of a prior commitment to
what is normatively Christian, one may be easily misled into supposing
that the same is true of the critical reflection on the validity of witness
that is also meant by "theology."

Whatever the reasons for it, however, this conventional alternative
against which I am arguing is open to a fatal objection. To the precise
degree to which it understands and performs theology as direct service
to the act of witnessing, it is forced to deny the essential nature and task
of theology as critical reflection. I do not mean by this, naturally, that
its denial has to be explicit, or that those who opt for it may not continue to think and speak of theology as "critical reflection." My point,
rather, is strictly logical: whatever it may be called, being reflection that
is of direct service to witness just because it is done by believers within
the limits of normative witness precludes theology's also being reflection that is critical only because it does not *assume* the validity of any
of the claims that witness expresses or implies, but rather *questions* the
validity of all of them.

Of course, it is also only logical to recognize that the claim of any
witness to be appropriate can be validated only by testing its agreement
with some witness taken to be normative. But aside from the fact that
given the plurality of positions previously referred to, what is taken as
normative must itself be problematic, whether or not the other claim of
witness to be credible is also a valid claim can never be settled simply by
appealing to normative witness. There always remains the question of

the credibility of normative witness itself; and if believers as such must indeed claim its credibility, the validity of their claim can never be validated by a process of reflection that directly serves their witness and therefore cannot even begin without already assuming its validity.

On the contrary, any process of reflection sufficiently critical to be able to validate this claim, as well as the other claims of witness to be appropriate and fitting, can be of service to it only indirectly. This, if you will, is the price that must always be paid for critical reflection if it is the genuine article. It can validate the claims on which it reflects only insofar as it is sufficiently independent also to invalidate them. Consequently, if theology is properly understood as critical reflection on witness, it must be independent enough to invalidate the claims to validity that witness expresses or implies. But then the only service that theology can possibly perform to the servant task of a ministry whose whole meaning is witness is the indirect service allowed for by this kind of independence.

5. The Theologian as *Servus Servorum Dei*

Indirect as it must be, however, the service of theology to the servant task of pastoral ministry is nonetheless essential, and that precisely because it is indirect. That this is so should be clear enough from what has already been said. But any doubt about it can be removed by simply recalling the meanings we recognized in the term "the servant task."

Applied to the pastoral ministry, this term means either the task of witnessing both explicitly and implicitly at the general or special level or in a specialized form, or else the task of witnessing implicitly only as general, special, or specialized ministry. In either case, the task can be performed only by bearing a valid witness, a witness whose own at least implicit claims to be adequate to its content and fitting to its situation are valid claims. But clearly the only way to validate these claims is by just that process of critical reflection that is properly meant by "theology." It follows, therefore, that the service that theology alone is able to provide is essential to the task of witnessing that is the servant task of pastoral ministry.

It is possible, naturally, that the need for theology's service may be less urgent in some situations than in others. As in the case of other speech acts, the validity claims expressed or implied by the act of witnessing may not have become problematic, or not problematic enough to require moving to the level of critical reflection to validate them (cf. Habermas 1976, 253). In that event, the obligation assumed in making them can be discharged immediately, at the level of performing the act itself, simply by appealing to the standard praxis of ministry and to normative witness or by invoking what is generally accepted as common human experience. As long as these procedures suffice to answer such questions as may arise about whether witness is fitting to its situation or adequate to its content, theology as such may hardly seem necessary and may not be supposed to perform any essential service. But let the situation change enough so that questions persist even after following these procedures, and the need for critical reflection if the act of witnessing is still to be performed becomes only too apparent. At the same time, it becomes evident that the service of theology as alone able to provide such critical reflection is an essential service.

Another variable we need to recognize is that theology's service cannot be exactly the same to all the different tasks of witnessing that may be meant by "the servant task of pastoral ministry." Depending on the different senses in which this term can be understood, theology also must be understood to have a somewhat different task. Thus, for example, in any of the three senses in which it means the task of witnessing implicitly only, theology's service in critically reflecting on the adequacy of witness to its content will need to come primarily from that part of systematic theology that is properly distinguished as "moral theology" because it focuses attention on the expression of faith through action, secular as well as religious. Or, again, the service of theology as practical theology cannot be simply the same when it reflects on the fittingness of witness to its situation at the two levels of the general and the special ministry. But having recognized these, as well as such other differences as may be relevant, we may still be confident that the service of theology is, after all, one. Because for all their differences the different tasks of witnessing are deeply united, theology's service to each of them is the same essential service of validating their claims to be valid and thus to perform the servant task of pastoral ministry.

This all assumes, of course, that theology, in fact, provides this service of critical validation. But to avoid any misunderstanding, I should acknowledge that not everything that is called "theology" may actually go toward validating the claims of witness to be both adequate and fitting. Here too theology is like other forms of critical reflection in that it may always go wrong not only in one direction, but in two. Not only may it be made to serve the task of witnessing directly, thereby ceasing to be critical reflection in more than name only, but it may also become so remotely related to what is really at stake in witnessing as no longer to have much, if anything, to do with validating the claims to validity that are thereby expressed or implied.

For various reasons, this second way of going wrong is particularly likely in the case of professional theology, especially when it is pursued in an academic, as distinct from an ecclesial, context. Given the high degree of specialization, not only of academic theology itself, but also of the other secular forms of reflection on which it depends, much of the work routinely done by theological specialists may have little, if anything, to do with validating the claims of witness. Moreover, academic theology is like any other highly developed field of reflection in generating its own inertias, which over time may make for a considerable gap between the theological questions being pursued by theologians in the academy and those that are most urgent to both lay and professional ministers, as well as to other professional theologians who pursue their reflection in the church. But there is another, still more fundamental reason why not only professional theology, but lay theology as well, may no longer be essential to the task of witnessing. Before one can validate any claim to validity, one has to analyze accurately the kind of claim it actually is. Consequently, there is always a risk in any process of critical reflection, including theology, that one will confuse the claim one is supposed to validate with some other, logically different kind of claim. But in that event, all that one may proceed to do by way of giving reasons for or against the claim will be simply irrelevant to validating it.

No one acquainted with the modern history of theology will be a stranger to this confusion. But for it, the long and still continuing conflicts between religion and science and faith and history could never have arisen. The lesson to be learned from these conflicts, however, is once again that not everything that passes for theology is properly that — whether because it is not really critical reflection or, as in this case, because it is critical reflection on something other than the claims to validity expressed or implied by the Christian witness. On the contrary, wherever theology really is critical reflection, and critical reflection on precisely these claims, the service it performs to the task of bearing this witness could not be more essential.

Recognizing this, I do not hesitate to speak of the theologian as "servant of the servants of God." From at least the time of Gregory the Great, this title has been applied to the office of the Pope as primate of the universal church; and an appropriate title it is, considering the saying of Jesus in the gospels that "whoever wants to be first must be last of all and servant of all" (Mk 9:35). It is applied just as appropriately, however, to any other office of special ministry, if one holds, as I do, that the whole point of any such office is in one way or another to be of service to the servants of God who constitute the general ministry of the church. But if the argument of this essay is sound, the title is just as appropriate for the office of the theologian, whether lay, professional, or academic. Although in this case the service to God's servants is but the indirect service of critical reflection, it alone can make good their claims to fulfill their servant task.

– 5 –

Christian Theology
and Theological Education

I

This essay is a response to Joseph Hough and John Cobb's *Christian Identity and Theological Education* (1985). More exactly, it offers an interpretation and evaluation of the argument of this book from the perspective of what I take to be the proper question of Christian systematic theology.

Pending subsequent discussion of the nature of Christian theology, suffice it to say here only this. If, in general, historical studies ask about what human beings have thought, said, and done in all situations already past, while practical studies ask about what human beings are to think, say, and do in some situation still future, systematic studies ask what human beings would be justified in thinking, saying, and doing in this or any other situation of the present, whatever may have happened in the past or ought to happen in the future. Assuming, then, that Christian systematic theology is a systematic study in this very general sense, one may say that the question it properly asks about theological education, just as about anything else, is the question proper to it as this kind of study. It is not the historical question about what has already been thought, said, and done about theological education, nor is it the practical question about what ought still to be thought, said, and done about theological education in the upcoming future; it is, rather, the systematic question about what it would be right to think, say, and do about theological education here and now in this present, even as in any other present in which such thinking, saying, or doing might be required.

That Hough and Cobb's argument is in significant part addressed to this systematic question seems reason enough to try to interpret and evaluate it as I propose to do. On the other hand, I fully recognize that this question is not the only or even the primary question that their book addresses. Aside from what they have to say to the historical question about theological education, much of their argument is addressed to the practical question about it; and precisely this part is what they themselves evidently take to be primary when they state the eminently practical purpose of the book: "to make realistic proposals for revising theological curricula appropriate to the Christian faith in the present situation" (Hough and Cobb 1985, vii). There is every good reason, then, why their proposals should be considered, above all, from the perspective of the proper question of Christian practical theology, although I must leave it to others to pursue this and other questions that can and should be pursued in an adequate discussion of the book.

To avoid any misunderstanding, I would add two further comments. The first pertains to what I have said or implied about the differences between the questions proper to Christian systematic, and to Christian practical theology, respectively. As real and important as these differences seem to me to be, I in no way suppose that there are not also close relations between the two questions that are equally real and important. On the contrary, I assume that there is one such relation that has to be taken into account in defining the proper scope of this essay — namely, that the question about the proper question of Christian practical theology is itself a question proper to systematic theology. I assume, in other words, that it is Christian systematic theology that properly asks what we would be justified in thinking, saying, and doing in this or any other present situation about Christian theology in general, as well as about Christian historical, systematic, and practical theology in particular. But this means that all that Hough and Cobb have to say systematically, either about theology and any of its disciplines or about the theological education cognate therewith, falls within, not outside of, the scope of the systematic question that I shall be pursuing.

The second comment has to do with what is and is not meant by the statements I have made about Christian systematic theology's properly asking what it would be right to think, say, and do about theology or theological education not only in this, but also in any other present situation. The possibility of misunderstanding here arises from a possible confusion of the situation *in* which systematic theology asks its proper question with the situation, or the aspect of the situation, *about* which it asks its question. Certainly, from my standpoint, nothing is more obvious about human existence than its thoroughgoing historicity. Everything about it is historically conditioned and situationally located relative to some particular society and culture with distinctive links to the past and peculiar possibilities for the future. But then the same is true of all the questions that human beings ask, whatever the nature of the questions and regardless of the level at which they ask them. In this respect, any pursuit of the proper question of Christian systematic theology, including this one, can take place only in some present situation to which it is and remains relative both in defining the question and in formulating any possible answer. But fully recognizing this is in no way inconsistent with saying, as I have said, that what Christian systematic theology properly asks about is nothing peculiar to this or any other present situation, but something that one would be justified in thinking, saying, and doing in any situation whatever, no matter what else one might have reason to think, say, and do. Consequently, to maintain that Christian systematic theology has this distinctively different relation to the situation on which it reflects need not mean, and, so far as I am concerned, emphatically does not mean, that it is not every bit as relative to the situation in which it reflects as either of the other theological disciplines or any other form of human reflection.

2

I turn now to the first of my two tasks: an interpretation of the systematic understanding of theological education for which — or, at any rate, from which — Hough and Cobb argue. The point of the qualification is simply to underscore what has already been acknowledged — namely, that the controlling purpose of their book is not systematic but practical. Accordingly, if one takes "arguing" to mean not simply developing a certain line of thought, but building a case so as to validate a certain thesis, then one could quite reasonably say, I think, that Hough and Cobb's systematic understanding of theological education is more what they argue from than what they argue for.

Be this as it may, the question is what they mean systematically by "theological education." Not surprisingly, they have nothing to say directly about the generic concept "education" taken simply by itself. Judging from what they say or imply about theological education in particular, we are no doubt safe in assuming that they take education in general pretty much in the conventional sense as the act or process of teaching and/or learning knowledge or skill. If we stick close to their explicit statements, however, the place to begin in answering our question is the distinction they make between two senses of the more specific concept.

The first is what they call the "basic sense" of "theological education," which they define simply as "the education of all Christians in the faith." Such education, they hold, "is the right and need of every Christian," even as "it is the responsibility of the entire church." But this basic sense of the term is to be distinguished from another sense because within the context of the church's general education of all of its members in the Christian faith — what Hough and Cobb speak of as "this encompassing theological education" — it has made special provisions for the preparation of its leaders. In this second sense, "theological education," as they understand it, means "the special education appropriate to church leaders" (4f.).

Their further elaboration of this distinction is by way of a critical discussion with Edward Farley's account in his book *Theologia* (1983), in developing which they in part follow the lead of Friedrich Schleiermacher. With Farley, they agree that it is indeed in *theologia*, rightly understood, that theological education in the first and basic sense has "its basis and unity," in fact, that *theologia* is "the basis of unity of *all* theological education." At the same time, they question whether Farley's understanding of *theologia* is correct. For one thing, his account of it, being overwhelmingly concerned with method, is "too abstract and formal to provide guidance for theological education." What is wanted, they argue, is not merely "a particular way of approaching the understanding of faith," but rather "the faith itself," or, as they otherwise put it, "the understanding of faith." They also find reason to doubt whether the understanding of faith that Farley's method would be likely to yield would connect doctrine closely enough to practice to be sufficiently informed by consciousness of the global context of Christian existence to be an adequate understanding. Consequently, in endorsing his claim that the renewal of theological education requires "the recovery of *theologia*," they make clear that for them this means "the clarification of Christian identity as the basis for Christian practice," or, as they also put it rather more broadly, "reflective understanding, shared by members of a Christian community regarding who they are and what they are to do given their concrete world-historical situation" (3ff., 18).

Since this is the kind of clarification or understanding that is rightly taken to be *theologia*, it is the basis of unity of all theological education, special no less than basic. But unlike Farley, Hough and Cobb do not infer from this that the special education proper to church leaders needs nothing else to unify it. On the contrary, they follow Schleiermacher in arguing that the unity of such special education, insofar as it is distinct from theological education in the basic sense, is "teleological," in that it "is constituted by the aim to help educate professional leaders for the church." Although *theologia* is as essential to it as to basic theological education — in fact, Hough and Cobb hold, "leaders require an especially full and reliable understanding of *theologia*" — its distinctive difference as special theological education derives from its primary purpose to educate professional church leadership (4f.).

The question now is whether this is the only ground of its difference from basic theological education. That the answer is not entirely clear is due in part, certainly, to Hough and Cobb's primary interest in special theological education, and in the primarily practical rather than merely systematic nature of their interest. Just as this explains why they pay no direct attention to the generic concept of education, so it also explains why they do not do much more than I have already indicated in developing the basic sense of "theological education." But there is a further reason insofar as they define the scope of *theologia* more narrowly in some contexts than in others. Thus, as I already noted, it sometimes

seems to be restricted to a clarification of Christian identity as the basis for Christian practice, while at other times it is extended to cover
a reflective understanding by Christians not only of who they are, but
also of what they are to do, and even that quite concretely, as specified
to their given world-historical situation. Because of this indefiniteness as
to the scope of the term, there remains some question whether or not
the special theological education appropriate to church leaders includes
anything beyond *theologia*, except whatever necessarily follows from its
being constituted as special by the aim to help educate such leaders (5).

There are a couple of passages, however, that I take to clarify how
Hough and Cobb intend to account for the difference between basic
and special theological education. Arguing in one of them that practical theology as they eventually define it — as including both "practical
thinking" and "reflective practice" — is "especially needed by professional leaders," they nonetheless allow that "the practical Christian
thinking which it signifies is important for all Christians and [that] the
distinctiveness of professionals is only that they have special responsibility to help others in this thinking." This means, I take it, that whether
the scope of *theologia* is defined more narrowly or is defined broadly
enough to include practical Christian thinking, education in such thinking properly belongs to theological education in the basic sense in which
it is the right and need of every Christian just as much as it belongs to
special education for church leaders. To be sure, Hough and Cobb go on
to say that the other component of practical theology, reflective practice,
"is a particular responsibility of the professional" and that, since they
have "somewhat arbitrarily" defined the practical theologian as "one
whose reflective practice is primarily in the church," this second component "does distinguish the professional church leader from most other
equally faithful Christians." But they do not say even this without further allowing that "many church members will be called on to engage in
reflective practice in their own professions," even though "the extent to
which they should be expected to be involved in reflective practice with
respect to their roles in the church must be limited" (91f.). Moreover, as
they explain in another passage, what they mean by "practice" is "every
Christian's practice of Christian vocation. The vocation of church leaders is the same as that of all Christians, namely, to live as Christians in
their vocational settings. The only difference is that church professionals
exercise their special calling within the church" (84). But if this really is
the only difference, then not only other Christian professionals, but all
Christians whatever, each being alike specially called to practice in some
vocational setting, have the need for and the right to theological education in some kind of reflective practice and practical Christian thinking
as well as, or as already included in, *theologia*.

In my interpretation, then, the only reason Hough and Cobb give for the distinctive difference of special theological education from basic is that it is united by the aim to educate leaders for the church and therefore necessarily includes instruction and training in the more specialized kind of practical Christian thinking and reflective practice required of such leaders. But if this is the only ground of difference, special theological education differs from basic, not as a different kind of education, but as a special case of the same kind. In the special case, just as in general, it is education of Christians in the faith, or, more exactly, in the understanding of faith and in the thinking involved in practicing it, both "thinking *about* practice" and "thinking *in* practice" (90). Any difference in the special case derives solely from its proper aim to educate Christians who are specially called to practice their faith as leaders of the church, and thus to lead their fellow Christians in understanding and practicing the same faith.

Before proceeding to an evaluation, I want to make two further points about Hough and Cobb's concept of theological education.

The first has to do with the considerable importance they give to Christians' understanding the world as the context of their lives. Given the primarily practical interest of their book and their concern, accordingly, with the particular situation in which Christians are now called to live, they understandably speak of "the global context," indeed, of "the global context of threatened catastrophe" (106). The systematic insight here, I judge, is that the understanding of faith and the thinking in faith to which all theological education is ordered, necessarily include an understanding of the world in and for which faith is to be lived. Because Christians as such are concerned with "the indivisible salvation of the whole world," they cannot adequately understand their own identity as Christians or rightly think about the practice to which it commits them without understanding their concrete situation in the world from the perspective of their Christian identity and thinking about its implications for their commitment to Christian practice (102). If Hough and Cobb insist, therefore, that developing such understanding is integral to special theological education of church leaders, then, again, this is not because understanding the context of their lives does not belong to the theological education of all Christians, but only because it is of particular importance to those who bear special responsibility for leading the church in understanding its mission and carrying it out.

The second point concerns the kind of understanding and thinking with which Hough and Cobb take theological education to have to do. If it is correct to say that they recognize only one kind of theological education of which the education of church leaders is a special case, the reason they do so, presumably, is that they see all theological education as developing only one kind of understanding and thinking. In fact, they see it developing the kind of understanding and thinking that

are immediately involved in any Christian's self-understanding and life-
praxis — or, in the terms they generally use, "identity" and "practice."
This means, I assume, that while all theological education is of Christians by Christians, the questions to which it is addressed are universally
human. They are the questions typically asked in one way or another by
any human being about who she or he authentically is and then, given
some answer to this question, about what she or he is now to think, say,
and do in order to be and remain her- or himself.

Of course, this need not mean that theological education is the only
way in which these questions of self-understanding and life-praxis are
addressed in the Christian community. Hough and Cobb are quite clear,
indeed, that the worship of the church has a fundamental role to play in
the formation of Christian identity and of the commitment to Christian
practice (see, e.g., 74ff., 114ff.). Furthermore, when they express their
position more exactly, they represent theological education as such as
education in "the understanding of faith," as distinct from "the faith
itself," and thus as developing an understanding of Christian identity, as
distinct from Christian identity, and the thinking involved in Christian
practice, whether thinking *about* it or thinking *in* it, as distinct from
such practice itself (4, 84, 90). Even so, they leave no room to doubt that
the understanding and thinking that theological education directly serves
are sufficiently of a piece with Christian identity and practice themselves
to be only inadequately distinguishable from them.

Thus they tell us that even in the special case of theological education
for church leaders, the purpose of historical courses in Bible and church
history is "forming identity" (108).* In the same vein, they fully accept
"the seminary's responsibility for the Christian formation of students"
and raise questions about adding special courses on Christian discipleship only because they prefer "to have the commitment to discipleship
structure the entire curriculum" (114, 116). Finally, I may mention their
judgment about the kind of faculty who are wanted to teach in theology and ethics in theological seminaries. Because "the major task" of
these disciplines "is to encourage students to think globally as Christians
about the issues of the day,... the need in the seminary is for practical Christian thinkers.... [W]e need faculty who will reflect on these
questions as Christians" (105f.).

3

Extended as it is, this interpretation is far from having considered all
that Hough and Cobb have to say systematically about theological ed-

---

*The text as printed reads "identifying formation," but the authors have confirmed my
reading of what they mean to say.

ucation. But it is time now for me to evaluate their argument on the assumption that I have correctly understood their answer to the systematic question. In doing so, I shall also continue to assume my own understanding of this question as the perspective for my evaluation, although I hope that as the discussion proceeds, this understanding will become increasingly explicit.

I want to begin by stating three things that I judge to be essentially sound in Hough and Cobb's understanding of theological education, together with the reasons for my judgment.

First of all, they seem to me to be entirely justified in holding that what they call "theological education" in the first or "basic" sense is the right and need of every Christian and the responsibility of the whole church. Clearly, to be a Christian at all, one must have some understanding of Christian identity and be somehow engaged in thinking about Christian practice. But just as clearly, anyone who is a Christian both needs and has the right to be educated in such understanding and thinking, even while sharing the responsibility to provide education in them for all of her or his fellow Christians.

Second, Hough and Cobb have good reason for claiming that "the special education" that they understand to be appropriate to church leaders is exactly that. If to be a leader of the church is to bear special responsibility for helping one's fellow Christians in understanding their Christian identity and in thinking about their Christian practice, essential to one's preparation for leadership is special education in just such understanding and thinking. No less essential, however, is special education in how to think both *about* and *in* one's own special practice as a leader of the church.

Third, Hough and Cobb are quite right in assuming that anything that could be properly called "theological education" must in some way be of service to the kind of understanding and thinking that are immediately involved in Christian self-understanding and life-praxis. However theological education is to be understood, it evidently exists to serve Christians both in their general calling as Christians and in the special calling of some of them as leaders of the church. But it seems clear that theological education can perform this service only by somehow developing the understanding and thinking that are constitutive both of Christian existence as such and, in a special form, of church leadership.

If this much all seems to me to be basically sound, however, there is one fundamental point where I must give a contrary evaluation. This is Hough and Cobb's further assumption that what they call "theological education" is what is properly so called. In my judgment, there are good reasons for thinking this assumption to be mistaken; and in the remainder of my response I wish to explain these reasons as fully as limits allow.

The basic issue here is what is properly meant by the term "Christian theology." To get at this issue, I recall Hough and Cobb's statement both in the Preface and at the conclusion that the book itself is an example of the practical theology that it recommends (viii, 130). Faced with the problem arising out of their own Christian practice as theological educators of how to educate the church's leaders, they have undertaken to think about their practice precisely as Christians, on the basis of an understanding of their identity and with an awareness of the global context of their work. In doing this, however, as the book itself makes clear, they either express or imply certain distinctive claims to validity. They claim, for one thing, that the statements they make are true or credible, in the sense of being worthy of belief. But then they further claim that their understanding of Christian identity and of its implications for practice is appropriate, in that it faithfully recalls the memories that constitute Christian identity. Finally, they also claim that the proposals they make are fitting to the situation in and for which they make them.

They are not unaware, naturally, that their claims are problematic. Not only do they regard a quest for total agreement as hopeless, but they also allow that Christians have sometimes distorted their identity instead of faithfully preserving it (4, 27f.). In fact, they are expressly critical of the church in North America because it is currently in danger of losing its identity by conforming to "expectations established for it by a bourgeois society that stems from the Enlightenment" (93).

But what is to be learned from this about practical theology as they understand and practice it? It seems to me two things are to be learned. In the first place, like any other case of the kind of understanding and thinking that are immediately involved in Christian self-understanding and life-praxis, it necessarily makes or implies the distinctive claims to validity to which I have drawn attention; that is, it claims to be credible and appropriate as well as fitting. But then, in the second place, it is perforce practiced in a situation in which other Christians, themselves also understanding and thinking *as* Christians, either have made or are in prospect of making identically the same validity claims for different and even contrary ways of understanding and thinking about Christian identity and practice.

To take these two lessons seriously, however, is to realize that there is both the possibility and the necessity — if not, indeed, the urgency — of yet another kind of understanding and thinking than that represented by what Hough and Cobb call "practical theology." It is the kind, namely, that is only mediately or indirectly involved in Christian self-understanding and life-praxis because it has immediately and directly to do, not with making or implying these claims to validity, but with critically validating them.

My contention is that it is this other kind of understanding and thinking, which the practical theology of Hough and Cobb's book it-self makes both possible and necessary, that is properly called "Christian theology." But, then, as I understand theological education, it properly has to do with developing *this* kind of understanding and thinking — or, better, this is what it *directly* develops, since it thereby performs an indispensable service in also developing *indirectly* the understanding and thinking that are immediately involved both in Christian existence and in leadership of the church (see above, pp. 52–65).

In support of this alternative way of deciding the basic issue, one may appeal to the fact that the word "theology" and its cognates are not exclusively used in the broad sense in which Hough and Cobb use them. That they are commonly so used is obvious enough. Just as the term in general is often meant in its literal sense of thought and speech about God without any further restriction, so it is frequently used in a Christian context to cover all that Christians think, say, and do about God in understanding who they are and in thinking about what they are to do. Correspondingly, "theological education" can be used as broadly as it is by Hough and Cobb, so that it is equivalent, in effect, to "Christian education." On the other hand, as ordinary speakers commonly use these terms, they are not strictly equivalent: Christian education is one thing; theological education, something else. One reason for this is that the word "theology" has long since come to have a stricter, more proper sense, meaning not all thought and speech about God, but only some of it — namely, such as functions in reflecting more or less critically on all of it. Thus, in the specific sense of "Christian theology," what is often meant is just such critical reflection on all specifically Christian thinking and speaking, even as in the corresponding sense of "theological education," the term refers to the act or process of developing this kind of critical reflection.

But if these considerations remove any ground in the ordinary use of terms for objecting to my alternative, they scarcely do anything more. This is clear from the fact that any number of theologians today could readily agree that Christian theology in the strict and proper sense refers, not to the "first act" of Christian faith itself, but to a "second act" of critical reflection in relation to faith. For many, if not most, of those who share in this consensus, however, theology's relation to faith is not simple but complex, because it is not only, as they say, a reflection *on* faith, but also a reflection *in* faith. Insofar as it is critical, then, it neither is nor can be critical of faith itself, in the sense of critically validating the claim to truth or credibility that any understanding of Christian faith makes or implies. At least this validity claim must be privileged and exempted from critical reflection; and it is a fair question whether this must not also be true of the other claim to appropriateness that is made or implied by some particular understanding of faith, but for also privileging which reflection *in* faith would be empty of any specifically Christian meaning. In any case, if this is all that is meant by "critical reflection," then Hough and Cobb's practical theology is certainly "critical." But so far as I am concerned, any reflection on faith that must be in this sense a reflection *in* faith, including their practical theology, is not properly critical reflection at all, because it is not a matter of critically validating claims to validity, but only of making or implying them.

In the final analysis, then, the question is not whether we may properly use the term "theology" and its cognates in a strict as well as a broad sense; the question is what we are to mean as and when we so use them. Are we to mean only such "critical reflection" as is possible to Christians understanding and thinking *as* Christians? Or are we to mean the critical reflection that is necessary if Christians' claims to truth or credibility, not to mention appropriateness and fittingness, are themselves to be critically validated? However one answers this question, two things, at least, must be taken into account.

First of all, anything less than the second, more radical kind of reflection cannot be fully appropriate to the kind of understanding and thinking that are immediately involved in Christian self-understanding and life-praxis. As I have already pointed out, all such understanding and thinking necessarily make or imply the same three claims to validity that are evident in Hough and Cobb's own practical theology. Thus, by its very logic, any instance of Christian witness, as I should prefer to call the expression of this understanding and thinking, makes or implies the claims to be credible, appropriate, and fitting in the general senses previously explained. One may confidently say this, at any rate, assuming that any analysis of the meaning of Christian witness as wholly noncognitive is seriously defective. Provided that the truth claims that Christians certainly appear to make or imply in bearing their witness are, in some respect at least, really that, there is no good reason to doubt that the "depth grammar" of their witness has the essential threefold structure that I have suggested. But this means that no critical reflection on Christian witness can be fully appropriate to the logical structure of such witness that exempts its claims to credibility from critical validation. On the contrary, to insist that theology in the strict sense includes critically validating this, as well as the other claims distinctive of Christian witness, is simply to take this witness at its word in thinking out what critical reflection would have to be in order to be fully appropriate to it.

The second thing that must be taken into account is what critical reflection has come to mean given contemporary historical consciousness and the experience of radical pluralism. In societies and cultures that for long periods are relatively stable and more or less isolated from significantly different social and cultural patterns, the validity of claims to truth as fundamental as religious claims typically are is not likely to seem in need of critical validation. Although the claims in fact *are* problematic — no less so, indeed, than any other human claims — the underlying plausibility structures are sufficiently intact and unchallenged that the claims are not experienced *as* problematic. But in a situation such as ours has now become, marked by rapid social and cultural change and encompassing a plurality of societies and cultures striking in their differences, there is a heightened consciousness of the historicity and the relativity of all social and cultural forms, including those of religion. In this sort of situation, religious claims to truth are likely to seem even more problematic than most others, and at least as problematic as they actually are. Consequently, the felt need for the critical validation of these claims if they are to be accepted as valid is acute enough that no reflection on the validity of the Christian witness can credibly claim to be fully critical that exempts its claim to truth or credibility from such validation. On the other hand, to hold that theology in the strict sense critically validates all the claims of Christian witness, including its claim to be credible, is simply to take seriously our own situation in determining what theological reflection has to be if its claim to be fully critical is still to be accepted as credible in this situation.

But if this is what is properly meant by "Christian theology" in the strict sense of the words, there is no mistaking the difference between it, on the one hand, and all forms of Christian witness, on the other. Making or implying claims to validity is one thing, critically validating such claims, something else. And this is true even if the concepts and terms in which the two functions are performed are not different but the same. However similar their conceptual and terminological forms, there remains, in Charles Wood's phrase, "a functional distinction" between, on the one hand, actually bearing Christian witness with its several claims to be appropriate, credible, and fitting and, on the other hand, critically reflecting on this witness so as to validate these several claims (Wood 1985, 24f.). By the same token, the theological education cognate with Christian theology thus understood is also different from all forms of Christian education, including what Hough and Cobb call "theological education." Instead of directly serving Christian witness and the understanding and thinking that it expresses, such education serves them only indirectly by directly serving the understanding and thinking that are necessary if their distinctive claims to validity are to be critically validated.

This is not in the least to say, however, that theological education is not the right and need of every Christian and the responsibility of the whole church. On the contrary, precisely in being called to bear witness to the truth as it is in Jesus in and for the world, each Christian is also at least implicitly called to engage in critical reflection on the validity of her or his own witness and of the witness of the church as a whole. Consequently, she or he has the right and need to be educated not only in the Christian faith and life, but also in the critical reflection on Christian witness that can alone make good its claims to validity. At the same time, each Christian shares in the church's common responsibility to provide for the properly theological education and formation of all of its members, even as for their properly Christian education and formation.

On the other hand, there is a difference between this basic or, as I call it, "lay" level of theological education and the advanced or "professional" level of such education that is appropriate to those whose special calling is to leadership of the church. Just as all who are so called need an especially full and reliable *Christian* education, so they also need an especially full and reliable *theological* education — in the strict sense of being specifically instructed and trained in the knowledge and skills necessary to critically interpreting and validating the church's witness. As a matter of fact, next to their identity or self-understanding as Christians and their commitment to Christian practice, there is no more important requirement of professional church leaders than such strictly theological knowledge and skill. For if not the very heart of church leadership, then certainly its very mind, is a fully developed capacity for self-criticism and the disposition to practice it such as only theological education and formation at a relatively advanced level can provide.

To say this, however, is not to imply, as Hough and Cobb do, that the only goal of advanced or professional theological education is to prepare leaders of the church. In my understanding, advanced theological education also has the goal of preparing leaders of the academy, in the sense of persons sufficiently instructed and trained to conduct the process of critical theological reflection itself as well as the process of formal teaching and learning that such reflection makes both possible and necessary. Thus I find it appropriate to distinguish between two related but distinct forms of professional theology: the ecclesial or generalized form that it typically takes in the case of those whose special calling is to leadership of the church; and the academic or specialized form that it typically assumes in the case of those who are specifically called to leadership of the academy. As for the different kind of reflection *in* practice that each of these forms requires, I accept Hough and Cobb's own principle that education in it must be a joint task of the theological school or seminary *and* the institution in which the practice is located, which in the case of academic theology must be the academy, even as in the case of ecclesial theology it can only be the church (Hough and Cobb 1985, 95, 127).

There remains, finally, the whole matter of the theological disciplines and what is to become of them as they are presently understood and practiced. Without going into details, let me say simply that just as

Christian theology as such is rightly understood as critical reflection on Christian witness with its distinctive claims to validity, so the particular disciplines of theology are correctly understood as playing distinct but interrelated roles in critically interpreting Christian witness and critically validating its claims. In my view, this means that one can and should distinguish between the three main disciplines of practical, systematic, and historical theology. Practical theology asks and answers the question as to the validity of the claim of witness to be fitting to its situation. Systematic theology, including what is sometimes distinguished as moral theology, inquires as to the validity of witness's claim to be adequate to its content because it is both appropriate to Jesus Christ and credible to human existence. In conducting this inquiry, systematic theology is perforce dependent, in somewhat different ways, on both historical theology, including biblical theology, and philosophical theology. But whereas philosophical theology is properly conceived as an independent secular discipline, historical theology integrally belongs to Christian theology itself, because the Christian witness on which it reflects is historically given and the only conceivable norm for the appropriateness of this witness is the normative witness of the Christian community, which is likewise accessible only to historical inquiry. So far as the future of the theological disciplines is concerned, my difference from Hough and Cobb's proposals is sharp and clear. What is called for, as I see it, is not the transformation of the theological disciplines into so-called practical theology, but, on the contrary, the transformation of the so-called theological disciplines into appropriate forms of fully critical reflection such as have just been defined (cf. Ogden 1992c, 1–21, 69–93, 94–101; Wood 1985, 37–55).

Early in their argument, Hough and Cobb affirm that "what is needed today as a basis for reforming theological education is a strong conviction about who we are as a Christian people" (Hough and Cobb 1985, 4). I have argued, alternatively, that what is needed is rather a clear understanding of what Christian theology is as critical reflection on the validity of Christian witness. However the issue between these arguments is to be decided, it is evidently a fundamental issue that anything less than just such critical reflection will not be able to decide.

– 6 –

Theology in the University

The Question of Integrity

It is not too much to say that the fate of professional theology in the modern world is very much tied up with theology's being typically located in the university. Whereas in the ancient world a theologian was generally a bishop, and in the medieval world, usually a monk; in the modern world, since the Reformation and the Counter-Reformation of the sixteenth century, a theologian has typically been a university professor.

Of course, even much academic theology has continued to be done outside the university in freestanding schools and seminaries all through the modern period right up to the present. But somewhat as even rural areas in an urban society such as ours are, in their way, urban in culture, so even nonuniversity schools of theology have generally been importantly determined in their culture by university theology. One indication of this in recent North American theological education is that the faculties of nonuniversity schools of theology are commonly appointed from persons whose graduate study in theology has been done in universities.

In the course of the modern period, however, universities themselves have undergone fundamental change — from the pattern established by the great medieval universities, in which theology not only had an integral place but was also, as the phrase went, "queen of the sciences," to the so-called secular universities of today, where theology is either completely excluded or else enjoys only residual status, its place, relative to other fields and disciplines, being at best ambiguous, doubtful, and insecure. Of a piece with this change is that modern universities have become increasingly self-conscious about their autonomy as academic institutions and about the freedom that properly belongs to their members, especially the relatively permanent members that make up their faculties. In this connection, individual faculty and the professoriate collectively have also become more and more professionalized, particularly with the establishment of organizations like the American Association of University Professors (to which I shall refer hereafter as the AAUP).

The upshot of all this is that in North America, at least, it is now universally held within the academic community that institutional autonomy and academic freedom define the university. Indeed, already well before the founding of the AAUP in 1915, William Rainey Harper, president of the newly formed University of Chicago, argued that

> When for any reason, in a university on private foundation or in a university supported by public money, the administration of the institution or the instruction in any one of its departments is changed by an influence from without, when an effort is made to dislodge an officer or a professor because the political sentiment or the religious sentiment of the majority has undergone a change, at that moment the institution has ceased to be a university, and it cannot again take its place in the rank of universities so long as there continues to exist to any appreciable extent the factor of coercion. . . . Individuals or the state or the church may found schools for propagating certain special kinds of instruction, but such schools are not universities, and may not be so denominated. (quoted in AAUP Report 1988, 54*)

Considering that this understanding of the nature of the university has become ever more widely accepted in North American higher education, we should not be surprised that even church-related universities now commonly understand themselves accordingly. This had become clear already a generation ago from the well-known typology employed in a report of the Danforth Commission on Church Colleges and Universities (Pattillo and Mackenzie 1965, 66–69; cf. AAUP Report 1988, 53f.). According to this typology, church-related institutions of higher learning tend to fall along a spectrum defined on one end by the "defender of the faith" type of institution and on the other end by the "non-affirming" type. Institutions of the first type seek to entrench their students in a particular religious position and therefore limit their autonomy and academic freedom accordingly. Institutions of the second type, by contrast, are so lacking in any explicit religious commitment as not only to enjoy unlimited academic freedom and autonomy, but also to be barely distinguishable from secular colleges and universities. Distinct from both of these more extreme types, however, is the "free Christian (or Jewish)" type of institution, which, while it is explicitly confessional in its commitment, understands its autonomy as an institution and the academic freedom of its members to be indispensable to its proper service to the faith it confesses. Its distinctive mission or vocation precisely as a church- (or synagogue-) related institution is to be a fully free and autonomous university or college. If many Protestant institutions have long since conformed to this third, intermediate type, it

---

*For reasons that are made clear below, I am indebted to this report throughout the essay and owe a special debt to the work of Matthew W. Finkin, who not only drafted the report but also did the historical research lying behind it.

is significant that even Roman Catholic universities and colleges have increasingly come to understand themselves in the same way ever since the
1960s and the changes in Roman Catholic theory and praxis sanctioned
by the Second Vatican Council.

In the course of these changes in the self-understanding of the university, however, the place of theology has become increasingly uncertain.
Given the usual way of understanding and practicing it, as thinking and
speaking performed in direct service of the church and its witness, theology has been typically viewed as not being really of the university, even
if it happens to be in the university. Here, at least, the principles of institutional autonomy and academic freedom that are now understood to
define the university can no longer apply and must, in the nature of the
case, be suspended. This is so even if it is recognized only tacitly, rather
than openly, under the guise of a tendentious redefinition of what such
autonomy and freedom are supposed to allow.

Significantly, even the AAUP has developed principles and policies
that have at least appeared to allow for certain exceptions to its otherwise strict insistence on academic freedom and institutional autonomy as
definitive of the university. Thus, in its 1940 *Statement of Principles on
Academic Freedom and Tenure,* which is still binding, there occurs what
has come to be referred to as "the 'limitations' clause." According to this
clause, "Limitations of academic freedom because of religious or other
aims of the institution should be clearly stated in writing at the time of
the appointment." Developments during the 1970s and 1980s, however,
finally forced the AAUP to reexamine this clause so as to determine exactly how it should be understood and applied. The developments to
which I refer are the growing number of cases involving church-related
institutions in which issues of academic freedom have once again arisen,
and which have therefore come before Committee A, the AAUP's instru-
ment for investigating and disposing of all such cases. Often enough, as
it happens, these cases have directly or indirectly raised the question of
theology in the university.

Recognizing this, the members of Committee A, meeting in June
1987, authorized appointment of a four-member subcommittee, including theologians, to review the whole matter of the limitations clause and
its recent application to particular cases, and then to report back to the
committee. As it turned out, I was the Protestant theologian who was
asked to serve on this subcommittee, the Roman Catholic theologian being my friend and former colleague at the University of Chicago, David
Tracy. Our final report was approved for publication by Committee A at
its meeting in June 1988 and published in the September–October 1988
issue of *Academe,* together with some critical reactions and an invitation to readers generally to submit additional comments. There is no
need here to say anything about the procedure we followed in conduct-

ing our review or about the course of our deliberations in arriving at the substance of our report. It will be sufficient to summarize its two main conclusions, which are directly relevant to the theme of this essay.

We concluded, first of all, that when the limitations clause is interpreted, as it should be, in the context out of which it was formulated and in relation to the long history of discussion of which it was a part, its purpose is not what it has often been supposed to be both by institutions invoking it and by Committee A in applying it to particular cases. Thus, for example, in the early 1960s, a Roman Catholic institution, Gonzaga University in Spokane, Washington, had permitted the termination of appointments of faculty members upon the commission of a "grave offense against Catholic doctrine or morality." The AAUP committee investigating the case observed in its 1965 report that the 1940 *Statement of Principles* recognized "the propriety of limitations, suitably indicated, on academic freedom because of the religious aims of the institution," although the committee was critical of the lack of specific guidance that had been provided by the institution's statement of this particular limitation. Whereupon Gonzaga University, exercising, as it claimed, "its right under the 1940 *Statement*" to specify the limitation more exactly, revised its faculty handbook to include the following statement: "Intelligent analysis and discussion of Catholic dogma and official pronouncements of the Holy See on issues of faith and morals is encouraged. However, open espousal of viewpoints which contradict explicit principles of Catholic faith and morals is opposed to the specified aims of the University." With this, the investigating committee declined any further critical comment, although it did go on to criticize other portions of the handbook in some detail (AAUP Report 1988, 53).

The same understanding of the purpose of the limitations clause was emphasized in the 1967 AAUP report of a Special Committee on Academic Freedom in Church-Related Colleges and Universities. Although this report rightly recognized that the clause has to be understood in its context and against its historical background, it went on to allow that "[a]t some point in the scale of self-imposed restrictions a college or university that comes under them may, of course, cease to be an institution of higher education according to the prevailing conception." Having thus introduced the notion of a scale of restrictions, some of which are, but others of which are not, inconsistent with the idea of an academic institution, the report went on to observe that some of its later statements further defined the "area of acceptable restriction." It then supplied guidelines for demarcating this area of acceptability, saying that any limitation or restriction must be "essential" to the religious aims of the institution (AAUP Report 1988, 52f.).

As a result of our close review of the context and history of the limitations clause, we became convinced, and argued in our report, that, contrary to this understanding, it in no way intends to legitimate or render acceptable restrictions on academic freedom, provided only that they are essential to "the religious or other aims" of the institution. Crucial for our alternative understanding was a gloss on the history of the discussion given by Committee A in its report for 1939, at a time when negotiations for the 1940 *Statement of Principles* were all but concluded:

> There are a few institutions of the proprietary or sectarian type which carefully specify in advance that which is to be affirmed and taught concerning certain subjects and which pledge in writing members of their faculties to uphold by precept and example the points thus made clear. The present officers of this Association have felt that such institutions were free thus to restrict members of their faculties and have wasted little time or sympathy on complainants who, having thus definitely pledge [*sic*] themselves by formal contract, have later wished both to retain their appointments and to recover the freedom we seek to defend for other teachers and scholars. The difficulty is not with the few institutions which are thus frank and precise in their agreements, but with those which covet for themselves classification with the freer colleges and universities and yet would impose upon members of their faculties an obligation to conform to certain of the beliefs and practices of the administrative officials of the institution or of the supporting organization. To repeat, this Association would not deny to a group which desires to do so the right to support an institution for propagating its views. It merely insists that such an institution ought not to be represented to the public as a college or university for the promotion of the liberal arts and sciences, in which scholars and teachers are free to seek and impart truth in all of its aspects. Furthermore, such an institution ought to be careful to stipulate in advance of employment the particulars in which it insists that members of its staff adhere to prescribed doctrines and practices. Otherwise, it must be assumed that a member of its staff is free to engage in the normal activities of a teacher and scholar. (quoted in AAUP Report 1988, 54)

In the light of this and other clear indications to the same effect, we concluded that the AAUP's position at the time of the 1940 *Statement of Principles* and its limitations clause rested on the same presuppositions contained in its founding *Declaration of Principles:* (1) that any institution has the uncontested right to impose or accept limitations upon its own autonomy and the academic freedom of its members; but (2) that any institution exercising this right thereby forfeits any moral right to proclaim itself an authentic seat of higher learning and assumes the moral responsibility of publicly declaring itself the proprietary institution it in fact is, including stipulating in advance the limitations it places on academic freedom (AAUP Report 1988, 54f.).

The second of our two conclusions had to do with "professional education," and, specifically, theological education, in the university. Contrary to the prevailing view that theology, at least, can only be an exception to the principles of academic freedom and institutional autonomy, we concluded that theology's right to be in the university depends on its being in fact of the university, and therefore bound by essentially the same principles binding on any other field or discipline, department or school.

> [T]here is no principled basis to distinguish professional clerical education from professional education generally.... A school of law endowed by its creators to train students as *laissez-faire* or Marxist lawyers, and measuring its faculty against a requirement of faithfulness to the doctrines thus set down, has every right to exist, but it has no right to class itself as a seat of legal learning on a par with free institutions. Neither would a school of law with commitments to religious orthodoxy. To the same effect, if theology is an academic discipline, it must be treated as any other discipline. Higher education is not catechesis, and this is no less true for professional clerical education than for any other professional calling. (AAUP Report 1988, 55)

But is any wrong done by allowing an unfree school of theology a place in an otherwise free university? Such is the last question raised in the second section of our report, and this is how we answered it:

> [I]t is difficult to maintain that an entire university forfeits its status simply by housing a component that requires creedal orthodoxy as a consequence of its singular religious mission. But a wrong it is. It is a wrong to the individual scholars so constrained, who are denied the liberty of inquiry and expression ostensibly afforded their colleagues in other disciplines, and who, if their later inquiries lead them to fall afoul of consecrated authority, must forfeit their posts. It is a wrong done to colleagues in other disciplines, who may never be secure that their academic freedom will indeed be insulated, for the power to muzzle, once permitted within a university, may prove difficult to constrain — especially given shifts in denominational doctrine and leadership. Consequently, it is a wrong done to the institution, for it must labor under a cloud of suspicion that the teachings and writings of its faculty may not be truly free. In sum, the housing of an unfree school within a free university is a contradiction: it may be *in* the university but, be-

ing unfree, it is not *of* the university, and it has no business being there. (AAUP Report 1988, 55f.)

I am well aware that this second conclusion, like the first, reflects nothing more than the thinking of a four-member subcommittee, and that while our report was subsequently approved for publication by Committee A, it still had to be critically received and possibly amended by the professoriate generally, including, presumably, the theologians belonging thereto. But whether, or with whatever refinements and amendments, it eventually becomes AAUP policy, I do not have the least doubt that the understanding it expresses of theology's right to a place in the university is the understanding that is bound to prevail — if, indeed, it does not already prevail — throughout the academic community. Sooner or later it will be clear to all that what is at stake in theology's presence in the university is the integrity of the university. Either theology is an academic field or discipline essentially like every other and therefore bound by the same principles of academic freedom and institutional autonomy; or else, being a restriction on these principles, or an exception to them, theology has no moral right to be reckoned on a par with the other academic fields and disciplines and is therefore not an integral part of the university.

In point of fact, however, theology continues to be generally understood and practiced in the churches and even by many, if not most, academic theologians, in such a way that its right to a place in the university is anything but secure. That this is so is made particularly clear by the recent and well-publicized case arising from Professor Charles E. Curran's being denied the right to continue to teach Roman Catholic theology at the Catholic University of America. Because this was one of several such cases that our subcommittee had to consider, I had already studied it in some detail before being appointed to the AAUP committee responsible for investigating the case. By the time this further responsibility was discharged, however, I had occasion to read the statements by Professor Curran and his counsel that sought to explain and justify his position against that taken by Catholic University and its chancellor. The crux of his defense is that the only Church teaching that he ever questioned or dissented from in his own teaching and scholarship as a theologian falls into the category of noninfallible teaching. In other words, at no point had he ever questioned or dissented from the infallible teaching of scripture and dogma as interpreted by the teaching office of the Church. What is striking about this defense, however, is its clear implication that if Professor Curran had ever dissented from, or even questioned, such infallible teaching, his right to teach at Catholic University would have been forfeited and could have been legitimately denied him — provided, at least, that this would have been the finding of his scholarly peers proceeding in accordance with academic due process. In short, at the crucial point of principle, Professor Curran's understanding and practice of theology was no different from that of the Cardinal Archbishop of Washington, who, acting *ex officio* as chancellor of the university, had initiated the proceedings to withdraw his canonical mission as a Roman Catholic theologian. But it is just this understanding and practice, accepted by theologian and chancellor alike, that our subcommittee found to be incompatible with the academic freedom and institutional autonomy definitive of the university.

The same point becomes clear in another recent case involving Southeastern Baptist Theological Seminary in Wake Forest, North Carolina. Like any number of other institutions related to the Southern Baptist Convention, Southeastern Baptist had come under the control of a new board of trustees, most of whose members belonged to the extreme fundamentalist majority then dominating the convention. As a result of this development, the faculty at Southeastern Baptist organized themselves into a chapter of the AAUP and entered the complaint that because their trustees had now denied their proper role in the appointment and promotion of faculty and had subjected them to new doctrinal restrictions, their academic freedom as well as the autonomy of their institution had been violated. But without questioning that there were, indeed, serious violations of academic freedom and due process in this case, and that the trustees of the seminary clearly did change the rules on persons already appointed to the faculty, I am most struck by the fact that even before the fundamentalist takeover, the so-called academic freedom of the faculty and the autonomy of the institution had been severely compromised by restrictions in the form of required subscription to stated articles of faith. In other words, from the standpoint of the second conclusion in our subcommittee report, Southeastern Baptist Theological Seminary and its faculty had never enjoyed real institutional autonomy and academic freedom to begin with. Of course, being a freestanding seminary, it is not located in a university. On the other hand, the action of its faculty and their appeal to the principles of academic freedom and institutional autonomy provide a good example of the point I made earlier, that even nonuniversity schools of theology have come to be increasingly determined by the culture of the university and of the academic theology done within it.

Obviously, there are complexities even in such relatively clear-cut cases as these that call for a more nuanced treatment than I have given them here. But I am satisfied that even if all the relevant complexities were taken into account, the bottom line would not be significantly different. It is simply a fact that as theology is still widely understood and practiced, not only in the churches, but by academic theologians themselves, it remains an undertaking that cannot be an academic field or

discipline on a par with every other in the strict and proper sense of
the words. Far from being subject to the same academic freedom and
institutional autonomy by which the university as such is now defined,
theology is, in fact, a restriction on, or an exception to, such freedom
and autonomy.

Of course, apologists for the usual understanding and practice of
theology frequently argue that academic freedom and institutional autonomy are, in effect, analogical concepts that have somewhat different
meanings in different contexts, or as applied to different academic fields
or disciplines. Indeed, these apologists reason, such freedom and autonomy are never absolute, because they are always subject to certain
limitations. No scholar-teacher is free to ignore the overriding obligation to tell the truth, and the autonomy of any academic institution is
circumscribed by the well-being of such other communities as it exists
to serve. But then if we reject, as we must, unlimited freedom and autonomy, we must also realize that our concepts of them in fact have a
range of meanings depending upon particular context and application.
We are then in a position to recognize that what these concepts mean as
applied to the church-related institution and to the theologian-scholar-
teacher need not be simply the same as in any of their other applications.
On the contrary, the institution's autonomy in such a case allows for its
freely acknowledging church authority, and the academic freedom of the
theologian may very well include fidelity to, and respect for, the teaching
office of the church.

The objection to this argument, however, is that it is a futile attempt
to have it both ways. Even if one grants that institutional autonomy and
academic freedom are never absolute and that they may, indeed, have
a range of meanings, still, what they are supposed to allow cannot be
redefined beyond certain definite limits. If an institution yields to church
authority in any properly academic decision or proceeding, it thereby
forfeits its autonomy as an academic institution. If a theologian's fidelity
to, or respect for, the teaching office of the church in any way limits
what she or he can teach or publish as a proper conclusion of theological
inquiry, then her or his academic freedom consists in nothing but the
words. The prevalence of such argument, however, is clear evidence of
the situation in which we find ourselves, thanks to the way in which
theology for the most part continues to be understood and practiced in
both the church and the academy.

My conviction is that this situation is particularly unfortunate because there is good reason to believe that the conventional understanding and practice of theology that create it are as unnecessary as they are
problematic. Through the efforts of a number of theologians working
out of different ecclesial traditions and cultural contexts, there has already emerged a clear alternative, from which it follows that theology

need not be in any way a restriction on, or an exception to, academic freedom and institutional autonomy, but may be every bit as subject to them as any other field or discipline rightly claiming a place in the university (see, e.g., Küng and Tracy 1989; Wood 1985; 1994; Griffin and Hough 1991).

The key to this alternative understanding and practice is to distinguish clearly and sharply, although without in any way allowing a separation, between Christian faith and witness, on the one hand, and Christian theology, on the other. The basis for this distinction is that, in general, it is one thing to make or imply claims to validity by means of our various thoughts, acts, and statements; while it is another, very different, though also closely related, thing to reflect on our claims critically to see whether or not they are really valid. Thus Christians can believe and bear witness to their faith only by making or implying several such claims to validity, to the effect that their witness is not only fitting to its situation, but also adequate to its content, and therefore both appropriate to Jesus Christ and credible to human existence. But in the pluralistic circumstances in which they typically bear their witness and thus make or imply these claims, the question naturally arises as to whether or not the claims are valid. It is simply a fact that some or all of the same claims to validity are made or implied by others, Christians and non-Christians, for contrary forms of faith and witness. Thus the very act of bearing Christian witness establishes both the possibility and the necessity of a certain form of critical reflection whose task is to validate (or invalidate) the several claims to validity that that act either makes or implies. If one holds, then, as those arguing for the alternative understanding and practice of theology typically do, that it is just this form of critical reflection that is properly meant by the phrase "Christian theology," one is free to understand and practice Christian theology consistently and without qualification as simply another form of the same critical reflection that takes form in some way or other in any academic field or discipline.

This is so, at any rate, if one assumes, as I do, that the whole point of any such field or discipline, whether in the humanities and sciences or in the various professional areas (engineering, law, business, medicine, and so forth), is somehow to advance essentially the same process of critical reflection in a deliberate, methodical, and reasoned way — that is, by so reflecting on the claims to validity made or implied in some area of life-praxis as to validate (or invalidate) them. My contention is that when Christian theology is understood and practiced as it should be, it is not just another way of bearing Christian witness that is rightly subject to the teaching office of the church, but rather a distinct form of essentially the same process of critical reflection embodied in one way or another in all the other academic fields and disciplines.

This means, of course, that theology's service to the church and its witness, while both real and important, can never be direct, but must always be indirect, in essentially the same way in which all of the other forms of critical reflection can be of only indirect service to the other areas of life-praxis that they exist to serve. It could not possibly be otherwise if theology is, in fact, a genuine form of critical reflection. For no form of reflection can be really critical unless it is free not only to validate the claims to validity on which it reflects, but also to invalidate them. But this qualification implies that its service to the particular area of life-praxis that it exists to serve can only be indirect. Therefore, theological reflection also can be genuinely critical only if its service to Christian witness is always indirect and it remains free to invalidate all claims of witness, even when they are made or implied by the teaching office of the church. This point explains, in turn, why the principles of academic freedom and institutional autonomy must apply as fully to theology as to every other field or discipline in the university. If the whole point of theology is to reflect critically on the validity claims made or implied by Christian witness, it must be fully subject to these principles and so in no way a restriction on, or an exception to them.

It is not my purpose in this essay, however, to develop and defend further this alternative understanding and practice of theology for which I have argued elsewhere (in the preceding essays as well as, especially, in Ogden 1992c). My purpose here, as indicated by my subtitle, is simply to clarify the question of integrity that is raised by theology's continuing to be present in the university.

I could not accomplish even this, however, without making one final point. Clearly, theology's being in the university raises the question of the university's integrity as an academic institution that is fully free and autonomous. But no less clearly, in my view, it also raises the question of the integrity of theology itself. Whatever else is to be learned from the long history of Christian theology, one thing seems certain: it is always wrong for theology simply to adjust its claims (including, not least, such claims as it may make about itself) to the understanding and practice of the world around it. This means in the present case that how theology is to be understood and practiced can never be responsibly determined simply by theology's looking to the modern university and the principles by which it is defined. On the contrary, theology must also look to its own essential nature as Christian theology, fully realizing that it is at least possible that those who continue to defend the conventional understanding and practice of theology are right: it cannot be understood and practiced in accordance with its own nature unless it is recognized openly or tacitly to be a restriction on, or an exception to, the defining principles of academic freedom and institutional autonomy. I do not hesitate to say that if such persons prove to be right, I, for one, would feel obliged to give up my alternative understanding and practice, even though, in my case, this would mean giving up theology altogether as no longer a defensible undertaking.

Obviously, this is not what I and a number of other theologians expect finally to come of our efforts. But I trust that the point I am making is clear: if the only theology that could be of the university as well as in it would be Christian theology in name only, then the question of integrity — of theology's integrity as well as the university's — would not really have been answered after all.

Part II

Theology and Christology

– 7 –

Concerning Belief in God

I

In our society and culture, the traditional and still predominant form of religious belief is theistic — specifically, the monotheistic religious belief of Judaism and Christianity as well as of classical Hellenism. This form of religious belief is constituted explicitly as such by the foundational belief in the reality of God. Consequently, for any of us who have been socialized and acculturated into our society and culture, whether into its traditional forms or into one or the other of their more or less radical revisions, the most important question concerning religious belief is almost certain to be the question concerning belief in God. Because all the other religious beliefs and practices in our social and cultural context presuppose an answer to this question, one must be concerned with it, above all, if one is to engage seriously in religious inquiry of the sort that I propose to pursue in this essay.

I stress that my concern is with belief in God from the standpoint of religious inquiry, because this is not the only standpoint from which one may find oneself concerned with such belief. Belief in God is also a proper object, not only of the inquiries constitutive respectively of philosophy and metaphysics, but also of the inquiries necessarily pursued by such human sciences as psychology, sociology, and anthropology, as well as by history. Even so, my concern here is not as a philosopher or metaphysician, much less as a human scientist or historian, but as a theologian and student of religion — both of whom engage, in somewhat different ways, in what may be properly distinguished as religious inquiry.

Of course, I have no intention of separating the present inquiry as religious from any of the other inquiries from whose standpoint belief in God is also in some way a proper object of study. As a matter of fact, I shall be explaining in due course why religious inquiry concerning belief in God necessarily implies both philosophical and metaphysical inquiries concerning the same belief. But contrary to David Hume's famous dictum that any things that can be distinguished can also be separated, it is possible — and in some cases necessary — to distinguish things without separating them. And so we may, and even must, distinguish the present inquiry as properly religious, without thereby separating it from any of the other inquiries that in their own ways are also properly concerned with belief in God.

Before explaining further what I understand by religious inquiry and what can be said about belief in God from its standpoint, I want to comment briefly on why such belief typically becomes a question for us. To grow up in our society and culture, I have said, is in one form or another to internalize its traditional religious beliefs, including, above all, the belief in God that is constitutive of the radically monotheistic religions of Judaism and Christianity. In the case of those of us who have been raised in church or synagogue, this internalization is most likely to have taken the form of a positive acceptance of a more or less traditional belief in God, while in the case of others of us, this internalization may very well have taken the form of a negative rejection of traditional belief in God because of a positive acceptance of some more or less radically revisionary ultimate belief. But in either case, continuation in the process of maturing involves being confronted with questions about the truth of our religious beliefs. Although none of us could live humanly at all without being socialized and acculturated, and thus internalizing in some form or other the beliefs of some human group, none of us can become a truly mature human being without critically appropriating our inheritance of beliefs once the question of their truth is raised in our minds. To try to repress this question once it has arisen is to live dishonestly or insincerely, whatever our particular beliefs.

The question of truth is bound to arise, however, as soon as we recognize, as we must, that all our religious beliefs are controversial, and that this is so in several different respects, or at several different levels: as between different traditions or movements within religions (e.g., Reform, Conservative, and Orthodox in the case of Judaism, or Protestant, Roman Catholic, and Orthodox in the case of Christianity); as between different theistic religions (e.g., Judaism, Christianity, and Islam); as between theistic religions and nontheistic religions (e.g., the three monotheistic religions just mentioned and, say, Theravada Buddhism or Zen); and, finally, as between religious and nonreligious ultimate beliefs (e.g., any of the religious beliefs previously referred to and the ultimate beliefs, say, of Marxism, or scientism, or some other form of modern secularistic humanism). As a matter of fact, a different but no less important kind of controversy is evident today in all of the major religious traditions. I refer to the often embittered controversies between traditionalist interpretations of the traditions and their more or less revisionary reformulations — such as, for example, the controversy in the contemporary Christian community between those who still interpret the Christian life as simply a matter of moral responsibility within the given social and cultural order and those who see the tasks of Christian love as including the specifically political task of transforming the structures of society and culture so as to overcome existing oppression and achieve greater justice.

Whatever the kind or level of controversy, there is nothing to be done by any of us who wish to become mature persons in our religious beliefs once the question about their truth has arisen than to try to find a reasonable answer to this question. This requires us to engage in what I mean by "religious inquiry," by joining with any and all others who are similarly moved in a cooperative search for truth in which the only constraint, just as in any other serious inquiry, is the constraint of the evidence and the better argument. Such inquiry is likely to occupy us to some extent all our days, even if, as we may hope, it will not take too long to find sufficient reason either to reaffirm our inherited beliefs or else to affirm some alternative beliefs, so that we may identify ourselves religiously in something like the same way in which we grow up otherwise by identifying ourselves morally, politically, aesthetically, and so on.

2

If we ask now about the question of the truth of belief in God, analysis discloses that it is essentially two questions — distinct and yet closely related: (1) What, properly, is to be understood by the term "God"? (or How is God properly conceived?); and (2) Is there sufficient reason to believe that when the term "God" is properly understood it applies to something real? (or Does God properly conceived also exist?). Obviously, it is the second of these questions that we are most likely to have in mind when we speak of the question of belief in God. But it is hardly less obvious that any answer to the second question depends on some answer to the first. As a matter of fact, not only does the question whether God exists depend for its answer upon how God is conceived, but the same is true of any answer to the crucial procedural question of the modes of reasoning or kinds of argument that are, and are not, appropriate to answering the question of God's reality. There are the very best of reasons, then, why we should take some pains in pursuing the first of our two questions concerning belief in God.

I trust it will seem reasonable, in the light of my opening comments about the traditional and still predominant form of religious belief in our society and culture, if I appeal to the foundational belief of traditional Jewish and Christian monotheisms in responding to our first question as to how the term "God" is properly understood, or how God is properly conceived. There can be no serious question that the term "God" is primarily a religious term, since it is first employed by religion, and its religious use always remains its primary use, however it may also come to be used in philosophy or metaphysics. Consequently, it is always to religion that we must finally appeal if we wish to understand the proper use of the term; and for reasons that should now be clear, this means that in our context it is to the foundational belief of Judaism and Christianity that we must look for an answer to our first question.

The difficulty, of course, is that this belief has been formulated over the centuries in both of these religious traditions in widely different ways; and therefore it cannot be simply identified with any of its formulations, but can be retrieved only by critically interpreting all of them. Without minimizing this difficulty, I believe one can argue — although I shall not develop the argument here — that Jewish and Christian monotheisms are constituted by essentially the same use of the term "God," and that this use suggests that the concept of God as it figures in both of these religions involves a certain characteristic duality or tension.

On the one hand, God is conceived in both religions to be a distinct individual who enters into genuine interactions with others — both acting on them and, in turn, being acted on by them. On the other hand, God is conceived in both religions to be strictly universal, in the sense that anything that is so much as even possible has its primal source and its final end in God. Thus if God is an individual, God is the *universal* individual, the one individual with strictly universal functions, whose action on others is an action on *all* others and on whom, in turn, *all* others somehow act or make a difference. Similarly, if God is universal, God is the only *individual* universal, the one universal that functions individually, not only by acting on all other things, but also by interacting with them, and thus also being acted on by them.

If it be objected that this concept of God that I find expressed in Jewish and Christian monotheisms is really an ideal type, I should readily agree that it has rarely if ever been expressed in such a way as to bring both of its essential aspects to clear and coherent expression. In the more religious and often mythological formulations of these monotheisms, the individual aspect — or the aspect of God as an individual — so predominates as to call into question the universal aspect — or the aspect of God as universal. On the other hand, there is something like the reverse difficulty in the more philosophical or metaphysical formulations of Jewish and Christian monotheisms, where the emphasis upon God as universal obscures or contradicts the aspect of God as an individual. In other words, there are two main ways of going wrong in thinking and speaking about the God conceived by these radically monotheistic religions, and both of these ways are illustrated many times over by the history of Judaism and Christianity. I could also express this by saying that the history of these two religions exhibits the possibility of two main types of intellectual idolatry: a *concrete* type, according to which God is thought and spoken of as an individual without taking sufficient account of God's universality; and an *abstract* type, according to which God is thought and spoken of as universal without doing justice to God's individuality (cf. Hartshorne 1970c).

But if God is properly conceived only as the universal individual, or the individual universal, more or less adequately attested in Jewish and Christian religious belief and practice, certain consequences follow that are of the utmost importance for answering the question concerning belief in God. On the one hand, it follows that an answer to this question is by no means entirely dependent on the fate of classical Jewish and Christian theisms at the hands of modern and postmodern criticism. There seems little doubt that the more metaphysical among the classical formulations of theistic belief tend to be determined by what I have called the abstract type of intellectual idolatry. By this I mean that they so think and speak of God as universal as either to deny or to obscure the genuine individuality of God. Thus, for instance, while God is said to act on all things and therefore to be externally related to them, and so to be in the strict and proper sense "absolute," God is also said to be in no sense "relative," because internally related to nothing, and so in no way acted on by other things, as any genuinely interacting individual perforce has to be. But then any predicate expressing or implying God's individuality, and hence God's interaction with others, such as the familiar personal predicates of loving others, knowing others, judging others, caring for others, and so on, must either be denied of God altogether or else be asserted of God only more or less unclearly or incoherently.

The truth, I suspect, is that the classical formulations of theistic belief are neither clear nor coherent, since they continue to assert the personal predicates that are certainly characteristic of primary religious belief and practice in a theistic religious context. But as serious a criticism as it may be to say this, it is, after all, a criticism of the classical *formulations* of theistic belief, not of this *belief itself*. Provided one so expresses the concept of God as to take account of both of its essential aspects — and this is exactly what is attempted by all revisionary, especially all neoclassical, formulations of the concept such as those of many process philosophies and theologies — there is every reason to suppose that belief in God remains an open question, however devastating modern and postmodern criticism of classical theism may have proved to be.

On the other hand, it also follows from the concept of God whose propriety I am urging, that an answer to the question of belief in God cannot be settled by any strictly empirical or merely factual mode of argument, such as has again and again been insisted on by modern and postmodern critics of classical theistic belief. Ever since Hume, it has been widely supposed that statements about anything real or existent, and hence about any individual, can be true only empirically or factually, and thus only contingently, rather than necessarily. But if God is properly conceived only as the strictly universal individual, this modern supposition is exposed as involving, in effect, the concrete type of idolatry, and thus of begging the question of belief in God instead of rationally answering it. Otherwise put, if Hume's rule about the necessary contingency of all assertions about individuals calls the reality of God into question, the existence of religious traditions such as Judaism and Christianity, for which God is nothing if not the universal individual, is at least sufficient to challenge the unrestricted application of Hume's rule. Because God is properly conceived only as the strictly universal individual, the question of theistic belief, in the sense of belief in the reality of God, lies beyond the scope of all strictly empirical or merely factual modes of reasoning, and must be settled, if at all, by some very different kind or kinds of argument.

Nor are these the only procedural consequences that follow once appeal is made to the Jewish and Christian religious traditions for a proper concept of God as the universal individual, or the individual universal. For if the question of belief in God is thus shown to be independent both of the abstract idolatry of classical theism and of the concrete idolatry of modern secularism, it is just as certain that it cannot be settled by some merely fideistic appeal to particular religious traditions, but only by appropriate modes of inquiry and argument. By "fideistic" here, I mean the kind of position that proposes to answer all questions as to the ultimate justification of religious belief by appealing simply to the claims and warrants of some already given religious faith (the word *"fides,"* from which "fideistic" and its cognates are derived, being the Latin word for faith in this sense). Such a position has been taken again and again throughout Jewish and Christian history right up to the present time, when it is sometimes represented in a peculiarly sophisticated form by certain analysts of religious language. But not the least objection to any such fideism is that it is implicitly contradicted by the concept of God constitutive of radically monotheistic belief. If God can be properly conceived only as the strictly universal individual, then God must also be conceived as ubiquitous or omnipresent, and hence as immanent in anything whatever insofar as it is so much as even possible. But then God must also be conceived as somehow immanent in any and all possible beliefs or experiences, so that everyone must in some way or at some level believe in God or experience God, and no one could in every way or at every level disbelieve in God or fail to experience God.

In other words, belief in God, by the very meaning of the term "God" and by the very nature of such belief, must be somehow warranted not only by the particular faith and experience of those who explicitly believe in God in terms of some inherited religious tradition such as Judaism or Christianity, but also by any and all human experience and belief simply as such. Thus, contrary to the claim of fideistic accounts

of belief in God, including those of certain forms of contemporary analytic philosophy, if anyone is indeed justified in believing in God, then
no one could really be justified in not believing in God — or, alternatively, if anyone is indeed justified in not believing in God, then no one
could really be justified in believing in God.

3

To recognize this, however, is to realize the importance of asking about
the kind or kinds of inquiry whereby the question of belief in God can,
in fact, be properly answered. And so we are led to develop further what
has already been said about distinctively religious inquiry as a necessary
step toward any answer to the second of our two questions concerning
belief in God — the question, namely, whether the term "God," properly understood, has any application to reality, or whether God properly
conceived also exists. If we are to answer this question, or at least understand how one properly goes about answering it, we must understand
the kind or kinds of inquiry by which alone it is appropriately answered;
and as we have seen, this means that we must primarily understand the
kind of inquiry that is distinctive of religion, even if there may be other
kinds of inquiry that are also appropriate to answering it.

To pursue the question as to the nature of religious inquiry, then, I
would observe, first of all, that the constitutive question of such inquiry
is the primary explicit form of what I call "the existential question"
or, alternatively, "the question of faith." I speak of it as "the existential question" because it has to do with the ultimate meaning of our
very existence as human beings and therefore is and must be asked and
answered at least implicitly by anyone who exists humanly at all. Alternatively, I call it "the question of faith" insofar as I reflect on the
"basic supposition" underlying it (Christian 1964, 84–88). Like any
other question, it can be asked at all only because, or insofar as, one
supposes certain things to be the case. But in asking *this* question, what
one necessarily supposes to be the case is what is perforce supposed
by our basic faith simply as human beings in the ultimate meaning of
our lives — namely, that reality is ultimately such as to authorize or
make appropriate some understanding of ourselves as alone realistic and
therefore our only authentic self-understanding.

So far as I can see, at least this much in the way of faith is basic to
our very existence as human beings, because it is implicitly presupposed
as the necessary condition of the possibility of all that we think or say
or do. Even suicide, to the extent that it is the intentional act of taking
one's own life, necessarily presupposes faith in this basic sense of the
word. But if this is correct, such underlying faith in the ultimate meaning
of life is the basic supposition of the existential question; and it is this

to which I intend to call attention by speaking of this question as also "the question of faith."

The same question, however, may also be called "the religious question," assuming, as I do, that what is properly meant by "religion" is the primary form of praxis and culture through which the existential question, or the question of faith, is explicitly asked and answered. If this question is and must be asked at least implicitly insofar as we exist humanly at all, because the basic faith underlying it is a necessary condition of the possibility of whatever we think, say, or do, some answer to the question is necessarily implied by all forms of praxis and culture, secular as well as religious. The distinctive thing about religion, however, is that it not only *implies* an answer to the question, but also *explicates* such an answer — just this being its unique function as a primary form of praxis and culture alongside the other, secular cultural forms.

But if this explains why religious inquiry is possible, what makes such inquiry necessary? That it is necessary seems evident enough, both from the existence throughout human culture and history of particular religions and — as we noted earlier — from the various kinds and levels of controversy instituted by their existence. Yet if we ask for the reasons for the various religions, basic faith in the ultimate meaning of life, while certainly a necessary condition, is not sufficient. Religions come to exist, not simply in order to explicate our basic faith, but only because our basic faith becomes in some way problematic. Even though we have no alternative, finally, but to exist and to act in the faith that life somehow ultimately makes sense, how, exactly, we are to understand our faith is so far from being unproblematic as to be continually called into question. Why? Because our life is perforce lived under conditions that threaten to undermine any naive assurance we may have as to its ultimate meaning.

Thus, for instance, there are the inescapable facts that each of us must suffer and die, that we invariably involve ourselves in guilt, and that all our undertakings are continually exposed to the workings of chance. Or, again, there is the loneliness that overtakes us even in the most intimate of human relationships and, still worse, the gnawing of doubt and the threat of final meaninglessness when we recognize, as we must, that our religious beliefs, like all of our ultimate beliefs, are just the ones of whose truth we must always be the least certain at the level of explicit belief. And these conditions are only exacerbated in the case of those who must suffer the injustices and oppressions of the existing social and cultural order. Indeed, the deeper misery of the oppressed is the constant sense that they are excluded from participating in a meaningful human life of the sort that they are nonetheless compelled to believe in as soon as and as long as they exist humanly at all.

Of course, none of these conditions would pose the kind of problem it poses for us, but for our prior assurance that our lives somehow finally make sense and are worth living. This is why the question of faith, to which all religious concepts and symbols in one way or another mediate an answer, is never the question *whether* life is ultimately meaningful — any more than the question answered by a properly scientific assertion is *whether* the world has some kind of order. Rather, the question of faith and, in its explicit form, the religious question is also always only *how* the meaning that we are sure life finally has can be so conceived and symbolized that we can continue to be assured of it — just as the question of science is always *how* we are to understand the order that we are certain the world must have, so that we can sufficiently predict and control the future that we not only survive in the world, but also prosper in it.

Even so, all the negativities of our existence, insofar as we experience and reflect on them, challenge our basic faith, driving us beyond any simple understanding of it. In this way, the conditions of human life as we unavoidably lead it, again and again create the profound need for *re*-assurance, for an understanding of ourselves and the world in relation to the strictly ultimate that will enable us to make sense of the basic faith we inevitably have.

It is to just this need to make sense somehow of our basic faith in the ultimate meaning of life that religion generally, and hence each religion in particular, is the response. All of the various religions are so many attempts, under the pressure of this need, to solve the problem of understanding our basic faith, given the negativities of existence as we all, in fact, undergo it. How different religions, in particular, manage to do this, or with what radicality of insight, is, naturally, historically variable, depending upon which of the conditions of human life are taken to focus the problem and on the depth at which these conditions are grappled with and understood. Even so, the whole point of any religion is so to conceive and symbolize the great inescapabilities of life as to solve the problem of our existence as such: the problem of our having to believe somehow in the ultimate meaning of life under conditions that make such faith seem all but impossible.

The upshot of the preceding analysis, then, is this: the structure of religious inquiry is constituted by a single question that is neither merely metaphysical nor merely moral, but is distinct from both of these other kinds of inquiry, even while having aspects that respectively relate it to each of them. Accordingly, it can be described as the question about the meaning of ultimate reality for us, which asks at one and the same time about both ultimate reality and ourselves: both the ultimate reality that authorizes or makes appropriate some understanding of our existence as realistic and therefore authentic, and the authentic self-understanding that is authorized or made appropriate by what is ultimately real.

As such, the religious question has, on the one hand, a *metaphysical* aspect in which it is distinct from all properly metaphysical questions, even while being closely related to them. It is distinct from metaphysical questions insofar as it asks about the meaning of ultimate reality for us, while they ask about the structure of ultimate reality in itself. But it is also closely related to metaphysical questions insofar as any answer to it necessarily implies certain answers to them. This is so because it is only insofar as ultimate reality in itself has one structure rather than another that it can have the meaning for us that it is asserted to have in taking it to authorize or make appropriate one self-understanding rather than another as the authentic understanding of our existence. On the other hand, the religious question has a *moral* aspect in which it is both distinct from and closely related to all properly moral, including specifically political, questions. It is distinct from moral questions insofar as it asks about the authentic understanding of our existence authorized or made appropriate by ultimate reality, while they ask about how one is to act and what one is to do in relation to the interests affected by one's action. But the religious question is also closely related to such moral questions insofar as any answer to it has certain necessary implications for any answer to them. This is the case because it is only insofar as acting in one way rather than another is how one ought to act in relation to relevant interests that ultimate reality can have the meaning for us it is asserted to have in taking it to authorize or make appropriate one self-understanding rather than another as authentic.

Of course, as thus analyzed, the religious question might be said to be two questions rather than one, insofar as in asking it one asks about both ultimate reality *and* authentic self-understanding. But as true as this certainly is, there is an overlap between the two questions that speaking of them simply as two fails adequately to take into account. In asking about the meaning of ultimate reality for us, one asks about ultimate reality only insofar as it authorizes or makes appropriate authentic self-understanding, even as one asks about authentic self-understanding only insofar as it is authorized or made appropriate by ultimate reality. Recognizing this, I prefer to speak of the question constituting distinctively religious inquiry neither simply as two questions nor simply as one question, but rather as one question with two essential aspects, metaphysical and moral, each of which necessarily implies the other.

4

If this is the logical structure of religious inquiry, and if the standpoint from which it must perforce deal with belief in God is the meaning of ultimate reality for us, how our second question concerning belief in

God is to be answered should be clear enough. There is indeed sufficient reason to conclude that the term "God" properly understood actually applies to what is real, or that God, so conceived, also exists, insofar as belief in God can be shown to be the most appropriate way of answering the religious question, and thus solving the problem of our existence as such. In other words, the distinctively religious question of the truth of belief in God, given the understanding of "God" previously clarified, is the question of whether the strictly ultimate reality authorizing or making appropriate the authentic understanding of our existence is best conceived as God in this sense of the word, and hence as the one universal individual, or individual universal.

To establish that this is, in fact, the case is the objective of all arguments for God's reality or existence, insofar as such arguments are understood as belonging to properly religious inquiry. Thus, however many may be the ways of developing it, there is really only one such religious argument — to the effect, namely, that we exist humanly at all only because of our at least implicit belief in God and that as a consequence, this belief must also be affirmed explicitly if our explicit understanding of ourselves is to be both complete and consistent.

As for whether I myself take this religious argument for God's reality to be sound, my answer is affirmative on two conditions: provided one conceives God neoclassically as genuinely individual no less than universal, and provided one repudiates the secularistic insistence that God as individual can exist only contingently by maintaining, on the contrary, that God is genuinely universal as well as individual and hence exists, and can only exist, necessarily. In my view, in short, the truth of belief in God from the standpoint of religious inquiry depends upon so understanding the term "God" or so conceiving the God to whom it applies, that both the abstract and the concrete types of intellectual idolatry are overcome.

On the other hand, insofar as both of these misconceptions are overcome, belief in God seems to me to have a strong claim to be religiously true; for the two aspects of God as properly conceived, as individual and as universal, correspond exactly to the two demands implicitly placed on any truly profound answer to the distinctively religious question of the meaning of ultimate reality for us — the individuality of God constituting a ground of life's meaning such as only a genuine individual can possibly provide, and the universality of God constituting this ground as in principle unsurpassable, because God is the primal source and the final end not only of our own existence and of the world around us, but of everything else, possible as well as actual.

In sum: belief in God thus understood explicates an understanding of our basic faith as well as of all the negativities of our existence that enables us to reaffirm the faith we inevitably have, even while coming to terms with the inescapabilities of life that confound any less profound understanding of our existence.

5

I have two concluding comments. The first is that while a religious argument for belief in God such as I have just outlined is the primary way of going beyond any mere fideism by rationally arguing for theistic belief, it is not, in the nature of the case, the only way of giving reasons for such belief. I explained why this is so when I argued that the religious question, although distinct from both properly metaphysical and properly moral questions, nevertheless has two aspects that closely relate it to both of these other types of questions — in such a way, namely, that any answer to it necessarily implies certain answers also to them. Because this is so, however, there not only can, but also must, be both metaphysical and moral arguments for belief in God if such belief is, in reality, religiously true.

To be exact, there are and must be as many metaphysical arguments for God as there are transcendental concepts of completely unrestricted or strictly universal application — like the concept "God" itself, provided God is properly conceived as the universal individual or the individual universal. Because any such transcendental concept is and must be implied by any concept, including perforce any other transcendental concept, one can begin with any transcendental concept whatever — including the concept of God — and if theistic belief is true, validly infer therefrom to God's existence. As for moral arguments for belief in God, there is, so far as I can see, really only one such argument, however many may be the ways of developing and formulating it. It is the argument to the effect that if anything is morally binding on us at all with respect either to what we are to do or to how we are to act, then God must exist or be real as the only intelligible ground both of our obligation and of the other conditions that must be present in the very nature of things if fulfilling our obligation is to be possible or finally to make any sense.

But if there are, to this extent, moral as well as metaphysical ways of rationally arguing for belief in God, one may say that belief in God is also the proper object of philosophical as well as of metaphysical and moral inquiry. For while philosophy, in the broad classical sense as the love of wisdom — any and all wisdom, whether secular or religious — is more than metaphysics and morals taken simply as such, it essentially includes both of them and thus comprises within its own distinctive kind of inquiry the inquiries respectively distinctive of them. Thus if, as we saw earlier, modern secularism notwithstanding, belief in God cannot be appropriately a matter of scientific inquiry or of any other strictly empirical or merely factual mode of reasoning, it *is* the proper object, not only of religious inquiry, but also — in their respectively different ways — of metaphysical and moral, and hence of philosophical, modes of inquiry and argument.

My second and final comment is by way of emphasizing the necessary limits, not only of all arguments for belief in God, religious and otherwise, but also of belief in God itself. It lies in the nature of any deductive argument, including all arguments for belief in God, that one can always rightly refuse to accept its conclusion by successfully questioning either its formal validity or the material truth of one or more of its premises. For this reason, the most that any such argument can ever achieve is so to connect various assertions that one more fully grasps their meaning and thus understands the price one has to pay for asserting or denying any of them — in the way, namely, of denying or asserting the other assertions with which any one assertion is necessarily interconnected. Thus the function of any well-constructed argument for belief in God, whether religious or philosophical, moral or metaphysical, is to connect assertion of such belief with certain other beliefs or assertions so far less controversial that the absurdity of denying one or the other of them will seem too high a price to pay for denying the truth of theistic belief. In this sense, all arguments for belief in God have the logical structure of *reductio ad absurdum* arguments. They seek to show, in one way or another, that the only alternatives to such belief are either so much less clear or else so much less coherent that it is thereby established as the most reasonable way of terminating the inquiry giving rise to the arguments.

Naturally, the same may be said for any clear-headed argument *against* belief in God. It too will seek to show that affirming the falsity of such belief is more reasonable than the contrary, because it involves a much lower price in the way of more or less hopeless unclarity or no less hopeless incoherence than one must pay in opting for any other alternative.

But whatever the outcome of arguments for and against belief in God, such belief itself also has its limits in that *belief* in God is one thing; *faith* in God, something else. Certainly, from the standpoint shared by Judaism and Christianity, faith in God is primarily a matter of trusting in God and being loyal to God, as distinct from asserting — even sincerely asserting — God's reality. Faith in God, in a word, is existential; while belief in God as such is merely intellectual. This is why liberation theologians can say quite rightly, however one-sidedly, that according to scripture, to know God is to do justice.

Of course, to know God through faith necessarily implies the truth of theistic belief, and if such belief were finally to prove false or insupportable, faith in God would be exposed as an inauthentic, because unrealistic, response to the way things ultimately are. But this connection between faith and belief cannot be reversed; for one may very well believe in God, and do so ever so honestly or sincerely, even while neither authentically trusting in God as the sole ultimate ground of one's life nor authentically serving God as the sole ultimate cause one is called to serve by doing justice.

This is no doubt a disturbing reflection to those of us who are seriously concerned with belief in God and who are therefore only too likely to succumb to the existential idolatry of making the rightness of our beliefs an essential part of our basic faith in the ultimate meaning of life. But I submit that it can also be a profoundly liberating reflection. In becoming aware that the meaning of our life, finally, is not dependent on our having the right beliefs, but only on our continuing to trust and to be faithful, whatever we may be led to believe, we may be sufficiently free from ourselves and for others to really examine our beliefs — to ask, perhaps for the first time, just what they really mean and whether we have sufficient reason to continue to hold them.

– 8 –

The Metaphysics of Faith and Justice

I

Thanks to the political theologies and theologies of liberation, the question of faith and justice has now become a, if not the, central question of Christian theology. For all the discussion recently devoted to it, however, whether the question has as yet been adequately answered is far from certain.

One reason for this is that the proper relationship between faith and justice still remains highly controversial. Despite widespread agreement that faith by its very nature inevitably finds expression in moral action, whether or to what extent faith also demands to be expressed through specifically political action continues to be disputed. In fact, some theologians, faced with what they take to be the virtual identification of Christian faith with political action, have been so concerned with distinguishing faith and justice as at least to seem to argue for their separation. On the other hand, other theologians for whom a specifically political responsibility is the demand of faith itself so react against what they take to be misguided attempts to separate faith and justice as to give every appearance of simply identifying them.

But if this familiar polarization in theology continues right up to the present, it is not the only reason for doubting that the question of faith and justice has been adequately answered. Another reason is that up to now insufficient attention has been paid to the metaphysical aspect of the question and, in this sense, to what I mean by "the metaphysics of faith and justice." Of course, neither faith nor justice as such is a matter of metaphysical belief or reflection. But it is certainly arguable that both faith and justice necessarily have metaphysical implications, and that it is of the utmost importance theologically for these implications to be made fully explicit.

According to the Christian witness, faith is the kind of basic human attitude or disposition that can be formally characterized as an existential self-understanding, or understanding of our own existence, in relation to others and to the encompassing whole of ultimate reality. As such, however, faith is the only self-understanding that is not only explicitly authorized by Jesus who is said to be the Christ, but — as Christians claim in saying that this is who Jesus is — is also implicitly authorized by the whole of ultimate reality itself as our authentic self-understanding. Consequently, even though faith as such is an existential, rather than a metaphysical, matter, it necessarily implies certain claims about the ultimate reality of self, others, and the whole in its structure in itself as well as in its meaning for us; and the proper name for all such claims is precisely "metaphysical." But if this same faith has moral as well as metaphysical implications, including the specifically political implication of justice, then the justice that faith demands necessarily implies the same metaphysical claims as the faith that demands it. I conclude, therefore, that the question of faith and justice can be adequately answered theologically only insofar as attention is given to the metaphysical aspect of the question.

As it happens, however, the theologies that have made this question central in the current discussion have tended, on the whole, either to neglect this aspect of the question, or else to proceed more or less uncritically in explicating the metaphysics of faith and justice. Instead of thinking out the full metaphysical implications of the basic understanding to which they have come in reflecting on the meaning of faith and justice for our self-understanding and life-praxis, they have either settled for talking merely about the meaning of ultimate reality for us or else taken over traditional metaphysical ways of talking about the structure of ultimate reality in itself that are doubtfully consistent with their own basic understanding. At the same time, the other theologies that have contributed most in our time to explicating and justifying the metaphysical implications of the Christian witness seem to have been typically preoccupied more with theoretical questions of belief and truth than with practical issues of action and justice, and so have contributed only indirectly to clarifying and answering our central question. One may also wonder, perhaps, whether the rather marked speculative tendencies of some of these theologies have not kept such contribution as they have actually made from being clearly recognized in its bearing on the question.

In any event, the point of these broad generalizations, to all of which there are obvious exceptions, is only to explain why the argument I now propose to develop seems to me worth developing. Without exaggerating the need for what I shall do, I want to offer some theological reflections on the relationship between faith and justice and on what I take to be their necessary metaphysical implications.

2

Turning first to the relations between faith and justice, I wish to argue that even when "justice" is understood not merely in a generally moral, but in a specifically political, sense, the demand for justice is a demand of faith itself. Thus, in my understanding, the relation between faith and justice is a special case of the relation between faith and good works. Just as, in general, good works are distinct from faith and not to be identified with it, and yet are also demanded by faith and not to be separated from it, so justice, in its political meaning as right structures of society and culture, is both distinct from faith and demanded by it, and hence neither identifiable with faith nor separable from it. But if this understanding is correct, both poles in the familiar polarization on the question involve equally serious, even if precisely contrary, misunderstandings of how faith and justice are really related. My task now is to explain briefly why just this seems to me to be the case and why I hold, accordingly, that both of the usual alternatives can and should be overcome.

I noted earlier that faith in the sense in which the Christian witness understands it may be characterized formally as an existential self-understanding. But I immediately went on to add that it is the only self-understanding explicitly authorized by Jesus, whom Christians assert to be the Christ, the point of their assertion being that it is also the very self-understanding implicitly authorized as the authentic understanding of our existence by the mysterious whole of ultimate reality that they call by the name "God." If we ask now for the material content of this self-understanding, the only adequate answer is that it is an understanding of ourselves and all others as alike objects of the unbounded love of God, which is to say, of the inclusive whole of reality of which both the self and others are all parts. It is precisely the gift and demand of this unbounded love that are decisively re-presented through Jesus; and to understand ourselves as we are thereby explicitly given and called to do is to actualize the one possibility of self-understanding that is properly called "Christian faith."

It is of the essence of this self-understanding to have a distinctive double structure: it is both trust in God's love alone for the ultimate meaning of our lives and loyalty to this same love and to all to whom it is loyal as the only final cause that our lives are to serve (Niebuhr 1960, 16–23). Although in both aspects faith is a human response to God's love, its first aspect of trust is relatively passive, while its second aspect of loyalty is relatively active. Moreover, the priority of the first and more passive aspect of trust to the second and more active aspect of loyalty is absolute. It is precisely out of our acceptance of God's love in trust that we alone become sufficiently free from ourselves and all others to be truly loyal to God's cause. It is no less true, however, that if we truly trust in God's love, we cannot fail to live in loyalty to it. Thus, while the second aspect of faith is and must be strictly posterior to the first, there is nevertheless but one faith with two aspects, each of which necessarily implies the other.

To be loyal to God's love is to be loyal not only to God, but also to all to whom God is loyal; and this means, of course, everyone, both ourselves and all others. But to be loyal to another necessarily involves — if, indeed, it is not simply another word for — loving the other, in the sense of so accepting the other as to take account of the other's interests and then acting toward the other on the basis of such acceptance. So it is that the faith that can originate only by our trusting in God's prevenient love for all of us can eventuate only in our returning love for God and, in God, for all whom God loves.

But this means that the returning love that faith involves is like the prevenient love to which it responds in being, in its own way, unbounded. This it is, in the first place, because the love demanded from us, like the love given to us, covers the full range of creaturely interests. Because God's love itself is subject to no bounds and excludes nothing from its embrace, there is no creature's interest that is not also God's interest and, therefore, necessarily included in our returning love for God. This explains why the first commandment that we shall love God with the whole of our being can be fully explicated only by the second commandment that we shall love our neighbors as ourselves. But as the first commandment itself makes clear, our returning love for God is unbounded, in the second place, because it covers the full scope of our own responsibility. Because we are to love God with all our heart, with all our soul, with all our mind, and with all our strength, nothing of ourselves is to be withheld from our love for God and for those whom God loves. In this sense, all of our powers and all of the possible uses of our powers are governed by the one demand for love that is necessarily implied by the demand for faith itself.

To recognize this is to understand why the self-understanding of faith necessarily has properly moral implications. Clearly, if all our powers and all of the possible uses of our powers are governed by the demand for love, the whole sphere of action through which we actualize our powers must be at least indirectly governed by the same demand. But it is precisely the sphere of action, including both how we act and what we do, that is the proper concern of morals. Thus even though faith as such lies beyond the sphere of action in the sphere of self-understanding, it is nevertheless inseparable from action, and its necessary implications for action are properly moral. In general, we may say that these implications include everything that follows for human action — both how we are to act and what we are to do — from a love for God and for all others in God that is unbounded in the two respects just noted, and so covers both the full range of creaturely interests and the full scope of human responsibility.

Of course, just what these implications do include at any given time and place is a variable that depends not only on the given circumstances and possibilities of action, but even more importantly on some understanding of the range of relevant interests and of the extent of human powers for realizing them. But if changes in Christian morals are to this extent inevitable, what never changes is that the returning love for God in which faith by its very nature eventuates always has just such properly moral implications, and that they always pertain to acting in the situation in a distinctive way — namely, in such a way as to take account of all the interests affected by one's action in order to realize these interests as fully as circumstances and possibilities allow. Recalling, then, the classical definition of doing justice as giving everyone her or his own (*suum cuique*), we may summarize the argument up to this point by saying that the faith that works by love inevitably seeks justice and finds expression in doing it.

The question remains, however, whether this faith also demands justice in the specifically political sense of the word. Granted that faith does indeed imply doing justice in the generally moral sense of right action that gives each her or his own, what this does and does not imply depends upon some understanding of what belongs to those whose interests are affected by our action and of what we are able to do to realize these interests. But, clearly, the understanding of these matters that underlies the demand for justice in the specifically political sense is closely related to our distinctively modern historical consciousness, by which I mean our consciousness of ourselves as historical subjects who bear full responsibility for creating ourselves and one another in and through our creation of society and culture. In other words, we can experience the demand for political justice as we do only because we have now become aware that the social and cultural structures by which human existence is always limited are neither divine appointments, nor natural givens, but human creations. Thus we now recognize not only that we have the power in principle to transform these structures so that they more nearly allow for the realization of all relevant interests, but also that it is in the deeper interest of all creatures that there be a social and cultural order that frees each of them to realize its interests as fully as possible in solidarity with all the others.

The final conclusion of the argument, then, depends upon appealing not only to the moral implications of faith in any situation, but also to the understanding of ourselves and of our fellow human beings as the agents of history that is certainly pervasive of our situation today. On the other hand, once this understanding can be presupposed, we have the right to conclude that doing justice is a demand of faith itself, even in the specifically political sense of creating and maintaining right structures of social and cultural order. As a matter of fact, with the full consciousness of our own historical agency, we become aware that the justice that love inevitably seeks and in doing which it finds expression is, above all, political justice in this sense.

Of course, the love through which faith works must always continue to accept others and to act in their interests within society and culture as presently constituted. But with the change marked by historical consciousness, the first and most fundamental responsibility of love is for a just ordering of society and culture themselves — for so maintaining or transforming their most basic structures that they allow for the fullest possible realization of all relevant interests, thereby giving to everyone her or his own.

The real relation between faith and justice, then, resists both of the usual ways of viewing their relation as alike misunderstandings. Rightly understood, faith and justice are in principle different, because while faith is a matter of human existence, of authentic self-understanding in trust and loyalty in response to God's love, doing justice is a matter of human action, whether right action toward all others (its general moral sense), or creating right structures of social and cultural order (its specifically political sense). But this means that faith and justice can and must be clearly distinguished and can never be simply identified without being seriously misunderstood. At the same time, faith and justice are also in principle connected, just as in general, human existence is in principle connected with human action insofar as any understanding of ourselves cannot but have implications both for how we are to act and what we are to do. In fact, the deepest root of all human action is in the self-understanding that constitutes any human existence distinctively as such. This means that we can avoid the contrary but equally serious misunderstanding of faith and justice only if we recognize that they also can and must be integrally related and can never be simply separated. For this reason, but without in any way simply identifying them, we may say that the specifically political demand for justice is a demand of faith itself.

3

My task now is to pursue the question of the metaphysics of faith and justice as thus understood. Assuming that they are really related in the way I have argued, how do we make fully explicit what they necessarily imply about ultimate reality — not only in its meaning for us, but in its structure in itself?

To clarify this question, it is necessary, first of all, to ask just what is included under the term "ultimate reality," and how, accordingly, we properly understand the scope of metaphysics. According to a well-known definition of William James's, the real is "what we in some way find ourselves obliged to take account of" (James 1911, 101). Accepting this definition, we may infer that "ultimate reality" covers everything that we are all finally obliged to take account of insofar as we exist humanly at all, whatever other things we may or may not have to take account of in each leading our own individual human lives. In other words, ultimate reality includes everything necessary in our experience or self-understanding, as distinct from all the other things that we experience or understand that are merely contingent relative to our own existence simply as such. If we already presuppose, then, that the theistic religious language employed by the Christian witness in authorizing faith in God's love as our authentic self-understanding can be metaphysically justified, we can say — as I, in fact, have been saying already — that ultimate reality includes not only the self and others, but also the encompassing whole of reality that theists refer to when they use the name "God."

Significantly, it is this threefold differentiation of ultimate reality into self, others, and the whole — or self, world, and God — that underlies the understanding of metaphysics that has been conventional in the Western tradition since at least the seventeenth century. In this understanding, the scope of metaphysics includes both *metaphysica generalis*, or ontology, understood as critical reflection on strictly ultimate reality as such; and *metaphysica specialis*, comprising the three disciplines of psychology, cosmology, and theology, understood as critical reflection respectively on the three ultimate realities of self, world, and God.

My judgment is that this conventional scheme is still useful provided one avoids certain misunderstandings that an unthinking use of it may perhaps encourage. One such misunderstanding would be to suppose that there can be an adequate distinction between general metaphysics or ontology, on the one hand, and the discipline of special metaphysics called "theology," on the other. Given the concept of God necessarily implied not only by the Christian witness but by any radical theism, God is not merely one reality among others, but is in some sense reality as such. But if this kind of theism is metaphysically true, then ontology itself must be theology, even as theology can only be ontology. Much the same would be true of the distinction between ontology and cosmology as well if, as some forms of radical theism maintain, the concepts of God and the world are correctly understood only as correlative concepts. In that case, the constitutive concept of ontology, namely, "reality as such," would be strictly equivalent to the distinction or correlation between the constitutive concepts of theology and cosmology, "God" and "the world."

But whether the world as well as God is in some respect a strictly ultimate reality and therefore any adequate distinction between ontology and cosmology is also impossible, there is hardly any question that the self, at least, is in every respect contingent and hence cannot possibly be a strictly ultimate reality. To be sure, the self is ultimate in that it is necessary to our experience or understanding of ultimate reality, including the self; and it is for this reason, presumably, that psychology, understood as critical reflection on the self as thus ultimate, can be represented as the third discipline of special metaphysics. But we would certainly be

misled by the scheme that so represents it if we supposed that the self
is a topic of special metaphysics in the same way in which God is, and
perhaps the world is as well. Because the self, radically unlike God, exists only contingently rather than necessarily, its reality is not strictly
ultimate and it therefore falls within the scope of metaphysics only in a
broad, rather than in the strict, sense of the word (Ogden 1975).

So far as theology is concerned, however, it is metaphysics in the
broad sense that includes psychology that is most directly relevant. This
is clear enough from the foregoing theological reflections on the relation between faith and justice; for whatever else faith and justice may
be said to be, they have been shown to be possibilities of human existence and action, whose metaphysical implications necessarily include
claims about the reality of the self such as properly belong to metaphysical psychology. With this in mind, we may begin with some comments
on the psychology — or, as I prefer to say, anthropology — that must be
an integral part of any adequate metaphysics of faith and justice.

The comments here can be brief because the main point of such an
anthropology has already been made in explaining how faith and justice
are both distinct and inseparable, as I have argued they are. I refer to the
distinction I introduced between human existence or self-understanding,
on the one hand, and human action or life-praxis, on the other. Clearly,
if this distinction is valid, it is so only because the reality of the human
self in its essential structure in itself necessarily involves both of the moments that the distinction serves at once to distinguish and to relate in a
definite way. But if the reality of the self indeed has this duplex structure,
no anthropology that failed to attend to both of its essential moments
in their difference as well as their unity could adequately explicate the
anthropological implications of faith and justice.

Thus, if an anthropology were to advert to the fact that the self is
existence and therefore can and must understand itself, all the while ig-
noring that the self's possibilities are also always limited by social and
cultural structures, it would so understand the self that the demand for
justice in the specifically political sense could not be understood as a
demand of faith itself. On the other hand, if another anthropology so
focused on the social and cultural limitations of the self as either to ignore or to deny that the self nonetheless always bears responsibility for
understanding itself and leading its own unique life, it would be equally
unable to understand justice in either of its senses as ultimately grounded
in the self-understanding of faith.

These examples should suffice to indicate the range of philosophical resources of which, in my judgment, theology is well advised to
make use if it is to explicate and justify the anthropological implications of faith and justice in an adequate way. But since in other things
I have written on this question I have expressly stressed the importance

of existentialist philosophy, I would like to emphasize that I certainly do not think of it as the only important resource. As necessary as its analysis of the self as existence still seems to me to be to any anthropological reflection, the value of this analysis as well as its limitations are more likely to be justly appreciated when it is viewed together with the other post-Hegelian philosophies of human activity that Richard J. Bernstein has discussed in his book *Praxis and Action* (1971). Both Marxism and pragmatism, along with more recent analytic philosophies of action, help to make sure that the other moment of action or life-praxis in the self's essential structure will be brought out no less effectively than the moment of existence or self-understanding on which existentialist philosophy so sharply focuses.

Also important for the same reason are not only the contributions of so-called philosophical anthropology, especially, in my opinion, Michael Landmann's analysis of human beings as both the creators and the creatures of culture, but also the sophisticated philosophy of life-praxis that provides the foundation for the "critical theory" of Jürgen Habermas and, in a somewhat different way, for the "transformation of philosophy" proposed by Karl-Otto Apel (Landmann 1961; 1964; Habermas 1968; 1973; 1976; Apel 1973). Although theology must certainly do its own anthropological reflection and cannot rely on any of these resources without criticism, all of them are directly relevant to its task if it is both to explicate and to validate the understanding of the structure of the self that faith and justice necessarily imply.

As for the other, strictly metaphysical implications of faith and justice, I propose to explicate, first, what they necessarily imply for the essential structure of the reality of God. The comments I shall then go on to make about the structure of the world and of reality as such can be more easily made and understood once these theological implications have become explicit.

Faith, as we have seen, is by its very nature our human response of trust and loyalty to the explicit gift and demand of God's love both for ourselves and for all others. But if the meaning of God for us is the gift and demand of unbounded love that authorizes trust in this love and loyalty to its cause as our authentic self-understanding, the ultimate whole of reality that we call by the name "God" has to have a unique structure in itself. Just as it must be all-inclusive both of self and the world, and therefore strictly universal in scope and function, so must it also be genuinely individual in that it is a single center of interaction, both acting on and being acted on by itself and all others. Ordinarily, of course, universality and individuality are distinguishing properties, the most universal things being the least individual, and vice versa. But if the kind of trust in God's love and loyalty to its cause that are Christian faith are, in fact, authorized by ultimate reality in its meaning for us, the encompassing whole of reality in its structure in itself must be as individual as it is universal, and as universal as it is individual, and hence an exception to the rule by which individuals and universals are otherwise distinguished.

This conclusion can also be seen to follow from the demand of God's love as summarized in the two commandments that we shall love the Lord our God with the whole of our being and that we shall love our neighbors as ourselves. Clearly, if it is God whom we are to love with all of our powers, God must be one individual distinct from all others whose interests we can take account of and act to realize. At the same time, if all of our powers are to be exercised in our love for the one individual who is God, even while we are also to accept our neighbors as ourselves and act so as to realize all of their interests as well, God must also be strictly universal, in that there can be no interest either of ourselves or of any of our neighbors that is not somehow included in the interests of God.

The God implied by love for God as well as by faith in God, then, is not simply one individual among others, but is the one and only strictly universal individual. But this means that the inclusive whole of reality, which we experience as alone strictly necessary in contrast to the radical contingency both of ourselves and of all others, must also be distinctively dipolar in its essential structure. It belongs to the very concept of an individual, and hence to any individual whatever, that it is a center of interaction that both acts on itself and others and is, in turn, acted on by them. Therefore, even the universal individual called "God" must be conceived as having two essential aspects: a relatively more active aspect in which it acts on or makes a difference to both itself and all others; and a relatively more passive aspect in which all others as well as itself act on or make a difference to it. Thus the uniqueness of God in comparison with all other individuals does not lie in God's only acting on others and being in no way acted on by them, but rather in the strictly universal scope of God's field of interaction with others as well as with self. Whereas any other individual interacts with itself for a finite time only, God's acting on Godself and being acted on by Godself has never begun nor will it ever end. And so too with respect to interaction with others: whereas any individual other than God interacts with some others only, God interacts with all, not only acting on them, but also being acted on by them.

In both aspects, God as the universal individual is strictly unsurpassable; and only by being thus unsurpassable both actively and passively can God be the God necessarily implied by the distinctive double structure of Christian faith, which is to say, both the ground of unreserved trust and the object of unqualified loyalty. We may trust in God without reservation only because God is unsurpassably active, doing all that could conceivably be done by any one individual for all others as well as itself.

Likewise, we may be loyal to God without qualification only because God is unsurpassably passive, being open to all that could conceivably be done or suffered by anyone as something that is also done to God.

But if God can be worthy of our loyalty only by unfailingly suffering all that anyone could possibly do or suffer, what is it, exactly, that God must do in order to be worthy of the trust that is the irreversibly prior aspect of Christian faith? The answer to this question, in my opinion, is absolutely crucial if the implications of faith and justice for the reality of God are to be adequately explicated. If faith and justice are both distinct and inseparable, as I have held they are, then God must do both of two correspondingly distinct and inseparable things in order to be the ground of unreserved trust. On the one hand, God must so act to accept both the self and all others into God's own everlasting life as thereby to endow them with abiding significance. On the other hand, God must so act in the interests of both the self and all others as thereby to establish the cosmic order of natural law that sets the optimal limits of all other action, where by "optimal limits" is meant limits such that, were they to be set otherwise than they are, the ratio between opportunities for good and risks of evil would be less favorable than it in fact is.

Elsewhere I have argued that these two things that God must do to be worthy of our unreserved trust are what are properly meant respectively by the theological terms "redemption" and "creation" (Ogden 1989, 68–79). As such, they are the two essential aspects of the one work of God *ad extra* that is God's unbounded love for all others. But if faith in its first aspect of trust necessarily implies both of these aspects of God's work, the justice that is the demand of faith in its other aspect of loyalty especially implies the second. Both in its generally moral sense as acting rightly and in its specifically political sense of creating right structures of society and culture, justice implies that it realizes the same divine interest in the interests of all that is expressed by God's own work of creation. Even as God's work as Creator is in the deeper interest of every creature in a cosmic order that frees it to realize its own interests as fully as possible in solidarity with all of its fellow creatures, so acting rightly toward others and, even more so, creating right structures of social and cultural order are by way of realizing the same deeper interest, thereby carrying forward God's own work of creation. Thus the justice that faith demands necessarily implies the unsurpassable justice of God, who not only redeems all others from nullity and insignificance by accepting them without condition into the divine life itself, but also creates the optimal conditions of creaturely action, thereby doing all that anyone could possibly do in the interests of all others except what they must each do for themselves and for one another if it is ever to be done at all.

The question now is whether the reality of this God that faith and justice necessarily imply is their only implication that is strictly metaphysical. My answer is that it is not, because there is a certain respect in which the world, as well as God, must be said to be strictly ultimate. This is so, at any rate, if one holds, as I do, that the unbounded love of others whose gift and demand are decisively re-presented through Jesus is nothing merely accidental and contingent in God, but is God's very essence and is strictly necessary. Of course, the love of God for any *particular* others could only be contingent, assuming that God alone exists necessarily, all other individuals and events existing or occurring merely contingently. In this respect, God's love for others and the creation and redemption of them that are its two essential aspects must themselves always be contingent and so utterly free and gratuitous. But if God is not merely accidentally love of others and essentially love only of self — and this, I maintain, is what faith and justice necessarily imply — then that there are *some* others for God to love and that God, accordingly, is Creator of these others as well as their Redeemer are precisely not contingent but necessary. In this respect, the existence of the world, unlike that of the self, is strictly ultimate; and the concept "the world," understood as referring to the necessarily nonempty class of realities other than God, all of whose members exist or occur merely contingently, is strictly correlative with the concept "God."

If this is correct, however, there can no more be an adequate distinction between ontology and cosmology than between ontology and theology. To reflect critically on reality as such is and must be one and the same with reflecting critically on the distinction or correlation between God and the world — and conversely. Of course, there is the difference that whereas "God" is not only a concept but a name, designating the one universal individual who alone exists, and must exist, necessarily, "the world" refers to nothing individual, but only to a class, at least some of whose members cannot fail to exist or occur — namely, the class of all individuals and events other than God, any of which exists or occurs, and must do so, only contingently. But as important and even crucial as it is to appreciate this difference, the God implied by faith and justice necessarily implies at least some world of creatures other than God, even as any such world of creatures necessarily implies this one and only God as it sole primal source and its only final end.

So far as other implications of faith and justice for ontology and cosmology are concerned, they can be summarized for our purposes by saying that they are in every sense antidualistic, being in one sense monistic, in another sense qualifiedly pluralistic. They are monistic in the sense that any individual or event whatever, whether God or one of God's creatures, is of one kind of reality only, not of two or more kinds. This implication follows necessarily, I believe, from the concept of God as being strictly universal as well as individual, and hence as not being merely one individual among others, but the one individual whose existence is constitutive of reality as such. If God is indeed so conceived, then to be anything real at all is either to be God or to be a creature of God, whose difference from God cannot be absolute; for to be absolutely different from God would be to be absolutely different from reality as such, and so not anything real after all, but simply nothing. Thus it follows from faith and justice that there is only one kind of ultimate subjects of predication, and that no difference between any one such subject and any other can amount to an absolute difference in kind, whether it be a merely finite difference between one creature and another or even the infinite difference between any creature and God.

This means, among other things, that even the difference between human creatures such as ourselves and other creatures not similarly capable of self-understanding and moral action is at most a relative, not an absolute, difference. Consequently, there can be no ontological or cosmological justification for restricting the demand for justice to actions or structures pertaining exclusively to human interests. On the contrary, because all differences between creatures are relative only, the justice that faith demands requires that we act so as to take account of *all* interests, nonhuman as well as human, that can be affected by our action.

But if the implications of faith and justice are in this way attributively monistic, they are nonetheless substantively pluralistic, even if in a qualified sense. By this I mean that they imply not one, but many, ultimate subjects of predication. Although any individual or event is and must be ultimately of the same kind as any other, there are any number of such realities, each ontologically distinct from all the others. Above all, there is the unique ontological distinction between the self and others as all mere parts of reality, on the one hand, and God as the all-inclusive whole of reality, on the other. Even as each creature is ontologically distinct from every other, so each of them severally and all of them together are ontologically distinct from God. And yet, as I have indicated, the distinction between parts and whole, creatures and God, is unique; and for this reason, the substantive pluralism implied by faith and justice, real as it certainly is, is also qualified.

This already became apparent earlier when we took note of the important difference between the two concepts "God" and "the world." Even though these concepts are indeed correlative in that each necessarily implies the other, the symmetry they thus express between God and the world presupposes an even more fundamental asymmetry between them. For while God could not exist without the world any more than the world could exist without God, what God necessarily implies is not *this world or that* (since any world, unlike God, is merely contingent rather than necessary), but only *some world or other* — or, as I put it before, that the class of all individuals and events other than God not be an empty class. On the other hand, what any world necessarily implies is not merely *some God or other* (since the idea of more than one God is self-contradictory), but rather *the one and only necessarily existing God* but for which no world whatever would be so much as possible or have any abiding meaning (Hartshorne 1967, 64f.). Because of this profound asymmetry between God and the world, the ontology implied by faith and justice is indeed substantively pluralistic, but with an important qualification.

I hardly have to say, I think, that in my judgment the strictly metaphysical reflections of a certain form of process philosophy provide a unique resource for Christian theology. But I trust my argument has helped to make clear why the kind of neoclassical revisionary metaphysics developed, above all, by Alfred North Whitehead and Charles Hartshorne seems to me all but indispensable if the strictly metaphysical implications of faith and justice are to be explicated appropriately and validated as credible.

Having said this, however, I would emphasize that here too theology has to do its own metaphysical reflection and cannot afford to be uncritical in making use of this, any more than of any other, philosophical resource. To be sure, the situation here is not simply the same as it is with respect to the anthropology of faith and justice. In my opinion, at any rate, there is nothing inherently one-sided about this form of process metaphysics, nor is there any other revisionary metaphysics that is at all comparable in the overall adequacy of its strictly metaphysical positions. But aside from the fact that other kinds of metaphysics are concerned with the same problems and therefore can hardly fail to make some contribution toward further clarifying them, there are certain well-known difficulties with any speculative or categorial metaphysics that make it imperative to appropriate it critically. Specifically, there is the root difficulty of whether there can really be any such thing as proper metaphysical analogy, this being the kind of thinking and speaking on which any categorial or speculative metaphysics necessarily depends. Obviously, this is not the place to discuss so radical an issue (see, however, below, pp. 187–209; also Ogden 1992b, 127–147). But unless I am mistaken, it is one of the issues that Christian theology must not only discuss, but also resolve if it is to carry out its task of explicating and defending the metaphysics of faith and justice.

9

A Priori Christology
and Experience

I

If anything can be said to be "Christian doctrine," it is christology; so "the making and remaking of Christian doctrine" must at least mean, whatever else it means, the making and remaking of doctrine about Christ (see Coakley and Pailin 1993; cf. Wiles 1967; 1974). More broadly, it must mean the making and remaking of doctrine about Jesus who is said to be the Christ, as well as any number of other things that are functionally equivalent to "the Christ" and interchangeable with it.

To be sure, the distinction between "making" and "remaking" is hardly absolute, since what could reasonably be described from one standpoint as an instance of the first could be quite properly analyzed from another standpoint as a case of the second — and vice versa. Thus even within the comparatively short period of time documented by the New Testament writings, we find not only the making of christology, but the remaking of it as well, in the sense of reformulating still earlier thought and speech about Jesus in his decisive significance for human existence. But there are also good reasons for the not uncommon use of the distinction absolutely to designate two main phases in the whole long history of christological developments. The first phase, which is taken to be the making of christology, can be reckoned to include all the developments from the earliest Christian witness that is reconstructible from the writings of the New Testament to the classical definition of orthodox christology by the Council of Chalcedon. The second phase, then, is the remaking of orthodox christology that was carried out by the revisionary theologians of the late eighteenth and nineteenth centuries in their struggles to find a new, middle way between orthodoxy and the Enlightenment. Clearly, if the distinction between making and remaking christology is to be given more than a merely relative meaning, this use of it has a strong claim to express that meaning.

No less clear, however, is that the process of remaking christology that was begun by an earlier revisionary theology now has to be carried forward so as to include a remaking of this revisionary christology itself. In other words, from the standpoint of our own theological situation, the absolute distinction between making christology and remaking it is once again relativized. This is because both of the usual types of christology, revisionary no less than orthodox, have now proved to be incapable of solving the christological problem as it arises out of our theological situation today (cf. Ogden 1992b, 1–19).

One way of demonstrating this is to do the main thing I propose to do in the remainder of this essay — namely, to show that both orthodox and revisionary christologies are vulnerable to the same fatal objection to any proposed solution to the problem of christology. Having done this, I then want to show that a third type of christology, such as I should be willing to defend, is free from this objection and is therefore strong at the very point where the two usual types have been shown to be weak. In this way, I hope to indicate the remaking of christology, and thus of Christian doctrine, that now seems to me to be called for if Christian theology is to continue to play its proper role.

2

If we ask just what Christian theology's proper role is, my answer is that it is critical reflection on the Christian witness of faith so as to validate the claims to validity that bearing such witness necessarily makes or implies. This answer presupposes that Christian faith is a particular mode of human self-understanding, even as bearing witness to this faith by all that one thinks, says, and does is a particular form of human life-praxis. Precisely as life-praxis, however, bearing witness is a matter of leading one's life, or living understandingly, and therefore of necessity involves either making or implying certain distinctive claims to validity. Specifically, it involves two claims: that the *what* of one's witness, in the sense of what one thinks, says, or does to bear it, is adequate to its content; and that the *that* of one's witness, in the sense of the act of bearing it, is fitting to its situation. Actually, the first of these two claims is itself duplex in that it involves the two further claims that the *what* of one's witness is appropriate to Jesus Christ and that it is credible to human existence. Consequently, there are three claims to validity that bearing Christian witness either makes or implies and that may well need to be critically validated as and when they become problematic.

The proper role of Christian theology in general, as a field of critical reflection, is to provide such necessary validation. Central to playing this role is the discipline of systematic theology, whose task is to validate critically the claim of Christian witness to be adequate to its content and therefore both appropriate to Jesus Christ and credible to human existence. Systematic theology can perform this task, obviously, only by presupposing the critical interpretation of Christian witness that its sister discipline, historical theology (including biblical theology), has the task of providing, even as it must leave to its other sister discipline, practical theology, the further task of critically validating the claim of witness to be fitting to its situation. But if systematic theology neither is nor can be the only theological discipline, it is nonetheless at the center of Christian theology in critically validating the claims to validity that are perforce made or implied in bearing Christian witness.

Thus to understand its role, however, is not to imply that Christian theology is to be done merely critically and retrospectively, with a view only to such Christian witness as has already been borne. Of course, constituted as it is, as critical reflection on Christian witness, it would be neither possible nor necessary but for the prior existence of this witness and the continuing activity of bearing it. But the point is that bearing witness *is* a continuing activity and that the whole purpose of Christian theology, finally, is to perform a service necessary to bearing it validly. Consequently, Christian theology not only may, but also must, be done constructively and prospectively, as well as critically and retrospectively, with a view to the Christian witness of the future as well as to the Christian witness of the past. This means that systematic theology has to formulate as clearly and coherently as possible what any future Christian witness has to be if it is to be adequate to its content — what it must think, say, and do to be both appropriate to Jesus as Christians have experienced him and credible to the women and men who now need to hear it.

To do this, however, systematic theology must satisfy the specific requirements of both appropriateness and credibility as these arise out of our theological situation today. Of course, appropriateness and credibility themselves remain constant as the two criteria of adequacy, being as situation-invariant as the corresponding claims to validity that are necessarily made or implied in bearing Christian witness. But just what these criteria require is not constant, but variable, being as situation-dependent as human life-praxis generally is bound to be. Thus what is required today if Christian witness is to be appropriate depends upon what is now to be defined both in principle and in fact as the formally normative instance of Christian witness by which the appropriateness of all other instances has to be determined. Likewise, the requirements that must be met today if Christian witness is to be credible depend upon what is now to be accepted in fact as well as in principle as the truth about human existence.

In our theological situation today, an essential requirement of credibility is that any valid formulation of Christian witness (as well as, naturally, of Christian theology) must be capable in some way of verification by common human experience. I do not mean to imply by this that the requirement that Christian witness be verifiable somehow by experience is something completely new or peculiar to the immediate present. On the contrary, I hold that one of the lasting achievements of revisionary theology right from the beginning is to have shown that the credibility of Christian witness can be validated, finally, only by appeal to what anyone is capable of experiencing simply as a human being. Thus, for something like two hundred years, Christians and theologians, like their contemporaries generally, have been justified in rejecting all appeals to mere authority as in the nature of the case insufficient to validate the credibility of their witness and theology. Indispensable as such appeals certainly are to validating claims to appropriateness, they can do nothing whatever towards validating claims to credibility until such authority as they appeal to can in turn be verified by direct appeal to experience.

Because this is so, however, the problem of christology that arises out of our theological situation today is, in large part, the problem of validating the credibility of christological formulations in experiential terms. This is not the whole of the problem, because systematic theology, now as always, must also be concerned — and concerned first of all — with validating the appropriateness of christological formulations. And in this respect also, the specific requirements of the criterion, given our situation, make for certain problems, not least in validating the usual types of christology. But even after a christological formulation is validated as appropriate, there remains the question whether it is also credible; and in our situation today, the very least that "credible" can mean is "verifiable somehow in terms of human experience."

By the same token, the objection that it cannot be verified in experiential terms must be fatal to any formulation proposed to solve the christological problem. It would be fully credible, of course, only if it were to be, in fact, verified in some way by common experience. But unless it at least *can be* so verified, the question of whether it *is* verified and therefore "credible" in the relevant sense could not even be asked, much less affirmatively answered.

3

Having now clarified the significance of "experience" for my argument, I turn to the other main concept, "a priori christology." This concept as such has recently enjoyed a certain currency in Christian theology, thanks especially to the work of Karl Rahner. While I could readily appropriate much, if not all, of what Rahner means by it, my own use of it, at least for the purposes of this essay, is much more easily explained. To clarify what I mean by it, I want to consider first what is properly meant by "christology" simply as such, or by what I take to be the somewhat more precise term, "the constitutive christological assertion."

In its obvious literal sense, "christology" means *logos* about *christos,* or thought and speech (including the speech of actions as well as words) about Christ. But "Christ" here is evidently used not so much as a concept or a title as a proper name — to refer to the particular person Jesus whom the thought and speech of christology are all about. This is clear from the fact that, as we noted at the outset, the term "christology" is commonly used more broadly to refer to any thought and speech about Jesus who is said to be the Christ, even where what is asserted about him may be formulated in terms other than the particular concept or title "the Christ." Thus even where Jesus is said to be such different things as the Son of Man or the Lord, the Word of God or even God, we unhesitatingly recognize clear cases of "christology" in this broader sense of the word.

Moreover, it is evident from the New Testament and the church's creeds that predicating such honorific titles of Jesus is not the only way in which Christians have formulated what they have to think and say about him in their witness and theology. They have followed no less frequently the different, if closely related, way of asserting his decisive significance by narrative formulations that have to do with his origin and destiny or the course of his earthly life, and that we can understand today only as mythological or legendary. Thus, whether Jesus is said to be conceived by the Holy Spirit and born of the Virgin Mary, or to be risen from the dead and ascended into heaven, the assertion thus formulated mythologically is clearly the same christological assertion that the various honorific titles otherwise function to formulate. And the same is true of the legendary formulations that are also familiar from the New Testament, when different authors think and speak of Jesus' precocity among the teachers in the temple (Lk 2:41–49), his faithfulness to his vocation and submission to God's will (Mt 4:1–10 par.; Mk 14:32–42), his godly fear and obedience (Heb 5:7–9), his exemplary endurance of suffering (1Pe 2:21ff.), and his being sinless and made perfect (Heb 4:15, 5:9, 7:26ff.; 1Pe 2:22). These formulations are also rightly reckoned to be christological because they clearly function to do what all christology properly does — namely, formulate what I call "the constitutive christological assertion." By this I mean the one assertion, however formulated, that Christians make or imply about Jesus that constitutes not only christology, but also the Christian witness of faith itself explicitly as such.

Because it is thus constituted by an assertion about Jesus, however, christology simply as such is by its very meaning a posteriori. Just as Jesus himself is a historical fact, so the assertion of his decisive significance, however formulated, must also be, in one important part, a historical assertion. And this means that it could not be made or implied as such at all except after the fact of his appearance in history and on the basis of particular historical experience, mediate or immediate, of this fact.

On the other hand, the christological assertion is like any other, historical or not, in asserting a certain predicate of its subject. Relative to its particular subject or any other of which it could be meaningfully asserted, the predicate as such is a priori. Not only what it means, but also what conditions need to be fulfilled in order to assert it truly of any subject, can, and in a sense must, be understood before the fact of this or that particular assertion of it, whether of Jesus or of someone else. This would be true, indeed, even if the christological assertion were nothing more than a historical assertion. But this it cannot be, because it does not assert that Jesus *was* thus and so, but that he *is* the Christ; or, in some functionally equivalent and interchangeable formulation, that he is of decisive significance for human existence. As such, it is also, in important part, what is commonly called "an assertion of faith," or, as I prefer to say, "an existential assertion." This I take to mean that although it could indeed arise only after the historical fact of Jesus' appearance and on the basis of particular experience of this fact, it also makes a certain valuation of Jesus in relation to the existential question that we human beings typically ask about the meaning of ultimate reality for us. To be exact, it makes a valuation of Jesus as himself the decisive answer to this existential question and therefore as the explicit primal source authorizing the authentic understanding of ourselves and others in relation to the strictly ultimate reality of the whole.

It lies in the nature of the case, however, that the existential assertion of christology can no more be truly made about Jesus than about anyone else, unless certain conditions are fulfilled that are necessary and sufficient for truly making it. In other words, the valuation that christology makes of Jesus is not merely a subjective preference, but rather necessarily implies an objective claim — to the effect that Jesus fulfills all the conditions that are necessary to anyone's being the decisive answer to the existential question and therefore of decisive significance for human existence. But this means that it must be possible to stipulate these necessary conditions a priori — before the fact of Jesus, even as before every other fact of which "the Christ" or any functionally equivalent and interchangeable christological predicate could be meaningfully asserted.

What I mean by "a priori christology," then, is just such a stipulation. Even as christology simply as such is the explicit assertion, in some formulation or other, of the decisive significance of Jesus, so a priori christology is the explicit stipulation, again, in some terms or other, of the conditions that need to be fulfilled in order to make or imply the same kind of assertion about any subject whatever.

Among the other implications of this comparison is that a priori christology can also be implied even when it is not made explicit. As a matter of fact, it belongs to the very logic of a christology simply as such that it necessarily presupposes *some* a priori christology. To assert or imply that Jesus is of decisive significance for human existence could not be meaningful at all unless it presupposed some stipulation of the conditions necessary to asserting this truly of any possible subject. But there are the best of reasons, then, for making this implied stipulation explicit as an a priori christology. For whether or not a proposed christological formulation can be critically validated as credible depends, finally, upon whether or not the a priori christology that it necessarily presupposes allows for at least its possible validation.

4

This bring us to the main task of my argument: to show that christological formulations of either of the two usual types are open to the same fatal objection to any proposed solution to the problem of christology today. I will consider the two types of christology separately, but will proceed in each case by taking the same two steps. After briefly characterizing each type, I will first explicate the a priori christology that it necessarily presupposes, and then I will explain why this a priori christology precludes even the possibility of critically validating the christology itself as credible, if this means, as it must mean today, verifying its formulations in experiential terms.

I begin with the type of christology that I call "orthodox." If the classical formulation of this type was provided, as I have said, by the Chalcedonian definition, it is arguable that the two main approaches to christology that the definition sought to hold together were already present in the New Testament writings themselves (cf. Chadwick 1983). These approaches can be characterized sufficiently for our purposes by nuancing the distinction I made earlier between mythological and legendary ways of asserting Jesus' decisive significance by narratives about his origin and destiny or the events of his earthly life. In point of fact, there was not simply one mythological way of doing this, but two. On the one hand, there was the presumably earlier and more traditionally Jewish way of representing Jesus as in every respect a human being, but a human being who had been specially sent or commissioned by God, or whom God had in some special way elected or adopted, whether by inspiring him with the divine Spirit or by raising him from the dead. On the other hand, there was the later, and more typically Hellenistic (and Hellenistic-Jewish), way of representing Jesus as himself in some respect a divine being, whether an ideal figure like the Jewish Wisdom or Word of God, whose only pre-existence was God's own, or, rather, a real figure somehow pre-existing alongside God, who could become incarnate as a human being to effect the salvation of all other women and men.

If the first of these ways was relatively strong in more clearly attesting to the full reality of Jesus' humanity, it was relatively weak in not so clearly witnessing that he was God's own decisive act of salvation. But the reverse was true of the second way, whose relative strength and weakness were exactly opposite, in that it more clearly witnessed to Jesus as God's own decisive act, even while less clearly attesting to his being really and fully human. Essentially the same was true, then, of the later, more fully developed forms of these same two approaches between which the Chalcedonian definition attempted to effect a consensus. On the one hand, there was the *logos-anthropos* christology of Antioch, which was strong in its witness to Jesus' humanity, even if weak in attesting to him as God's own act of salvation. On the other hand, there was the *logos-sarx* christology of Alexandria, which was strong in attesting to Jesus as God's own saving act, even though weak in witnessing to him as really and fully a human being. By holding these two christologies together, the Chalcedonian definition, in its way, summed up the whole development of christology that had begun even before the New Testament writings, thereby providing the guidelines for the church's witness to Jesus that it is arguably the proper function of doctrine as such to provide (cf. Norris 1966; 1980).

If we ask now what this orthodox type of christology necessarily presupposes in the way of a priori christology, the answer seems clear enough. It presupposes that, for any possible value of x, x can be truly asserted to be of decisive significance for human existence if, and only if, x is not only really and fully a human being but also actualizes God's unique possibility of acting decisively to save all other human beings. By God's "acting" here, I mean, just as orthodox christology clearly means, what is commonly understood to be a divine intervention. We rightly speak of such an intervention whenever God intentionally produces a state of affairs by causally altering the way things would have gone otherwise, if the only causes involved had been natural or nondivine. Orthodox christology evidently takes for granted that just as any special act of God would be an intervention in this sense, so the same must be true *a fortiori* of God's decisive act of salvation in the human being Jesus. This means, then, that the a priori christology that orthodox christology presupposes stipulates being just such a divine intervention as among the necessary conditions that any value of x must fulfill if she or he is to be truly said to be of decisive existential significance. If, and only if, a being who is really and fully human at the same time actualizes God's own possibility of intervening decisively for human salvation, can she or he be truly asserted to be the Christ or any of the other things that are functionally equivalent thereto and interchangeable therewith.

The great weakness of this a priori christology, however, is that nothing in common human experience could ever verify that any really and fully human being at the same time actualizes an intervention of God, much less God's decisive intervention for human salvation. For all experience could possibly show, any assertion to this effect about any human being whatever would be merely that — merely an assertion, unverifiable by appeal to experience and to be accepted, if at all, solely by appeal to authority.

This should not be confused with the objection that the general concept of God's intervention is either unclear or incoherent or without any basis in experience. There are, indeed, certain well-known difficulties with the concept, theological as well as philosophical, which have led many revisionary theologians to abandon it (cf., e.g., Wiles 1986). But other, more traditionalist theologians and philosophers continue to defend the concept as viable on the grounds that it is necessarily implied by any Christian witness or theology that is appropriate to Jesus Christ, and that the usual revisionary arguments against it do not, in fact, provide sufficient reasons for abandoning it.

Thus one of the most common objections against the concept is that divine intervention is incompatible with the strict naturalistic determinism widely held to be at once assumed by modern science and confirmed by its continuing successes. But as William P. Alston has effectively shown, this objection has little weight. Aside from the fact that appeals to what science is held to assume or confirm are really only appeals to authority, neither the procedures of science nor its results warrant the conclusion that "every event in the universe is strictly determined to be just what it is by natural factors." On the contrary, "all our evidence is equally compatible with the idea that natural causal determination is sometimes, or always, only approximate," and "particular divine actions would not jeopardize, or otherwise adversely affect, anything fundamental to science" (Alston 1994, 48f.).

As for the other common objection that the concept of God's intervention entails violating laws of nature, Alston replies convincingly that this all depends on how we think of laws of nature and that we have no good reason to think of them in the particular way that warrants the objection. The only such laws that we have reason to accept do not specify the sufficient conditions of certain outcomes without qualification, but only within "a system closed to influences other than those specified in the law." Thus, "since the laws we have reason to accept make provision for interference by outside forces unanticipated by the law, it can hardly be claimed that such a law will be violated if a divine outside force intervenes; and hence it can hardly be claimed that such laws imply that God does not intervene, much less imply that this is impossible" (50).

Alston recognizes, significantly, that it is one thing thus to defend the general concept of divine intervention, something else again to validate claims arising from applying it to particular cases. In this connection, he makes a brief response to the classical formulation of objections to such claims in David Hume's chapter on miracles in the *Enquiry Concerning Human Understanding*. He observes, first of all, that "it is not generally the case that alleged divine interventions go contrary to our experience"; and then, secondly, that "the likelihood of a report of miracle is profoundly influenced by one's background religious and metaphysical assumptions. If these include the principle that the world is created and governed by a being who has reasons to intervene from time to time, this will materially increase the probability of some such reports being correct, though it does not, of course, establish the correctness of any particular report" (51). Consistent with this concluding admission, Alston expressly disavows any concern "to determine how we should go about identifying divine interventions," assuring his reader that he is concerned "only to argue for the viability of the concept" (51f.).

Alston's sense of the limitations of his argument is fitting. Even if an alleged divine intervention does not generally go contrary to our experience, so as to justify a strong experiential argument against its occurrence, nothing simply in experience either does or can suffice to identify it as the divine intervention it is alleged to be. An occurrence *contra naturam* is, for all experience could ever show, simply that, since whether it is a divine intervention, or is to be explained instead by other forces likewise unspecified by the relevant laws of nature, can never be determined simply by appealing to experience. As for Alston's second observation, careful inspection discloses that it subtly begs the question. That a God conceived to be the all-good and all-powerful creator and consummator of all things *may have* reasons to intervene from time to time does indeed seem to follow. But from background religious and metaphysical assumptions that include the principle that the world is, in fact, created and governed by a God so conceived, it in no way follows that God actually *has* any such reasons sufficient to increase the probability of at least some reports of God's having so intervened being correct. Whether God, in fact, has such reasons can no more be decided by a principle included in one's background religious and metaphysical assumptions than can the question whether God has, in fact, intervened. Nor are we ever in a position to answer the first question any more than the second simply by what we can experience as human beings.

Viable, then, as the concept of divine intervention may be, there is not the least reason to suppose that we could ever be justified in so applying the concept through experience as to identify any particular divine intervention. There cannot be a valid inference from the general concept to a particular application, because *a posse ad esse non valet consequentia*.

But then, even if God did in fact decisively intervene, no assertion to this effect could ever be verified in experiential terms. Because this is so, however, any christological proposal of the orthodox type is open to the fatal objection that its formulations of the christological assertion cannot be experientially verified. The a priori christology that it necessarily presupposes explicates a condition for making the assertion truly that no experience could possibly verify as being fulfilled. Consequently, whatever may be said for the appropriateness of such a christology, its claim to be credible cannot be validated in the way in which our situation today requires.

5

The same is true of the other usual type of christology that I distinguish as "revisionary." Since I have already extensively criticized this type elsewhere, I will consider it more briefly here and refer the reader to other writings for fuller discussion (see Ogden 1992b; also below, pp. 210–229).

If there is any single formulation of revisionary christology that can be rightly regarded as classical, it must surely be that of Friedrich Schleiermacher in *Der christliche Glaube* (2d ed., 1830). But here too the type was already anticipated, in a way, in some of the christological formulations documented by the writings of the New Testament. I referred earlier to these writings as evidencing a legendary way, alongside the two mythological ways, of asserting Jesus' decisive existential significance by narrative formulations concerning his origin and destiny and the course of his earthly life. Whereas the mythological ways, as we have seen, both represent Jesus, in some terms or other, as God's own saving act, and hence as actualizing God's unique possibility of intervening decisively for human salvation; the legendary way thinks and speaks of Jesus, again, in different terms, as actualizing the unique possibility of a human being to exist authentically and even perfectly in relation to God — to be utterly and completely open to God and to both self and all others in God, and to lead her or his whole human life accordingly. It is significant, however, that this legendary way of representing Jesus, which is evident already from the New Testament, traditionally had its place only in the context provided by one or both of the other mythological ways. Thus, while the Chalcedonian definition undoubtedly continues the legendary way, also, by explicitly attesting to Jesus' sinlessness, the claim thereby implied for the perfection of his human existence is in no way independent of his being God's decisive intervention, but rather follows logically from it.

It is quite otherwise, however, with the revisionary christology of Schleiermacher and of all who have continued to follow his lead right

up to today (cf. Faut 1904). Here the legendary way of asserting Jesus'
decisive significance has been taken out of its traditional context in
one or both of the mythological ways and then pursued by itself as an
independent type of christology. This is evident from the fact that all references to God's unique intervention in Jesus are construed as equivalent
to references to Jesus' own unique perfection as a human being. Thus
Schleiermacher can say that "it is exactly one and the same to ascribe
to Christ an absolutely powerful God-consciousness and to attribute to
him a being of God in him" (Schleiermacher 1960, 2:45 [§94]). When
Schleiermacher speaks of "God-consciousness," he is simply referring to
authentic human existence, so as to formulate the ideal of human perfection as a God-consciousness that is "absolutely powerful." But however
this ideal may be formulated — and revisionary theologians have formulated it in many different ways — the claim typical of revisionary
christologies from Schleiermacher to the present is that Jesus is of decisive existential significance because, and only because, he actualized
this ideal in his own existence as a human being.

The reason for this, of course, is that revisionary christologies are all
of a single type precisely because they necessarily presuppose one and
the same a priori christology. They presuppose, to be explicit, that, for
any possible value of x, x can be truly asserted to be of decisive significance for human existence if, and only if, x is not only really and
fully a human being, but also actualizes her or his unique possibility of
attaining a perfect human existence. By "a perfect human existence,"
I understand the ideal, or unsurpassable, actualization of authentic existence — of what any human being is at least implicitly authorized to
be in every moment of her or his existence by God, in the sense of the
strictly ultimate whole of reality in its meaning for us. This means, then,
that a human being can be truly asserted to be the Christ, or any of the
other functionally equivalent and interchangeable things that Jesus has
been asserted or implied to be, if, and only if, there is no moment in her
or his entire existence in which she or he fails to actualize the possibility of thus existing authentically. In this sense, a sinless human existence
not only implies, but is also implied by, a perfect human existence; and
only the actualization of such an existence could warrant truly asserting
of any human being what christology asserts of Jesus.

But the great weakness of this a priori christology, also, is that no
such assertion about Jesus or anyone else could ever be verified by direct appeal to experience, as distinct from some authority, itself in need,
finally, of experiential verification. Nothing that any one human being could possibly experience could ever verify that another, equally
really and fully human, actualizes even authentic existence, much less
attains perfection or sinlessness. Consequently, even if a human being
did in fact attain perfection, no assertion to this effect could be veri-

fied experientially, but could be accepted as true solely on the basis of authority.

Once again, however, there is no need in saying this to object to the very idea of perfection, or to the possibility of someone's attaining it. Just as the concept of a divine intervention can be allowed to be viable, so the idea of a human perfection can also be accepted as sufficiently clear and coherent to refer to something at least possible. But this in no way meets the objection that experience cannot possibly determine whether any human being has attained a perfect existence. Even if one could judge from the thoughts, words, and deeds of a person, instead of only from the witnesses thereto of others, there would still be no way of inferring from what one can thus experience about the person to a self-understanding that in the nature of the case one cannot experience. Nor can such an inference be mediated by a warrant to the effect that, if one has, in fact, understood oneself authentically, or attained perfection, one will think, say, and do certain things, while avoiding certain other things. What the inference logically requires is the converse of this warrant, and for all that any experience could possibly show, its converse is nothing but the formal fallacy that it gives every appearance of being. Moreover, the data base that would be needed to infer the attainment of perfection so far exceeds what any human being could possibly experience of another, that any attempt to acquire it can be dismissed at once as a practical absurdity.

Because this is so, all christological proposals of the revisionary type are vulnerable to the same fatal objection that must be made to any of the orthodox type. Their formulations of the christological assertion are experientially unverifiable, because they too necessarily presuppose an a priori christology that stipulates a condition for making or implying the assertion truly that no experience could ever show to be fulfilled. Therefore, even if the claim of revisionary christologies to be appropriate could be critically validated, their further claim to be credible in terms of human experience could not.

6

If the argument to this point is sound, it should now be clear that both of the usual types of christology, orthodox and revisionary, are incapable of solving the christological problem as it arises out of our situation today. The question for Christian theology, then, and for systematic theology in particular, is whether there is some alternative proposal for solving the problem. Is there perhaps a third type of christology whose formulations can be critically validated as credible because they at least can be verified in some way by common experience?

The answer to this question depends, as we have seen, upon whether there is another a priori christology that allows for at least the possible experiential verification of any christological formulations necessarily presupposing it. This an a priori christology can allow only if fulfillment of the conditions that it stipulates for truly asserting the decisive significance of Jesus or of anyone else can be verified somehow experientially. I now want to show that there is such an a priori christology and that, therefore, there is also a type of christology whose formulations can be critically validated as credible in terms of human experience.

The a priori christology I have in mind stipulates the following as the conditions that need to be fulfilled in order to assert truly of anyone what christology asserts or implies about Jesus. For any possible value of x, x can be truly asserted to be of decisive significance for human existence if, and only if, x is not only really and fully a human being, but also decisively re-presents the meaning of ultimate reality for us and, therewith, our unique possibility of authentic existence. By "re-presents" here, I mean simply "makes explicit." My assumption is that the meaning of ultimate reality for us, including our unique possibility of existing authentically, is and must be presented implicitly to each and every one of us as soon and as long as we are human beings at all. But what is thus presented at least implicitly in all our human experience can also become present again, a second time, and, in this sense, be *re*-presented explicitly through specific persons and things and through the specific concepts and symbols by which we grasp and express their meaning.

There is the further possibility, then, that someone or something will not only thus make the meaning of our existence explicit, but will do so "decisively," by so answering our existential question as thereby to authorize our decision between all other re-presentations. In other words, if x *decisively* re-presents our possibility, x is not simply one authority among others, but rather functions as the explicit *primal source* of all authorities, because it explicitly authorizes them as well as the authentic understanding of ourselves and others in relation to the whole. This means that if, and only if, a being who is really and fully human at the same time decisively re-presents our authentic possibility, and thus functions as just such an explicit primal source of authority, can she or he be truly asserted to be of decisive existential significance.

The great strength of this a priori christology, compared with both of the others we have considered, is that whether or not this condition is in fact fulfilled is at least verifiable by human experience. That a person decisively re-presents our authentic possibility depends entirely on what she or he thinks, says, and does, and on what others think, say, and do, including, not least, the others who bear witness to her or his meaning for us. But all of this can be directly experienced, mediately if not immediately, and there is no need to depend upon authority to validate the credibility of formulations asserting or implying her or his decisive significance for our existence.

This is not to deny that there is an important difference between verifying that someone, in fact, re-presents a certain possibility of self-understanding and verifying that the possibility thus re-presented is, in truth, our unique possibility of authentic existence. To verify the second may also be — and I believe is — a matter, finally, of experience. But the experience required to verify it is not simply the particular historical experience required to verify the first, but is the existential experience of our own existence with others in relation to the whole. This means that it also requires properly metaphysical and moral procedures of verification that go beyond all of the procedures required to verify strictly historical assertions (cf. Ogden 1992a, 16–21; 1992b, 82–85, 127–168).

But in this respect, the other a priori christology is in no way different from the two usual accounts, both of which likewise involve their own metaphysical and moral presuppositions. After all, it would not make any sense to talk about a divine intervention were there not a God who has the possibility of intervening; and unless the strictly ultimate reality is a God of whom a human being can and should be conscious, there could be no meaningful talk of human perfection's being an absolutely powerful God-consciousness.

The great strength of the other a priori christology, however, is that once its metaphysical and moral presuppositions are shown to be true, whether Jesus or anyone else is of decisive existential significance can be verified forthwith by appeal to particular historical experience such as anyone might possibly have. It does not stipulate conditions that no one could ever possibly experience to be fulfilled, whatever her or his other background metaphysical and moral presuppositions.

That there is this other a priori christology, however, means that there is also a third type of christology whose formulations can be critically validated as credible because they at least can be verified experientially. According to these formulations, Jesus is of decisive existential significance, not because he actualizes either God's possibility of intervention or his own possibility of perfection, but because he decisively re-presents our possibility of authentic existence. That he in fact does this, however, is experientially verifiable, whereas the reasons formulated by the two usual types of christology are not. Consequently, the third type of christology can be critically validated as credible in terms of experience, and thus is strong at the very point at which the other two types are weak.

Of course, this is not the only point at which a proposal must be strong if it is to solve our christological problem. Today as always, such a proposal must be appropriate as well as credible, and this means appropriate to Jesus as Christians have experienced him ever since the constitutive experience of the apostles. Whether this third type of christology is appropriate in this sense is not a question I can answer here, any more than I have argued that it is, in fact, credible. But even in this respect it may validly claim a certain strength, relative to the orthodox and revisionary types. Whatever else the apostles and other Christians may have experienced Jesus to be and mean, they could not possibly have experienced what no person is ever in a position to experience about another, either immediately or mediately. Therefore, the usual types of christology can no more validly claim to be appropriate to Jesus as Christians have experienced him than to be credible to human existence as all of us experience it.

On the other hand, the third type can still prove to be as appropriate in terms of specifically Christian experience as it is credible in terms of human experience generally. There are good reasons, then, to look to it for the remaking of christology, and thus of Christian doctrine, that our situation today requires.

Part III

Theology of Religions

10

"For Freedom
Christ Has Set Us Free"

The Christian Understanding of Ultimate Transformation

I

This essay is written out of an ongoing theological encounter between Buddhists and Christians, in which participants on both sides have tried to identify fundamental topics that could fruitfully focus Buddhist-Christian dialogue. The topic of discussion to which this essay is a contribution is "transformation," which I have taken the liberty of formulating more precisely as "ultimate transformation." This I have done both because it is in a quite precise sense that transformation is of interest to both Buddhists and Christians, and because of the precedent established by the well-known working definition according to which "religion is a means to ultimate transformation" (Streng 1985, 2). Pending such clarification as can come only as my argument develops, suffice it to say here that my principal assumption in so formulating the topic is that Buddhists and Christians are alike interested in discussing precisely ultimate transformation, because at the center of their respective self-understandings is that unique change in human life that may be formally characterized as the transition from inauthentic to authentic existence.

Given this assumption, my task is to state summarily the Christian understanding of this transition. Of course, the only way that I or anyone else can do this is to offer someone's understanding of this Christian understanding — in this case, my own. And recognizing this, one may wonder why I have committed myself to state *the,* instead of simply *a,* Christian understanding of ultimate transformation.

There are, in fact, two reasons. In the first place, to claim to offer even *a* Christian understanding is either to beg the question of whether it really is a *Christian* understanding after all, or else to assume the identical burden that must be borne by anyone who would offer *the* Christian understanding. In the second place, I can only suppose that what brings Buddhists and Christians together in theological encounter is not simply that they are all human beings who must somehow ask and answer the existential question about the meaning of ultimate reality for us, but also that each of them is a Buddhist or a Christian who as such bears responsibility for giving a certain answer to this question that is not only or primarily her or his own, but also, and first of all, that of the religious community of which she or he is a part. For both reasons, then, I can carry out my task only by trying to state, not what I understand by ultimate transformation, but what I understand to be the understanding of it that is normative for the Christian community.

On the other hand, I do not take mine to be the merely historical task of describing how Christians have in fact understood the transition from inauthentic to authentic existence. As much as I agree that what is normative for the Christian community is indeed given historically — namely, in the witness of the apostles by which the community as such was constituted — I nevertheless insist on the difference between interpreting historically what Christians have thought, said, and done in actually bearing their witness, and stating systematically what they ought to think, say, and do if they are to bear it validly. Because it is just such a systematic statement that I take to be called for here, I can only suppose that if mine is a properly theological task at all, it is a systematic, rather than a historical, theological task.

In taking it to be properly theological, however, I also understand it to be significantly different from preaching or teaching or any other form of bearing Christian witness simply as such. Whereas all forms of Christian witness address others so as to summon them directly or indirectly to a Christian self-understanding, the proper task of theology is so to reflect on the claims to validity that are expressed or implied by such witness as to validate (or invalidate) these claims. More specifically, it is the proper task of systematic theology to validate the claim of any instance of Christian witness to be adequate to its content, in the twofold sense of being both appropriate to Jesus Christ and credible to human existence. Thus, insofar as it is constructive, systematic theology consists in a formulation of the Christian witness that answers to the theoretical questions about the appropriateness and the credibility of this witness, as distinct from the existential question about the meaning of ultimate reality for us, to which Christian witness itself is an answer. The same must be true, then, of the statement called for in this essay if it is to be the properly systematic theological statement that I judge it should be.

This implies, of course, that the questions that are proper to criticizing the adequacy of my statement are mainly two: (1) Is its formulation really appropriate to the understanding of ultimate transformation expressed or implied by normative Christian witness to Jesus Christ? (2) Is its formulation really credible to human existence as such, in terms simply of our common human experience and reason? Obviously, any of my readers who may be Buddhists have particular reason to press the second question, even as those who are Christians will particularly want to press the first. But only a little reflection makes clear that we each have a stake in seriously asking both questions, lest we fail really to understand ourselves and our partners in dialogue or allow ourselves to believe what is not really worthy of our belief. This is not to say, however, that I shall offer the kind of evidence and argument for my claims that would be necessary to validate their appropriateness and credibility. On the contrary, one of the limitations of a summary statement is that it can do little more than clarify the claims that only a more developed statement could validate.

2

As I said before, my assumption in formulating our topic as "ultimate transformation" is that the transformation that Buddhists and Christians are interested in discussing may be characterized formally as the transition from inauthentic to authentic existence. But a statement such as this cannot advance our discussion very far until its operative terms are themselves clarified or defined. The next step, then, is to explain what is meant formally by "the transition from inauthentic to authentic existence"; and this will require, in turn, at least some explanation of the whole terminology of which this term is a part and in which I, for one, find it helpful to think and speak about our topic.

I would emphasize that this step, or one very like it, seems to me to be necessary in making any contribution to Buddhist-Christian dialogue. If Buddhists and Christians are to think and speak together about one and the same general topic, they must all concern themselves with providing the formal terms in which this can be done. Therefore, if any of my readers finds my terminology less helpful for this purpose than I do, I can only invite her or him either to help me refine it or else to suggest a possible alternative.

I begin with the term "ultimate reality." According to a useful definition by William James, reality in general is "what we in some way find ourselves obliged to take account of" (James 1911, 101). Assuming this definition, I should say that "ultimate reality" refers to everything that we are all finally obliged to take account of insofar as we exist humanly at all, whatever other things we may or may not have to take account of in each leading our own lives as individual persons. Thus ultimate reality includes everything necessary in our self-understanding, as distinct from all of the other things that we understand that are merely contingent relative to our own existence simply as such. Whatever else it includes, then, ultimate reality includes our own existence as selves, together with everything that is in any way a necessary condition of the possibility of our existence, whether other human selves or the still larger world of subhuman and possibly even superhuman beings. Among the conditions that are thus necessary, obviously, is any reality that can be said to be "strictly ultimate," because it is a necessary condition of the possibility not only of human existence, but of any existence whatever. Thus strictly ultimate reality is what not only we, but any being that is so much as possible, is obliged somehow to take account of, if only in the completely general sense of being really, internally related to it and therefore dependent on it and affected by it.

Of course, it is in a much more specific sense than this that we as human beings are obliged to take account of ultimate reality, including whatever is strictly ultimate. Recognizing this, philosophers have clarified an emphatic sense of the term "existence," in which it refers not merely to the actualization of essence generally, but to the specifically human essence that can be actualized only by self-understanding. Insofar as we exist in this emphatic sense at all, then, we exist understandingly; and so we are obliged to take account of our own existence, as well as of anything else that is ultimately real, not only by being internally related to it, and so dependent on it and affected by it, but also by somehow understanding it. Lest this claim be misunderstood, however, we should note that the understanding of existence and of whatever else is ultimate that is of the very essence of our humanity may or may not become explicit, and so may remain only a more or less implicit understanding.

As it happens, however, the capacity and the necessity somehow to understand ourselves and anything else that is ultimately real allow for yet another and more momentous contingency: we may *mis*understand both our own existence and everything else that is ultimate, including that which is strictly so. For this reason, to exist humanly at all is to be faced with the existential question about the meaning of ultimate reality for us, although once again we should note that one may very well ask and answer this question implicitly more than as an explicit question. In any event, as the question about the meaning of ultimate reality for us, it asks at one and the same time about both ultimate reality and ourselves. Thus it has two essential aspects, metaphysical and moral, in which it is distinctively different from, even while being closely related to, both properly metaphysical and properly moral types of questions.

On the one hand, it is different from properly metaphysical questions because, while it indeed asks about ultimate reality, it asks about the meaning of ultimate reality for us, not about the structure of ultimate reality in itself. Even so, it is also related to metaphysical questions insofar as any answer to it necessarily implies some answer to them — the meaning of ultimate reality for us being correlated with the structure of ultimate reality in itself. On the other hand, it is different from properly moral questions because, while it indeed asks about ourselves, it asks about our self-understanding, not about our action. Still, it is also related to moral questions, insofar as any answer to it necessarily implies some answer to them — our self-understanding being correlated with how we are to act and what we are to do.

Notwithstanding its two essential aspects, the existential question is a single question. In asking it, we do not ask two different questions about ultimate reality and about our self-understanding; rather, we ask one and the same question about both — on the supposition that some understanding of ourselves is appropriate to ultimate reality in its structure in itself and, in this sense, is authorized by it. Therefore, while we do indeed suppose that ultimate reality is prior to our self-understanding, we ask about ultimate reality only insofar as it authorizes our self-understanding, even as we ask about our self-understanding only insofar as, being appropriate to ultimate reality, it is authorized by it.

To speak in this sense of an "authorized" self-understanding, however, is precisely what I mean by an "authentic" self-understanding; and seeing that we cannot exist humanly at all except by somehow understanding ourselves, I use the term "authentic existence" to distinguish that way of being human that is actualized by an authentic self-understanding. Correspondingly, I hold that any self-understanding that is really a misunderstanding, because it is not appropriate to ultimate reality, and, in this sense, is unauthorized, is properly called an "inauthentic self-understanding," and the way of existing that it actualizes, "inauthentic existence."

By "the transition from inauthentic to authentic existence," then, I mean either the process of, or an instance of, change from an inauthentic to an authentic understanding of ourselves. Accordingly, the import of my original assumption is that the ultimate transformation that Buddhists and Christians both claim to understand in their respectively different ways may be thought and spoken about formally as just such a change in self-understanding. Of course, it will be clear from what has been said that any self-understanding is closely related both to certain metaphysical beliefs and to certain moral actions. Therefore, it is at least possible that the change from an inauthentic to an authentic self-understanding may involve still further changes in what we believe, as well as in how we act and what we do. But even if we fully allow for this possibility, the implication of my assumption is clear: relative to this ultimate transformation in self-understanding, all other changes are at most penultimate transformations.

3

The question now is as to the material understanding of ultimate transformation that is expressed or implied by normative Christian witness (see Bultmann 1949; 1984b). It will be clear from my title that I shall be guided in answering this question by the theology — or, more exactly, christology — of freedom classically formulated by Paul (cf. Betz 1979). But if accepting Paul's guidance is only to be expected of someone who stands in my ecclesial and theological tradition, it in no way settles the question of the appropriateness of my answer. On the contrary, even Paul's theology is in principle exactly like my own in being the formulation for a particular situation of the witness of the apostles that is the sole primary norm of witness and theology alike. The question remains, therefore, whether or to what extent his theology itself is appropriate when measured by this norm, as well as credible in terms of his situation, if not also in terms of ours. In any event, we have seen that what is called for here is not an exegesis of Paul, but a systematic theological statement adequate for our situation today; and it is this that I intend to provide even if it is the tradition constituted by Paul's theological reflections that I shall follow in doing so.

The proper starting point for such a statement is the constitutive assertion of Christian witness that Jesus is the Christ, in the sense that through Jesus, the meaning of ultimate reality for us is decisively re-presented. I say "*re*-presented" here in order to bring out that, given what the term "ultimate reality" has been explained to mean, any meaning of ultimate reality for us that could be explicitly re-presented through Jesus must have always already been implicitly presented in our self-understanding simply as human beings. Nevertheless, because our self-understanding can be fully ours only insofar as it becomes explicit, and because it is always possible for it to be really a misunderstanding, there are good reasons why what is first presented in our existence itself should also be presented again, and so *re*-presented, through particular historical events. Moreover, given the plurality of such re-presentations as have in fact emerged in the course of history, there is equally good reason why there should be some *decisive* re-presentation whereby one can responsibly decide between conflicting claims. In any case, the assertion constituting Christian witness explicitly as such is that the event of Jesus is just such a decisive re-presentation — hence its qualification of this event by christological titles like "Christ" — and that therefore the meaning of ultimate reality that we always already understand, if only implicitly or by misunderstanding it, is none other than that which this event makes explicit.

In this sense, Christian witness is and must be "christocentric." But there is a difference between claiming that the only meaning of ultimate reality for us is that which is decisively re-presented through Jesus, and claiming that it is only in Jesus that the meaning of ultimate reality for us is constituted (see below, pp. 182–183). In my view, the kind of christocentrism that makes or implies the second claim is profoundly incompatible with the Christian understanding of human existence. Jesus is rightly said to be the Christ because he *defines* the ultimate reality he re-presents, not because he *confines* it — just as, by analogy, certain elements, once consecrated, are rightly said to be a sacrament because they *define* the grace they signify, not because they *confine* it. On the other hand, I take it to be also incompatible with a Christian self-understanding to allow any event other than Jesus or alongside him to be or to belong to the decisive re-presentation of the meaning of ultimate reality for us. Although a Christian, in my view, can and must allow that the same meaning may indeed be re-presented through other events, which for non-Christians may well be its decisive re-presentations, it belongs to the christocentrism proper to the Christian witness to take Jesus alone to be decisive — just as, by analogy, a Christian may very well allow that even the most ordinary meal may be a real means of grace for certain persons, and yet insist that it is solely the Lord's Supper rightly administered that is a proper Christian sacrament.

But if we start with the christological assertion thus understood, we proceed by asking about the answer to the existential question that is decisively re-presented through Jesus. What does this answer assert about the meaning of ultimate reality for us and therefore about our own authentic self-understanding?

Its assertion about the meaning of ultimate reality for us is determined by the logically prior assertion that the only strictly ultimate reality, which not only we but anything that is so much as possible is somehow obliged to take account of, is the reality of God, itself understood to be the utterly boundless love both of itself and of everything else. According to this answer, the sole primal source both of ourselves and of any even merely possible world of other persons and things is the same unbounded love that is also the sole final end of all things. This means that our self-understanding can be authentic only insofar as it is appropriate to this love, and so authorized by it — whence the assertion that we are to understand ourselves through faith in God's love.

By "faith" here is meant the relatively passive moment in our self-understanding that consists in trust — trust in the love of God alone as the primal source and the final end of our own lives as well as of everything else. I think and speak of such trust as "relatively passive" because while it is indeed a moment in our own self-understanding, it is that moment in which we accept the always already prior reality of God's love for us and for all other things as the only strictly ultimate reality. In other words, the trust that is the relatively passive moment in our faith corresponds to the aspect of God's love in which it is relatively active, and unsurpassably so, because it does all that any love could conceivably do for all others as well as itself. We can and should trust in God's love without reservation because it unceasingly acts not only to create a world in which it is possible for us and all other creatures to exist and to act in turn, but also to redeem this world from its bondage to decay by embracing each and every creature into God's own unending life.

But "faith" also means the other relatively active moment in our self-understanding that consists in loyalty — loyalty to God's love as the one integral cause that all existence and action are to serve, our own as well as all others'. This moment of faith is rightly thought and spoken of as "relatively active" because even though it too presupposes the pre-venient action of God's love as the only strictly ultimate reality and is possible at all only where there is a prior trust in this love, it is the moment in our faith that is the proximate ground of our own returning action. As such, loyalty corresponds to the aspect of God's love in which it is relatively passive, albeit unsurpassably so, because it accepts all that could be conceivably done or suffered by anyone, whether itself or any other. We can and should be loyal to God's love without qualification because it unfailingly suffers all that we or anything else could possibly do or suffer as something that is also done to God.

It is faith in God's love in this twofold sense of unreserved trust and unqualified loyalty that is decisively re-presented through Jesus as our authentic self-understanding. But this means that any other self-understanding in which something besides God's love alone is the object of our trust and loyalty and, therefore, is also taken to be strictly ul-timate is an inauthentic understanding of our existence. The term for such an inauthentic understanding in traditional Christian witness and theology is "sin," whose meaning is seriously misunderstood when, as commonly happens, it is used only in the plural to refer to moral trans-gressions. As true as it is that moral transgressions are the inevitable consequence of sin, sin as such, and properly so-called, is not a mat-ter of action, of how we act or what we do, but a way of existing — namely, that way in which we do not accept, but rather reject, the al-ways already prior reality of God's love for us and for all as the only strictly ultimate reality.

Of course, being strictly ultimate, God's love is such that not only we, but anything whatever, is obliged somehow to take account of it; and for this reason neither we nor anything else could ever simply reject it. But so to understand ourselves as to direct our trust and loyalty to anything alongside God's love is precisely to reject it as the only strictly ultimate reality. In this sense, sin is indeed the rejection of God's love, which may be described either negatively as "unfaith," with its two moments of distrust in God's love and disloyalty to it, or else positively as "idolatry," with its two moments of trusting in and being loyal to something besides God's love as the only reality that is strictly ultimate.

In the Christian understanding, then, ultimate transformation as either the process of, or an instance of, change from an inauthentic to an authentic self-understanding is the change from sin to faith, or from unfaith and idolatry to trust in God's love and loyalty to it alone as strictly ultimate. In the Christian tradition, the name generally given to this change is "salvation," although other terms, such as "redemption" and "regeneration," are sometimes also used to describe it. In the Protestant tradition, it has also been commonly spoken of in terms of "justification" and "sanctification." Insofar as these terms are not simply other metaphors for thinking and speaking about one and the same change — as they often are, not only for Paul, but also for Martin Luther — they usually refer to two different aspects of the one transformation effected by God's love insofar as it is accepted through faith. In the case of "justification," the reference is primarily retrospective, in that it has to do with overcoming the *guilt* of sin from the past; while in the case of "sanctification," the primary reference is prospective, because it has to do with overcoming the *power* of sin over the future (see Watson 1959, 259; also Flew and Davies 1950; and Gerrish 1982).

But however one describes it, the possibility of such change is constituted solely by God's prevenient love, which, being boundless, embraces each and every woman and man, even though they have previously rejected God's love through the distrust and disloyalty of idolatrously trusting and serving other gods besides God. To be sure, the decisive re-presentation of this possibility is through Jesus, who is said to be the Christ just because he is the love of God itself made explicit in a decisive way. But as we have seen, it is one thing to *re-present* our authentic possibility, something else again to *constitute* it; and as surely as the right kind of christocentrism demands that the first be attributed decisively to Jesus, it just as surely demands that the second be attributed solely to Christ, by which I mean the prevenient love of God that Jesus decisively re-presents and for which "Christ," like all other such christological titles, is a more or less adequate expression. Properly speaking, we must say that the only constitutive agent of ultimate transformation from sin to faith is Christ, in the sense of God's own prevenient love, which is decisively re-presented through Jesus only because it is implicitly presented in human existence as such.

It is just this understanding of ultimate transformation that Paul formulates when he says, "For freedom Christ has set us free" (Gal 5:1). In the nature of the case, the way of existing actualized by the self-understanding of sin is an existence in bondage — namely, to all of the things that we take to be strictly ultimate by making them the objects of the trust and loyalty that rightly belong solely to God's love. By trusting and serving our various idols, we deliver ourselves into dependence on them and to this extent are not free, but bound in our relations both to them and to everything else. On the other hand, the way of existing actualized by the self-understanding of faith is just as naturally an existence in freedom — namely, both from and for everything other than

God's love, in which alone we place our trust and to which alone we
seek to be loyal. By trusting and serving nothing besides God's love,
we are delivered from dependence on all other things and to this extent are not bound, but free in our relations both to ourselves and to
everything else. This means that in making possible the change from
a self-understanding of sin to a self-understanding of faith, God's love
frees us from existence in bondage to existence in freedom. And it is this
that Paul has in mind when he tells us that it is for freedom that Christ
has set us free.

Not the least merit of his formulation, however, is to bring out that
the existence *in* freedom that is actualized by faith is, as he says, also
existence *for* freedom. In fact, Christ sets us free from existence in sin
for existence in faith only insofar as we exist and act for the freedom
of others as well as ourselves. This is the clear implication of my earlier
statement that faith in God's love consists not only in trusting in it without reservation, but also in being loyal to it without qualification. For,
clearly, to be loyal to God's love is also to be loyal to all to whom it is
loyal, and this, naturally, is everyone. Moreover, as certain as it is that
there cannot be any such loyalty unless there is first an unreserved trust
in God's love, it is equally certain that such prior trust itself can be really
present only where there is also this unqualified loyalty to God and to
all whom God loves. This is the point Paul himself makes in the immediate context of formulating his christology of freedom by speaking of the
faith for which Christ sets us free as "faith working through love" (Gal
5:6). It is the very nature of such faith, he attests, that it can be passive
to God's love for us only by being active in our own love for others.

However formulated, the point is that we cannot ourselves be freed
from the bondage of sin for the freedom of faith except by participating
actively as well as passively in God's liberating love. So it is that the
gift and demand of our own ultimate transformation involve us in the
ultimate transformation of all other human beings who can in any way
be affected by our action, as well as in such penultimate transformations
as are thereby also given and demanded by God's love (see Ogden 1989).

4

The last step in the argument is to clarify in principle exactly what
penultimate transformations are involved in ultimate transformation.
This we may do by recalling, first of all, something on which we have
touched more than once in the preceding discussion — namely, that any
self-understanding, being at least implicitly an answer to the existential
question about the meaning of ultimate reality for us, is closely related
both to metaphysical belief and to moral action. Therefore, understanding oneself in a certain way always involves believing certain beliefs

and performing certain actions. But if this can be said formally of any self-understanding, it might well appear that among the other changes involved in one's ultimate transformation from sin to faith is a change both in one's beliefs about ultimate reality and in one's actions toward others.

The difficulty in drawing this inference, however, is that one's self-understanding is not only closely related to one's beliefs and actions, but, as was pointed out above, also different from them. Because of this difference, it is entirely possible for one to believe what faith believes and to act as faith acts even without having made the transition from sin to faith. Recognizing this, we must always allow that making this transition may not involve any change in what one believes or in what one does, but only in how one understands one's existence in believing and acting alike.

Nevertheless, self-understanding necessarily involves both believing and acting; and in many, if not most, instances, ultimate transformation involves penultimate transformations in beliefs as well as in actions, including the actions whereby we bear explicit witness to our faith and beliefs. This explains why, in the language of the tradition, one rightly says that faith must always find expression in good works — works of piety as well as works of mercy — even as sin inevitably expresses itself in sins — sins of impiety and irreligion as well as sins of moral transgression. Good works in this sense are always necessary because we can *exist* for the freedom of faith only insofar as we *act* for it — namely, by bearing witness to others in all that we say and do that it is for just such a freedom that they, too, have been set free.

The question that arises in our situation today — and that requires special attention in this discussion — is whether such penultimate transformations in individual beliefs and actions exhaust the changes that ultimate transformation involves. In his book *Until Justice and Peace Embrace* (1983), Nicholas Wolterstorff effectively argues for a negative answer to this question, employing in doing so a typology of religions in which he distinguishes "salvation religions" generally into two main types: "avertive" and "formative." Although religions of both types "look forward to salvation from what is defective in our present mode of existence," avertive religions typically acquiesce in what is defective and then turn away from it to unite with a higher reality, while formative religions typically seek to reform what is defective in obedience to a higher will (Wolterstorff 1983, 5). But even among religions that are dominantly formative rather than avertive, there can be important differences. Wolterstorff argues that even though Lutheranism was sufficiently different from the more avertive religion of medieval Christianity to be classified as formative, "the focus of its formative efforts was mainly on ecclesiastical structures and on individual 'inwardness' " (10). On

the other hand, "the emergence of early Calvinism represented a fundamental alteration in Christian sensibility, from the vision and practice
of turning away from the social world in order to seek closer union with
God to the vision and practice of working to reform the social world in
obedience to God" (11).

I have two reasons for directing attention to Wolterstorff's argument.
First of all, it makes clear that the "world-formative Christianity" that
he traces to early Calvinism, and that he himself wishes to advocate
as appropriate today, is certainly not the only understanding of ultimate transformation by which Christians have been guided. Even if
one would want to qualify his characterizations of the different types
of Christian religion, one could not seriously question that there have
been such types and that the differences between them have indeed had
to do with whether or to what extent ultimate transformation has been
understood to involve penultimate transformation of the social world.

But my second reason for considering Wolterstorff's argument is that
even his account of the relatively late emergence of world-formative
Christianity in early Calvinism is not completely free of anachronism.
Anyone acquainted with the contemporary movements in Christian theology called "political theology" and "theology of liberation" will be
familiar with an apologetic that seeks to show that already in the New
Testament and even earlier in the witness of Jesus himself, there is
an understanding of ultimate transformation as involving more than a
change of individuals — indeed, as more or less explicitly political. On
the other hand, exegetes and historians of early Christianity continue
to give compelling reasons for dismissing such apologetic as anachro-
nistic. The fact is that the understanding of the scope of human power
and responsibility that underlies our contemporary concern with poli-
tics can be read out of the New Testament only by first being read into
it. Something like the same reasoning, I believe, can be urged against
Wolterstorff's apologetic for early Calvinism. Even if he is surely right
in insisting that this type of Christianity stressed the active as well as
the passive moment in faith, and the need for faith always to find expression, not only in religion, but in all the rest of human life, one may
nevertheless question whether its understanding of the scope of human
power and responsibility was not still subject to constraints that are even
more obviously present in earlier types of Christianity.

My point, in short, is that an understanding of ultimate transformation as also involving penultimate transformation of social and cultural
structures depends not only on normative Christian witness, but also on
a distinctively modern historical consciousness. Wolterstorff himself recognizes this insofar as he reckons among the factors that account for the
emergence of early Calvinism "the drastic alteration in social relations
taking place in Western Europe in the sixteenth century." "In this situa-

tion," he allows, "it was only natural that people would begin to reflect on alternative social structures and that the idea of social structure as part of the givenness of their surroundings would begin to seem entirely implausible" (11). But how much more is this true after the bourgeois revolutions of the eighteenth century and the proletarian revolutions of our own?

What makes a world-formative Christianity indeed appropriate to our situation today is the historical consciousness that is ours as contemporary women and men. We are aware, as earlier generations were not, that even the most basic structures of social and cultural order are neither divinely ordained nor naturally given, but humanly created — by historical beings like ourselves who have the power and the responsibility to change them, given the moral demand implied by faith. Because this demand governs the whole of our action, we can understand ourselves both as Christians and as the historical beings we know ourselves to be, only by acknowledging our specifically political responsibility for social and cultural change.

So in the Christian understanding for which I have argued, the existence for freedom for which we are freed by God's love involves our action not only for the freedom of faith of all our fellow human beings, but also for their freedom from unjust social and cultural structures that oppress them and keep them in bondage. In this way, our ultimate transformation involves penultimate transformations in all the social and cultural orders for which we are responsible, as well as in our individual beliefs and actions.

Even so, having also argued that our ultimate transformation is one thing and all other changes, something else, I must insist on this final point: as surely as ultimate transformation does indeed involve social and cultural change, even the most radical such change can never be more than penultimate in relation to the freedom of faith for which Christ has set us free.

II

Problems in the Case for a Pluralistic Theology of Religions

The case for a pluralistic theology of religions has increasingly gained support from a number of Christian theologians, some of whom have contributed essays to a volume devoted to making this case: *The Myth of Christian Uniqueness: Toward a Pluralistic Theology of Religions* (1987). Because the discussion documented by this volume is close to the heart of contemporary Christian theology, the arguments advanced in it deserve careful criticism. With this in mind, I propose to consider the case for pluralism that is presented by three of its contributors: Gordon D. Kaufman, Rosemary Radford Ruether, and John Hick. If I am right, each of their essays confirms that there are more or less serious problems in making such a case.

Of course, to develop this criticism is to say nothing whatever about other logically independent lines of argument by which the case for pluralism might be made; and more important, one can develop the criticism without being in the least unsympathetic with the theological intentions of those who seek to make the case. But the point of theological criticism is to see to it that the arguments for claims are sufficient to support them, and we will all be more likely to realize our theological intentions if we are aware of the full range of alternatives between which reasoned choice can be made in our attempts to do so.

I. "Religious Diversity, Historical Consciousness, and Christian Theology"

The problem discussed in Gordon D. Kaufman's essay, as I understand it, is how "Christians are to take other faiths, other life-orientations, with full seriousness" (Hick and Knitter 1987, 4). This problem, as he views it, is of a piece with the general problem of how human beings can now learn to cope sufficiently with their religious and cultural diversity to be able "to live together fruitfully, productively and in peace in today's complexly interconnected world" (3). This general human problem raises special issues for Christians because of "the absolutistic claims about divine revelation and ultimate truth that have often been regarded as central to faith" (3). Kaufman contends that these claims demand "careful theological scrutiny" and that serious attention to the issues they raise "suggests that we must today become self-conscious about Christian faith in new ways — ways that will enable us to move toward some fundamental revisions of the tasks and methods of Christian theology" (3). "If we are to approach sympathetically, and enter into dialogue with, others of quite different commitments and convictions, we must find ways of relativizing and opening up our basic symbol system" (5). Specifically, Kaufman holds, "the complex of attitudes and consciousness that underlies modern attempts to engage in historical and comparative studies of human religiousness can provide a way to break through the tendencies toward absoluteness and self-idolatry that often obstruct interaction between Christians and others" (5). The purpose of his essay, then, is to explain these contentions and to justify them theologically.

I want to begin my criticism by saying that there is much in Kaufman's argument that I have no difficulty appropriating, both in its understanding of the problem and in its basic proposal for resolving the issues that Christians and theologians have to face in dealing with this problem. I particularly appreciate the way he situates the special Christian problem in the context of the larger human problem of learning to live in peace rather than in conflict, given religious and cultural diversity. In fact, he does a better job than most theologians have done in remembering that not only religious but also secular communities and traditions have resources for interpreting and orienting human existence and must, therefore, always be reckoned with in any of our attempts to come to terms with "the other ways of being human" (4). But with all of my appreciation for his argument and agreement with it, I also see some basic problems that need to be brought out for discussion.

One such problem is indicated by the kind of reasoning Kaufman offers for developing a Christian theology informed by "modern historical consciousness" (11). Such a development is needed, he argues, because "only as we find ways of stepping back from, and thus not remaining confined within, those features of our traditions (both religious and secular) that wall us off from others, can we hope to come into genuine understanding of and community with them. Building such community with others," he adds, "is the most profound religious necessity of our time. Promoting it, therefore, is the most important task to which Christian theology today can attend" (14). Unless I am mistaken, this is the only kind of case that Kaufman ever makes for his proposal; for while he does contend, as I noted earlier, that such a development is needed because of "the tendencies toward absoluteness and exclusivity in traditional Christian faith," such tendencies evidently demand to be counteracted only because of the same religious necessity that we should come to genuine understanding and community with others despite our particular traditions (5). But if I am right about this, Kaufman's reasoning is in principle defective as theological reasoning. So one must judge it, at any rate, if one believes as I do that any theological proposal must be justified, not only by the religious needs of the contemporary situation, but also by the normative witness of the Christian community.

A classic example of such justification is Rudolf Bultmann's case for demythologizing. Had Bultmann reasoned as Kaufman does, he would have concluded simply from the modern religious need for a demythologized formulation of the Christian witness to theology's having the task of providing it. But the fact is, of course, that Bultmann reasoned very differently, insisting that however necessary demythologizing may be if modern women and men are to be able to respond to the Christian claim, it cannot be undertaken "on the basis of a postulate that the New Testament proclamation must under all circumstances be made viable in the present. On the contrary, we simply have to ask whether it really is nothing but mythology or whether the very attempt to understand it in terms of its real intention does not lead to the elimination of myth" (Bultmann 1951, 22; 1984b, 9).

The defect in Kaufman's reasoning is that it omits entirely to ask the same kind of question about the absolutistic claims that have often been regarded as central to Christian faith. If the Christian witness really is nothing but such claims, then I for one should concur that it simply cannot meet a profound religious need of our time. But if we are to contend, on the contrary, that Christian theology has the task of addressing this need, I submit that this can only be because a serious attempt to understand the Christian witness in terms of its own real intention leads to the elimination of all absolutism, and insofar justifies the development that Kaufman proposes we undertake.

The problem indicated by his methodological reasoning, however, is evidently basic to his whole approach. Not only does he take theology's task to be set simply by the needs of its apologetic situation, but he also proceeds as though the only question theology has to ask is about the credibility of Christian claims. This becomes evident from his discussion of the conclusion to which one may be brought in criticizing Christian claims with "the sort of historical self-consciousness" that he advocates (Hick and Knitter 1987, 11). It is always possible, he allows, that one may conclude that "the basic Christian categorial scheme" itself "orders and interprets human life in a way no longer viable or helpful. Perhaps one or more of the principal categories requires drastic revision, drawing on ideas suggested by other religious or secular traditions. The theologian may even feel forced to conclude (as some have in recent years) that such central Christian symbols as 'God' or 'Christ' must be given up entirely, other images or concepts being given categorial status in their stead" (10, 12). But if this might seem to mean the end of Christian theology, Kaufman maintains otherwise. "There is," he argues, "an almost unlimited range of theological possibilities and permutations," including, one infers, the eventuality just considered. Even so, "for a theology that wishes to remain 'Christian'... the fundamental task is quite straightforward: to work carefully and critically through the proposals for understanding human life and the world presented by the Christian tradition (and by theological reflection on the tradition); to try to grasp our contemporary experience and life in terms of these categories, images, and concepts; and to reconstruct them in whatever respects are required to enable them to serve as the framework for a worldview that can provide adequate orientation for life today" (12).

Here too I can only judge that Kaufman's approach is defective. However unlimited the range of theological possibilities and permutations, it is certainly limited by the demand that any theology that wishes to remain Christian, like the witness on which it reflects, must not only be credible in terms of our contemporary experience and life, but also appropriate in terms of normative Christian witness. But this means that Christian theology also has the task, no less fundamental than that which Kaufman rightly assigns it, of determining whether the proposals it judges to provide adequate orientation for life today are also adequate expressions of specifically Christian faith and life.

The other basic problem that needs to be brought out is closely related and is raised by his specific proposal that Christian faith and theology be relativized and opened up by the very different perspective of "modern historical consciousness," and thus by what he refers to as "a historical conception of human existence," or "an understanding of human existence as historical" (8). Unlike other theologians who seek a solution to the problem of our traditional parochialism by moving to what they claim is a "universal position," Kaufman argues that "every position to which we might turn is itself historically specific" and that, therefore, "a universal frame of orientation for human understanding and life is no more available to us than is a universal language" (5). Accordingly, he acknowledges that the perspective of "modern historical understanding" that grows out of "modern Western historical thinking" is "like all other perspectives — particular, relative, and limited" (9, 14). Nevertheless, he insists that it is by precisely this perspective that Christian faith and theology now need to be informed, because it "enables us to break the grip of the absolutistic commitments that have characterized much traditional Christian faith and theology, thus enabling us to encounter other significant religious and secular traditions *in their own terms* instead of as defined by our categories" (14).

I have already commented on the defective theological methodology revealed by this reasoning. But no less striking is the arbitrariness of Kaufman's assumption that all other religious and secular perspectives, including the Christian, must submit to be judged by his understanding of human existence as historical. If the constitutive claim of Christian witness is valid, the truth it asserts cannot fail both to confirm and to be confirmed by any other religious or secular truth of the same logical type, including that of a historical conception of human existence. Therefore, even if one agrees, as I do, that Christian claims can be validated as credible only on the basis of our common experience simply as human beings, one has no reason to suppose that this requires submitting these claims to the judgment of some other religious or secular perspective, whose own claims to validity are merely that, unless and until they too are critically validated. On the contrary, pending the inquiry required to validate *all* claims to credibility, one has every reason to assume that traditional Christian views may be as much the source of critical judgment as they are its object; while any other perspective, like Kaufman's historicism, may be as much in need of criticism as it is the basis for making critical judgments.

And this assumption will seem all the more reasonable when one considers the implications of Kaufman's perspective. If we understand "human historicity" as it enables us to do, he argues, Christian faith, like every other faith, is seen to be one among the many perspectives or worldviews that human beings have imaginatively constructed in "their search for orientation in life" (9, 7). Thus "we now see the great theologians of Christian history... not simply as setting out the truth that is ultimately salvific for all humanity (as they have often been understood in the past), but rather as essentially engaged in discerning and articulating one particular perspective on life among others" (9). In fact, so far from being in a position to claim that our assertions are "directly and uniquely authorized or warranted by divine revelation," we theologians can now acknowledge "forthrightly and regularly that our theological statements and claims are simply *ours* — that they are the product of our own human study and reflection, and of the spontaneity and creativity of our own human powers imaginatively to envision a world and our human place within the world" (12).

If these and other formulations seem clearly to express the same subjective reductionism often associated with historical understandings of human religiousness, Kaufman is quick to reassure us — in a parenthetical sentence — that he does not mean that theological assertions "are not in some significant sense grounded in God, as 'ultimate point of reference'" or that there "are no ways at all in which the concept of revelation might be used to articulate that grounding" (12). But one hardly knows what to make of such reassurance when in the sentence immediately following one learns that all "religious activity and reflection," including Christian theology, are to be understood as "human imaginative response to the necessity to find orientation for life in a particular historical situation" (12).

In any case, the theological implications of Kaufman's perspective seem plainly inconsistent with the claim to universal salvific truth that is evidently constitutive of the Christian witness. For they do not require simply that this claim be critically validated; they preclude the possibility of its ever being responsibly made.

To this extent, then, there are good reasons for resisting Kaufman's proposal. And one can be even more assured in doing so because a solution to the problem he discusses in no way requires theology to submit to some other particular perspective, whether his own or any other. It requires only, but ineluctably, that theology acknowledge its claims for what they are: claims that can be critically validated as credible only in terms of our common human experience and critical reflection. To this extent, certainly, Christians can encounter other ways of being human, whether religious or secular, only, as Kaufman says, "on equal terms"; although I maintain that if Christian faith means anything at all, it means the confidence that the promise of truth issued by the Christian witness cannot fail to be redeemed by all such encounters and that, therefore, our theological statements and claims cannot be "*simply ours*" (4, 12; emphasis changed).

But whether this confidence is well placed ever remains a question; and Kaufman is surely right that in theology's attempts to answer it, the critical reflection provided by other perspectives, including the historicist, plays a necessary role.

2. "Feminism and Jewish-Christian Dialogue"

As I understand the argument of her essay, Rosemary Radford Ruether is concerned to counter "Christian claims to universalism," or, more generally, any claims, Christian or Jewish, that there is "a single universal biblical faith" (137f.). In her view, "the idea that Christianity, or even the biblical faiths, have a monopoly on religious truth is an outrageous and absurd religious chauvinism" (141). This is particularly evident, she believes, in the light of two contemporary challenges: on the one hand, the challenge coming from Jewish-Christian dialogue, which by its very nature exposes "the hidden particularism" behind both Christian and Jewish claims to universalism; and on the other hand, the challenge coming from feminism, which "looks back at the history of all religions as expressions of male-dominated cultures," again exposing the particularism behind the universalistic claims of Judaism and Christianity (138, 142). Ruether's purpose in her essay is to discuss the question that these two challenges sharply raise — namely, the question

of "particularism and universalism in the search for religious truth" —
although she is clear right from the outset that she will speak to the
question "from the Christian side," rather than pretending to some kind
of impartiality (137).

In turning to criticism of her discussion, I want to say, first of all, that
I too feel the force of these two challenges, and am therefore grateful for
her attempt to address the question that they raise for Christian theology. Moreover, there is much in her essay with which I can easily agree,
especially in the second part, where she seems to me to explain persua-
sively why "the feminist challenge to Christianity cannot find sufficient
response in the recovery of neglected texts in the Bible or in inclusive
translation" and why, as a consequence, "women must be able to speak
out of their own experiences . . . and, out of these revelatory experiences,
write new stories" (147). But if I thus find myself sharing many of
Ruether's theological intentions, I nevertheless have problems with her
argument.

The first — and, for me, the most serious — of these problems is that
I see nothing that makes her argument properly theological. By "theological" here, I mean, of course, "Christian theological," since Ruether
herself makes clear that it is "from the Christian side" that she wants
to discuss the question of particularism and universalism in the search
for religious truth. Aside from her one statement to this effect, however,
I see nothing either in the form or in the content of her argument that
would lead anyone to suppose that it is from the Christian side that
she develops it. For all she says to the contrary, the position from and
for which she argues is simply the religious or philosophical position of
a feminist theist, or a theistic feminist, for whom "true revelation and
true relationship to the divine is [sic] to be found in all religions," even
though all patriarchal religions and ideologies are intrinsically biased
and one-sided in their exclusion of women from shaping their traditions
and handling their sacred objects (141).

My point is not that Christians or Christian theologians could not
responsibly hold such a position, since it seems to me at least arguable
that they both could and should do so. My point, rather, is that they certainly would not be alone in holding it, and that if they were to hold it
responsibly as Christians or as theologians, they would need to find warrant for doing so in what Christians rightly acknowledge as normative
for the appropriateness of their positions.

If I insist on this point, however, it is not only because Ruether's essay
completely fails to take account of it, but also because in other contexts
she herself has insisted on the same point. Thus, in arguing for a principle or norm for judging the sexist distortions of the Christian tradition,
including scripture, she nevertheless allows that "one can stand within
this tradition and claim to be renewing it only if this principle is, at the

deepest level, the true principle of the Scriptures and tradition as well, in spite of all distortion by the sin of sexism. If this is not the true principle of the biblical and Christian tradition, then this tradition itself must be evaluated as irredeemable and must be transcended by a new vision that would include woman fully" (Ruether 1985, 28). I believe that Ruether is absolutely right about this and that her point is of the utmost importance for the many-sided dialogue between feminists for which she calls at the end of her essay.

Not only post-Christian feminists like Mary Daly, but also other Christian feminist theologians like Elisabeth Schüssler Fiorenza, argue for a very different understanding of the norm or canon of theological judgment—and do so, in Schüssler Fiorenza's case, at least, by expressly arguing against Ruether and other feminist theologians who still insist on finding their critical principle in Christian tradition itself (Schüssler Fiorenza 1984, 12f., 86, 167 n. 50; see also below, pp. 233–236). But if Ruether is right in still insisting on this, I submit that she has the best of reasons for arguing in an exactly parallel way in discussing the question of particularism and universalism in the search for religious truth. If her argument for what she calls "true universality" is to meet her own standards for a valid theological argument, it demands to be developed beyond anything she provides in this essay — enough beyond it, at any rate, to make clear that she would not argue for such a position at all unless there were warrant for doing so in what, at the deepest level, is the true principle of normative Christian witness.

A second problem I have with Ruether's argument is that the inference she draws concerning the equal integrity or adequacy of religions does not appear to follow from, or even to be consistent with, the basic assumption she takes to imply it. "True universality," she explains, "lies in accepting one's own finiteness, one's own particularity and, in so doing, not making that particularity the only true faith, but allowing other particularities to stand side by side with yours as having equal integrity. Each is limited and particular, and yet each is, in its own way, an adequate way of experiencing the whole for a particular people at a particular time" (Hick and Knitter 1987, 142). Part of what Ruether has in mind in saying this, presumably, is that each religion is like every other in being "a unique configuration of symbolic expressions" that incarnates some "way of symbolizing life and its relationship to the higher powers," or some one among "a broad spectrum of possible ways of experiencing the divine" (141f.). But more important for understanding her claim that all religions have equal integrity or adequacy is that "there is true relationship to the divine, authentic spirituality, and viable morality in all religious systems" (141). This is the meaning, Ruether holds, of her counterassumption to "Christian claims of universalism," to the effect, namely, that "the Divine Being that generates, upholds, and renews the world is truly universal, and is the father and mother of all peoples without discrimination" (141f.).

But does the assumption that "the Divine Being" is "truly universal" and the source of all peoples "without discrimination" really mean that "true revelation and true relationship to the divine is to be found in all religions"? I do not see how it could mean this — any more than I see how the universal presence of the world about which all judgments of fact are made could mean that there are true disclosure of the world and true relationship to it in all factual judgments. If we are justified in believing as we do that judgments about the world can be false as well as true, notwithstanding that the world is universally present in human experience, I fail to see why we would not be justified in believing the same thing about the symbolic judgments of religion concerning the truly universal reality of the divine. Had Ruether inferred from her assumption, not that there *is* truth in all religions, but simply that there *can be* truth in all of them, I, at least, would have no difficulty with her inference. But it is clear enough from the formulations already quoted that she says "is," and I see nothing to suggest that she does not mean what she says, except, perhaps, one reference to "the possibilities of truth in all religions" (142). That even this reference does not have to be taken as suggesting any other meaning, however, is clear from the reflection that if there actually is truth in all religions, then, of course, there are also possibilities of truth in them.

One may further ask, I think, whether Ruether's inference does not in fact contradict the assumption that she takes to mean it. If this assumption is properly construed, as I have construed it, as being in a broad sense theistic, then clearly any religion or ideology that denied or failed to affirm theism in the same broad sense could not possibly be equal in integrity or adequacy with any religion or ideology that affirmed it. Therefore, unless Ruether is prepared to claim that all religions and ideologies affirm her own theistic assumption, she can infer that they have equal integrity or adequacy only by implicitly contradicting this very assumption. I take it that her inference similarly contradicts her evident assumption of feminism, from which it follows that no patriarchal religion or ideology can be equal in integrity or adequacy with a religion in which women fully participate in shaping its symbols and controlling its sacred objects.

Considering the seriousness of this second problem, I can only wonder whether Ruether may really want to make a different point. She observes quite rightly that Christianity's judgment of other religions tends toward an unjust comparison of their practices with its own ideals. Against this she demands that "ideals must be compared with ideals, and practice with practice" (141). But what is the implication of this demand for fair comparison if not that all judgments about the truth or validity of religions must be a posteriori, not a priori? And does this not mean, in turn, that there is a sense in which all religions are indeed to be treated equally, pending the inquiry by which their respective claims to validity can alone be critically validated?

Certainly, if Ruether's point is the one indicated by these questions, I have no reason to take issue with her. Religious claims to validity are exactly that — claims; and they are equally in need of validation once they have become problematic. But, clearly, this point can be made without arguing as Ruether argues. In fact, if the real wrong is apriorism, the mistake of judging a priori that one's own religion is the only true faith cannot be corrected by the no less a priori and, I should think, equally mistaken judgment that all religions have equal integrity or adequacy.

This leads directly to a third and, for the purposes of this criticism, final problem in Ruether's argument. Although the term she chooses to describe her answer to the question of particularism and universalism is "true universality," her right to use this term is far from clear, given no more than she says in developing her answer. "*True* universality," one assumes, is to be contrasted with "*false* universality"; and in context this could hardly be anything other than the claim that Ruether is concerned to counter, to the effect that one's own particularity as a Christian is the only true faith. But what does she set over against this claim, which she regards as not merely false but "outrageous and absurd" (141)? Her only alternative is to call for allowing other particularities to stand side by side with one's own Christian particularity "as having equal integrity" (142). But where is there any universality in this, as distinct from simply a relativistic acquiescence in the plurality of particularities that it certainly appears to be?

Assuming, as I would like to do, that Ruether really does mean to affirm a true universality, I can only urge her to develop her argument more fully so as to remove any doubt about her intentions. One way of doing this, for which I am prepared to argue, would be to clarify the difference between claiming that one's own religion is the only true faith, and claiming instead that any other religion must also be true just insofar as it both confirms and is confirmed by the truth in one's own. Of course, even this second claim is only that, and is therefore as much in need of critical validation as the corresponding claim for any other particular religion. But I submit that it is different enough from the claim that Ruether and I are both concerned to counter to justify describing it as "true universality."

3. "The Non-absoluteness of Christianity"

By his own account, John Hick's essay is a theological treatment of "the question of the place of Christianity within the wider religious life of

humanity" (34). As he sees it, there has been a marked development
in ways of answering this question since, roughly, the First World War.
Prior to that time, the usual answers, whether Catholic or Protestant,
were based on "the medieval assumption...of a Christian monopoly of
salvific truth and life" (16). During the last seventy years, however, this
traditional Christian exclusivism has tended to erode, whether because
of "more accurate knowledge and more sympathetic understanding" of
the other great religious traditions, or because of a "new awareness of
the pernicious side of Christian absolutism in history" (17, 20). Thus
many, if not most, thinking Christians have been gradually moving from
"an intolerant exclusivism" to a "benevolent inclusivism," according to
which not only Christians, but all human beings whatever, are somehow included within the salvation of which "the Christ-event is the sole
and exclusive source" (22). In Hick's view, however, such inclusivism
still involves an a priori assumption of the superiority of Christianity as
Christ's continuing agency in the world. Therefore, he sees us as having reached a critical point in the whole development, at which it may
either halt with Christian inclusivism or else proceed to its "logical conclusion" in "a pluralist understanding of the place of Christianity in the
total life of the world" (16, 32). The purpose of his essay, then, is to
argue us across "this theological Rubicon" so as to complete the movement from exclusivism to pluralism (16, 22f.). This he attempts, in part,
by pointing to resources already provided by the Christian tradition for
those who would now assert "the non-absoluteness of Christianity."

If this is an accurate understanding of Hick's argument, certainly
there is much in it with which I thoroughly agree. I too believe that
the question of "Christianity's place within the total religious life of the
world" now demands theological treatment, and that any answer to it
that is likely to prove adequate will have to be found somewhere on
the other side of the old exclusivism as well as of any inclusivism involving the same a priori assumption of the superiority of Christianity
(16). But beyond thus agreeing with what I take to be some of Hick's
main contentions, I especially appreciate his approach to the question.
He seems to me to be exactly right in thinking of the development for
which he argues as but one of three parallel developments that are now
called for in Christian theology — the other two being carried forward
by liberation theology, on the one hand, and feminist theology, on the
other. I take him to be no less right, however, in looking to the Christian
tradition itself for the warrants, as well as the resources, for carrying
out these necessary developments. Even so, I want to raise the question whether there may not be yet another way of crossing over from
Christian absolutism than the one for which he argues.

The first and basic problem here is whether pluralism in the sense
in which he understands it is, as he claims, the "logical" (or "natu-

ral") conclusion of the trajectory whose path can be traced "from an exclusivist to an inclusivist view of other religions" (16, 22). By "pluralism," I take it, he means the kind of theological position from which "the Christian tradition is...seen as one of a plurality of contexts of salvation — contexts, that is to say, within which the transformation of human existence from self-centeredness to God- or Reality-centeredness is occurring" (23). Thus for the pluralist, "Christianity is not the one and only way of salvation but one among several" — "*one* of the great world faiths, *one* of the streams of religious life through which human beings can be savingly related to that ultimate Reality Christians know as the heavenly Father" (33, 22). In Hick's understanding, then, pluralism entails asserting not only that there *can be* several ways of salvation, of which Christianity is but one, but also that there actually *are* these several ways.

But how, if at all, is this assertion the logical conclusion of the movement away from exclusivism? Granted that there is indeed a difference between the exclusivist claim that there is no salvation outside the church or Christianity and the inclusivist claim that all human beings are somehow included within the salvation accomplished solely by Jesus Christ, still what both positions assert in common is, as Hick puts it, that "the Christ-event is the sole and exclusive source of human salvation" (22). In other words, they agree in asserting that there *cannot be* several ways of salvation of which Christianity is but one, because, unlike all other religions, it alone is established by the one and only event of salvation. But, then, it is this assertion that one must contradict in order to go beyond inclusivism by drawing the logical conclusion of the movement away from exclusivism. To contradict it, however, clearly does not require one to assert that there actually *are* several ways of salvation of which Christianity is only one. All that one needs to assert is that there *can be* several such ways, even if, as a matter of fact, Christianity should prove to be the only way of salvation there is. But this assertion can be made by any christology for which the decisive significance of Jesus Christ is not that he *constitutes* salvation, but that he *represents* it — namely, by making explicit in a decisive way the gift and demand of God's love, which is the sole and sufficient source of human salvation. Because the meaning of God's love for us is always implicitly presented in human existence as such, it can always become more or less fully explicit in any human religion, whether or not there is any religion in which it in fact does so.

I submit, therefore, that pluralism in Hick's sense is not the logical conclusion of the movement away from Christian absolutism that he claims it to be, but an independent assertion to be considered on its merits. The real theological Rubicon does not run between exclusivism and inclusivism, on the one hand, and what he means by pluralism, on the other; it runs, rather, between two fundamentally different kinds of christologies: those that claim a constitutive significance for Jesus Christ with respect to human salvation, and those that understand his significance for salvation, however decisive, to be representative only.

As for the question of pluralism, suffice it to say that in my view — even as, presumably, in Hick's — any answer to it must be a posteriori and at least in part empirically justified. So far as my own experience in such matters goes, I am not yet at the point at which I can assert that there are in fact several ways of salvation of which the Christian way is but one. Of course, I do not dispute the claim that human beings generally evidence a deep desire for some kind of ultimate transformation and that not only Christianity, but each of the great religious traditions, offers itself as the means for just such a transformation, as Hick says, "from self-centeredness to Reality-centeredness" (23). But this claim I take to be purely formal, in that it allows for a wide range of material differences between one religion and another in understanding transformation. And my own experience of the actual differences between religions, as subtle as they have sometimes proved to be, fully confirms Clifford Geertz's observation that "what all sacred symbols assert is that the good for man is to live realistically; where they differ is in the vision of reality they construct" (Geertz 1973, 130). But, be this as it may, the possibility of pluralism in Hick's sense I understand to be securely grounded in the completely universal reality of God's love, which is savingly present throughout all human existence; and so I have every reason to look for more evidence of the actuality of pluralism than I have so far been able to find.

This is not to say, however, that I would think to look to what Hick takes to be the appropriate kind of evidence — namely, "the fruits of religious faith in human life," and thus the extent of individual and social transformation effected by particular religions (Hick and Knitter 1987, 23f.). In my opinion, to expect this kind of evidence to settle the issue of the relative superiority or inferiority of particular religions is no less mistaken than to expect to settle the issue of the relative truth or falsity of empirical beliefs by considering the number of persons who sincerely hold them. It seems to me that in dealing with this issue, Hick slips into the not uncommon confusion of the *validity* of particular religions with their *effectiveness*. This distinction is ordinarily made, of course, in discussions of the sacraments and, perhaps, means of salvation more generally. But if one holds, as I do, that the different religions themselves can be viewed at least analogically as different means of ultimate transformation, one can reasonably claim that all questions about their relative superiority or inferiority are questions about their relative validity or invalidity as sacraments of ultimate reality in its meaning for us — keeping in mind that the relative effectiveness or ineffectiveness of each of them depends upon its being appropriated by the existential self-understanding of individual persons in accordance with an appropriately generalized form of the rule, *nullum sacramentum sine fide.*

In this case, the evidence appropriate to judging their relative superiority or inferiority is not only such empirical-historical evidence as is required to determine what are, in fact, their normative forms, but also such metaphysical and moral evidence as is required to determine the truth and rightness of their necessary implications for belief and action respectively. Thus, if I am to assert not only the possibility of religious pluralism, but also its actuality, I must have evidence for concluding that there are, in fact, one or more religious traditions other than the Christian tradition whose normative understandings of authentic existence are equally valid with that of normative Christianity when they are fairly compared with respect to their necessary implications for both metaphysical belief and moral action.

This leads directly to the third and last problem I wish to raise with Hick's argument — namely, whether the "inspiration christology" to which he appeals as pointing the direction for theology today is the most adequate, if not the only, kind of representativist christology open to those who would make the crossing away from Christian absolutism (32). It seems clear that what he claims for this kind of christology is not that it is required by the religious pluralism for which he argues, but only that it is "compatible" with such pluralism (32). But since he does not consider any other possibilities, he evidently thinks that this is the most adequate answer that can be given to the christological question by those who are prepared to follow the movement away from exclusivism to its logical conclusion.

By his own admission, however, any such "inspiration christology" is open to the most serious objections. Aside from the fact that, as he himself long since showed elsewhere (see Hick 1958; 1966), it can continue to talk of God's becoming incarnate in Jesus Christ only by radically redefining the meaning of "incarnation," it involves anyone who tries to defend it in the following dilemma: either one construes it in such a way that it is at least a plausible interpretation of the inspiration christology expressed in the New Testament itself, in which case one can assert the uniqueness of Jesus that is undoubtedly intended by that christology only a priori and not on the basis of historical evidence; or else one persists in justifying one's christological assertion by historical evidence, in which case the unavailability of the requisite evidence forces one to interpret the New Testament's own christology of inspiration in an altogether implausible way, according to which Jesus is not the uniquely inspired Son of God, but simply one more human being, more or less instrumental in the transformation of other individuals and societies (cf. Hick and Knitter 1987, 31f.). Of course, the full force of this dilemma is obscured by Hick's proceeding as though the point of his inspiration christology and that of the New Testament were the same — despite the fact that, if anything is clear from the historical study of New Testament christology, it is that the two ways of thinking make radically different kinds of claims.

But I have no intention of restating a case that I have presented elsewhere and that Hick has already had an opportunity to come to terms with (see Ogden 1992b and Hick 1984). I simply want to make the point that one can very well join him in crossing over from a constitutivist to a representativist christology without having to shoulder the burdens of his particular way of doing this. In addition to a representativist christology that can be historically responsible only by allowing that Jesus Christ is nothing more than one example of Christian faith among others, there can be a representativist christology for which Jesus Christ is nothing less than the primal Christian sacrament.

I conclude, therefore, by pressing my question: Is Hick's the only or the most adequate way for theology now to assert "the non-absoluteness of Christianity"?

– 12 –

Is There Only One True Religion or Are There Many?

I. The Challenge of Pluralism

Among the many ways of formulating the Christian claim is to assert that the Christian religion is the true religion. In fact, throughout most of their history, Christians have generally asserted or implied that the Christian religion is the only true religion. But if this assertion may be fairly taken as typical of Christian witness, it has also long been more or less problematic in Christian theology — and for theologians charged with the responsibility of critically reflecting on this witness.

One thinks, for instance, of what the aged Augustine, determined to clarify his earlier writings and to retract any errors in them, had to say about his treatise, "Of True Religion":

> Again, in the same chapter, I said 'That is the Christian religion in our times, which to know and follow is most sure and certain salvation.' I was speaking of the name here, and not of the thing so named. For what is now called the Christian religion existed of old and was never absent from the beginning of the human race until Christ came in the flesh. Then true religion which already existed began to be called Christian. After the resurrection and ascension of Christ into heaven, the apostles began to preach him and many believed, and the disciples were first called Christians in Antioch, as it is written. When I said, 'This is the Christian religion in our times,' I did not mean that it had not existed in former times, but that it received that name later. (Augustine 1953, 218f.)

Just what Augustine's clarification or retraction comes to may not be entirely certain. But it makes clear enough that he was no longer willing to endorse any simple identification of the true religion with the Christian religion such as many Christians both before and since have asserted or implied in advancing the Christian claim.

One generalization that can be safely made about Christian theologians today is that more and more of them are evidencing the same unwillingness. Far from endorsing the claim that the Christian religion is the only true religion, they are increasingly asking whether this can possibly be a valid Christian claim. The principal reason for this is that an ever larger number, not only of theologians, but also of Christians generally, are now making or implying another very different, indeed, contrary claim. According to them, the Christian religion is but one of many religions, or logically comparable ways of understanding human existence, some or all of which may be as true as Christianity. Thus, from the standpoint of Christians and theologians who make or imply this contrary claim, the Christian religion may indeed be the true religion, but only in the sense in which the same may be said of other religions or comparable ways of existing as human beings. Because of this insistence that there are many true religions rather than one, the name by which this claim has now come to be generally known is "pluralism." And it is because of pluralism in this sense that Christian theologians today have increasingly had to ask whether the monism typical of most Christian tradition can any longer be accepted as valid.

Of course, in some senses religious pluralism is nothing new. If the word "pluralism" is understood, as it often is, simply as a synonym for the word "plurality," religious pluralism has always existed, since there has always been a plurality of religions in the world in which Christians have had to bear their witness and to reflect theologically on the validity of their claims in doing so. Until quite recently, however, the many religions, like the many cultures with which they are of a piece, lived for the most part in mutual isolation. Only with the revolutions of the recent past, especially the technological revolution in transportation and communication, has this isolation finally been broken through, to the point where the many religions and cultures are now compelled to live with one another as next-door neighbors in a single global village. It is this enforced proximity of each religion and culture to every other that is the really new thing about religious and cultural plurality in our situation today.

On the other hand, the word "pluralism" is also properly understood to mean, not simply the state or condition of plurality, but the belief or doctrine that affirms and advocates plurality as a good thing. And in this sense too, religious pluralism is not entirely new. At least since the Renaissance, theologians have spoken, in Nicholas of Cusa's words, of "one faith in the diversity of religions"; and already at the beginning of the nineteenth century, in the theology of Friedrich Schleiermacher, there was a clean break with the claim that Christianity is the only true religion. But what does seem to be new to our century, especially the second half of it, is the growing number of Christians and theologians who are proposing a pluralistic theology of religions. Out of their experiences of religious plurality, and thus a keener and more informed sense both of the strengths of other religious traditions and of the weaknesses of their own, they have come to affirm and advocate such plurality as a good thing — not, as they believe, in spite of their Christian commitment, but because of it. More and more of them are religious pluralists precisely as Christians and theologians; and this is why the challenge they pose to Christian witness and theology is new, and importantly new at that.

My concern as a theologian and in this essay is to address the question that this challenge has now made theologically central: Is there only one true religion, or are there many? Clearly, if the proponents of religious pluralism are correct, the older options between which Christians and theologians have typically chosen in answering this question cannot be theologically valid insofar as they alike imply religious monism in asserting that there is only one true religion. But the issue for theology is whether religious pluralists are right about this, and whether their new option can itself be theologically validated; or whether, on the contrary, their assertion that there are many true religions is, in its way, problematic enough that it too is vulnerable to the challenge of some more adequate option.

Obviously, there are severe limits to what can be done to settle this issue in a single essay. In fact, the most I can hope to do is to clarify the issue itself and, to this end, to take account of all of the main possibilities for answering our question. With this in mind, I now want to look more closely at the first answer to the question against which the challenge of pluralism is directed.

2. The Other Usual Options: Exclusivism and Inclusivism

Up to this point, I have spoken of this position simply as "religious monism" so as to contrast it explicitly and directly with religious pluralism. But in actual fact, pluralism is a challenge not merely to one, but to two ways of answering our question — ways that are significantly different, even though they alike claim that the Christian religion is the only true religion. If we are to clarify the issue before us, we need to take account of both of these other options and to understand the difference as well as the similarity between their two answers.

We noted at the outset that Christians have typically claimed that the Christian religion alone is the true religion. This they have claimed for the very good reason — from their standpoint — that no other religion even can be true in the same sense in which this can be said of Christianity. Although all religions make or imply the claim to be formally true, and hence normative for determining all other religious truth, the only religion whose claim to this effect can possibly be valid is the religion established by God in the unique saving event of Jesus Christ. Since only the Christian religion is thus established, it alone can validly claim to be the formally true religion.

For many, if not most, Christians, this kind of religious monism has been understood exclusivistically, in that they have denied the possibility of participating in the true religion, and thus obtaining salvation, to any and all non-Christians. The classical formula for such exclusivism is the dictum that goes back to the Latin church father Cyprian: *extra ecclesiam nulla salus* — "outside of the church there is no salvation." Some interpreters have held that this formula strictly applies only to the Roman Catholic form of exclusivism, since Protestant exclusivists have typically claimed instead that there is no salvation outside of Christianity (Hick and Knitter 1987, 16f.). But this seems to me to be a misleading way of stating the relevant difference, since in both cases salvation is possible only in and through the visible church and its proclamation. However, in the case of Roman Catholics, who have classically identified the visible church with their own institutional church, exclusivism has meant that there is no salvation, because no participation in the true religion, outside of the Church of Rome. In the case of Protestants, by contrast, exclusivism has meant that no one could expect to belong to the invisible church of the chosen except by belonging to the visible church of the called through membership in some true institutional church. In both cases, exclusivism is the option that not only asserts Christianity to be the only true religion, but also holds that Christians alone, as participants in the true religion through their membership in the visible church, obtain the salvation that God established the church to mediate.

From late antiquity through the nineteenth century, Christians in the West typically exercised this option of exclusivism in one or the other of its different forms. Throughout this period, they widely believed that Christianity was destined to spread throughout the world, eventually displacing all of the other non-Christian religions; and firm in this belief, they increasingly gave themselves to the missionary outreach that led to modern Christian expansion. But exclusivism has never been the only option open to Christians; and since roughly the First World War, which in this as in other ways was the real end of the nineteenth century, there has been a growing movement away from it. This has happened in part, no doubt, because of increasing knowledge, as well as extensive first-hand experience, of other religious and cultural traditions, especially of the other axial religions, or so-called world religions. But ever since the Second World War and the breakup of the European colonial empires in Africa and Asia, many Christians have also become more and more aware of the negative impact of exclusivism on the non-Christian majority of the world's population. Having served only too often to sanction the acquisitiveness and violence of Western imperialism, exclusivistic claims are now seen to be profoundly ambiguous if not yet totally discredited.

The upshot is that for some three quarters of a century, and increasingly during the last thirty years or so, Christians have been moving away from traditional exclusivism toward a more inclusivistic way of claiming that theirs is the only true religion. To a considerable extent, this has happened by their retrieving an alternative theological tradition that, ever since the New Testament, has made the possibility of salvation independent of participation in the true religion through membership in the visible church. In any case, clear evidences of the emergence of such inclusivism are to be seen on the Roman Catholic side in the theological developments leading up to the Second Vatican Council and its official statements about the church and the relation of the church to non-Christian religions; and on the Protestant and Orthodox side in the parallel developments taking place in the World Council of Churches Subunit on Dialogue with People of Living Faiths and Ideologies.

If we ignore certain differences in nuance and formulation, these developments have all led to a way of answering our question that is significantly different from that of exclusivism. According to this answer, the possibility of salvation uniquely constituted by God in the event of Jesus Christ is somehow made available to each and every human being without exception and is therefore exclusive of no one unless she or he excludes her- or himself from its effect by a free and responsible decision to reject it. Since salvation itself is thus universally possible, and in this sense is all-inclusive, there is also the possibility of all religions being more or less substantially true insofar as this salvation becomes effective in human beings, thereby transforming their self-objectification in the explicit forms of religion as well as in praxis and culture generally. Thus, not only can all individuals be saved by the salvation constituted by Christ, but all religions, also, can be more or less valid means of this salvation to those who either are not or cannot become members of the visible Christian church.

At the same time, Christian inclusivists continue to maintain that Christianity alone can be the formally true religion, since it alone is the religion established by God Godself in the unique saving event of Jesus Christ, and therefore it alone expresses normatively the religious truth that is represented at best fragmentarily and inadequately in all other religious ways. Thus, while according to Christian inclusivism, non-Christians can indeed be saved because or insofar as they accept Christ's salvation as it is made available to them anonymously and unknowingly through the means of their own religions, Christians alone are related to the same salvation explicitly and knowingly in the way that it is the abiding mission of the visible church to bring about in the life of each and every person.

Notwithstanding its significant difference from exclusivism, then, inclusivism is, in its way, monistic rather than pluralistic in its understanding of true religion. For it too, there not only is, but can be, only one true religion, in the sense that Christianity alone can validly claim to be formally true. Recognizing this, one of its most astute critics, John Hick, dismisses inclusivism as anomalous — "like the anomaly of accepting the Copernican revolution in astronomy, in which the earth ceased to be regarded as the center of the universe and was seen instead as one of the planets circling the sun, but still insisting that the sun's life-giving rays can reach the other planets only by first being reflected from the earth!" (Hick and Knitter 1987, 23).

We will return to a consideration of inclusivism in the concluding section of this essay. Meanwhile, having distinguished it from exclusivism, we have now taken account of all three of the usual options for answering our central question. In addition to the relatively new and challenging option of pluralism, there are the two older options of exclusivism and inclusivism, both of which are now being challenged in their monistic answers to the question.

3. The Case against Exclusivism

Not surprisingly, pluralists are particularly keen to distinguish their position from that of inclusivists, which they consider anomalous and unstable. In their view, either inclusivists must fall back on the exclusivism from which they have turned away, or else they must push ahead to the pluralism that alone offers a consistent alternative. For all of their sharp criticism of inclusivism, however, pluralists are more than willing to accept its help in overthrowing the common enemy of exclusivism. In fact, the combined opposition that their alliance with inclusivists makes possible means that exclusivism has now become an increasingly embattled position. Even so, the theological issue is whether this development is justified. Does exclusivism deserve to be overthrown? How strong is the case against it?

My judgment is that the case against it is exceptionally strong — as strong, in fact, as a theological case is likely to be. Without going into all that might be said against it, I want to focus on what I take to be *the* objection — namely, that by establishing in effect a double standard for obtaining salvation, exclusivism creates a form of the problem of evil that is insolvable.

According to the presuppositions of exclusivism, the predicament of human beings universally is a consequence of their sin, understood not merely as moral transgression, which is rather the result of sin, but as the deeper refusal of a human being to live, finally, in radical dependence upon God, solely by God's grace. Thus, while each and every person is created good and in God's own image, all human beings so misuse their freedom as to sin in this deeper sense of the word. In thus deciding for existence in sin, however, they forfeit their original possibility of existing in faith; and they have no prospect of ever actualizing this possibility unless God acts preveniently to restore it to them. But it is just this that God has in fact done in sending Jesus Christ and in thereby establishing the visible church with its proclamation of salvation. Anyone who is encountered by this proclamation is once again restored to the possibility of faith, her or his sin notwithstanding; and actualization of this possibility through acceptance of the proclamation is salvation from sin and liberation from the human predicament.

It is just as true, naturally, that everyone else remains trapped in this predicament and without prospect of salvation. And this is the great difficulty; for it means, in effect, that the human predicament of some persons is radically different from that of others. Since the life and death of Jesus Christ and the establishment of the Christian proclamation are events occurring at a particular time and place in history, only persons living after these events and somehow capable of being encountered by the proclamation have any possibility of being saved from their sin. But then the predicament of all other persons is not simply a consequence of their sin, in the sense of something for which they themselves, through the misuse of their freedom, are each individually responsible; it is also the predicament of having unfortunately had to live at the wrong time or in the wrong place, a matter of fate rather than freedom, in no way their own responsibility.

To be sure, in the classical formulations of exclusivism in orthodox theology, this difficulty is considerably mitigated. These formulations not only allow that the Christian proclamation was already present prophetically to Israel and through the Hebrew scriptures, and hence was available to everyone included in the old covenant, but they even assume that the gospel was first proclaimed to none other than Adam and Eve themselves, through the so-called *proto-evangelium* of Genesis 3:15, and in this way was already made available to the whole human race. But claims such as these have now lost all plausibility. There is no evidence whatever of the writers of the Hebrew scriptures consciously prophesying Jesus Christ, much less of the gospel's ever having been universally disseminated to all women and men. Moreover, as the sciences have continued to date the origins of distinctively human life ever earlier in the history of our planet, it has become ever clearer that, if exclusivism were true, the overwhelming majority of the human race would have been the victims of an egregious double standard. Through no fault of their own, all but a tiny minority of human beings who have lived and died would have been allowed to remain in their sin, with despair of ever being saved from it the only realistic attitude to their condition.

To recognize this, however, is to realize that exclusivism creates an acute form of the problem of evil to which there is no available solution. By "the problem of evil" here, I mean the trilemma generated by three assertions so understood that, while any two of them can be affirmed consistently with one another, the addition in any case of the third immediately yields a self-contradiction. The three assertions are:

1. God is omnibeneficent or all-good.

2. God is omnipotent or all-powerful.

3. Evil of some kind or in some form is real or exists.

On the assumption that on exclusivism's own premises, the vast majority of human beings remaining in their sin would clearly be some kind or form of evil, the reality or existence of this evil would compel one to deny either that God is all-powerful or that God is all-good. This is so, at any rate, unless the evil in question could be accounted for by some decision or agency other than God's consistently with God's still being all-powerful.

In the case of other forms of evil — such as, for example, the evil of sin or the moral evil committed by human beings or other beings also created with moral freedom — such a "free-will defense" of the all-goodness and all-powerfulness of God is at least available. But in this case, there is no possibility of arguing in this way; for as we have seen, the fact, if it were a fact, that by far most human beings, having once forfeited the possibility of existing in faith, would then have no prospect of ever actualizing it, would be due, not to their own decision or agency, but to God's. Specifically, it would be due to God's abandoning them to their predicament instead of so acting as to liberate them from it, as God would have done for at least the few human beings who are in a position to become Christians.

In sum, the only available solution to the problem of evil is of no avail in dealing with the implication of exclusivism. If exclusivism were true, the only inference from the fact that by far most human beings could have no hope of salvation would be either that God is not good enough to want them to be saved or that God is not powerful enough to do all that anyone could conceivably do to save them, except what they must do themselves — for themselves and for one another. Either way, the understanding of God necessarily implied by Christian faith, as at once unsurpassably good and unsurpassably powerful, could no longer be upheld.

Recognizing this, we may confirm my judgment that the case against exclusivism is unusually strong. We may also insist over against exclusivism that if the Christian understanding of God as unsurpassable in both goodness and power is really to be maintained, no woman or man can ever be without the possibility of existing in faith as soon and as long as she or he is a human being at all.

4. Difficulties with the Case for Pluralism

If the argument of the preceding section is sound, we have good reason to look to some option other than exclusivism for an answer to our question. It is by no means obvious, however, that it is to pluralism that we should look. We have seen, to be sure, that pluralists are wont to claim over against inclusivists that their position is the only consistent alternative to exclusivism. But there are difficulties with their argument for pluralism, not the least of which is why this claim itself should be thought valid (cf. above, pp. 154–168).

To see why I say this, we need to recall just what it is that Christians and theologians who argue for pluralism understand by it. According to at least one of them — namely, the same John Hick whose criticism of inclusivism I have already quoted — the term "pluralism" refers to the kind of theological position from which "the Christian tradition is...seen as one of a plurality of contexts of salvation — contexts, that is to say, within which the transformation of human existence from self-centeredness to God- or Reality-centeredness is occurring." Thus, for pluralists, "Christianity is not the one and only way of salvation but one among several" — "*one* of the great world faiths, *one* of the streams of religious life through which human beings can be savingly related to the ultimate Reality Christians know as the heavenly Father" (Hick and Knitter 1987, 23, 33, 22). In this understanding, then, pluralism entails asserting not only that there *can be* several ways of salvation of which Christianity is one, but also that there actually *are* these several ways.

Hick claims that this pluralistic assertion is the "logical" (or "natural") conclusion of the trajectory whose path can be traced "from an exclusivist to an inclusivist view of other religions" (16, 22). But how valid is this claim?

In the earlier discussion of exclusivism and inclusivism as both forms of religious monism, I noted that the reason for their claim that Christianity alone *is* the true religion is the, for them, very good reason that it alone *can be* formally true. Because in their views the only religion that can be true in this sense is the religion established by God in the unique saving event of Jesus Christ, they can confidently assert that the Christian religion alone is true in this sense because there simply cannot be many ways of salvation of which the Christian way is only one. But then this is the assertion, common to both monistic views, that has to be countered if there is to be a complete break with monism, whether exclusivistic or inclusivistic. To counter it, however, in no way requires one to assert with pluralism that there actually *are* many ways of salvation of which Christianity is but one. All that one needs to assert is that there *can be* these several ways, even if, as a matter of fact, Christianity should turn out to be the only way of salvation there is.

For this reason, Hick's claim is unfounded. Pluralism is not the logical conclusion of a consistent movement away from exclusivism, but is an independent assertion to be evaluated on its merits. Exclusivism and inclusivism could both be invalidated without in any way validating pluralism as the answer to our question.

Nor can validating it ever be easy by the very logic of such an answer. Whether any religion at all is true must, in the nature of the case, be more or less difficult to determine. Naturally, to be a religious believer at all is one and the same with claiming, either explicitly or implicitly, that one's religion is true. But aside from the fact that this is simply one more claim to religious truth whose validity also has to be determined along with that of every other, all that its being validated would entitle one to affirm a priori about the truth of any other specific religion is that it either can or cannot be true. Thus, even assuming that, from a Christian standpoint, not only exclusivism but also inclusivism could be known to be invalid, the most that a Christian could possibly know, prior to actually encountering the many religions and rightly interpreting them, is not that they in fact are true, but only that they at least can be true.

Of course, it is not particularly difficult to undertake the empirical-historical study of religion, or of specific religions, and to do this, as we say, comparatively. In this way, one can learn, for example, that after a certain amount of social and cultural development, human beings quite generally seem to feel the need for some sort of radical transformation of their own individual existence in relation to ultimate reality. Thus not only Christianity, but all of the other axial or world religions as well, are evidently addressed to this need and present themselves as the means of just such ultimate transformation. But learning only this about the axial religions entitles one to make no more than a purely formal statement about them — to the effect that they all exhibit the same essential structure both in focusing the existential problem on the individual person's misunderstanding of her- or himself and in seeking to solve it by radically transforming her or his self-understanding. Such a statement in no way excludes, but obviously allows for, a wide range of material differences, not excluding substantial contrariety and contradiction, between one religion and another in their respective understandings of human existence. And if my own experience of interreligious dialogue is any indication, it remains exceedingly difficult, even after the most extensive study and first-hand experience of another person's religious claims, to know just where, or even whether, one's own religion expresses the same religious truth.

There are still other difficulties, however, pertaining to the evidence and argument that at least some pluralists offer to support their claim that there are many true religions or ways of salvation. Thus Hick, notably, assumes that the evidence appropriate to validating the claim is provided by "the fruits of religious faith in human life," and so by the extent of individual and social transformation effected by the different specific religions (Hick and Knitter 1987, 23f.). But among the other difficulties of this assumption is the further assumption on which it rests that the ultimate transformation called for by Christianity and the other axial religions can be validly inferred from the so-called fruits of religious faith in individual and social life. Whatever may be the case in other religions, at least according to Christian teaching, any such inference is cut off; for while faith and love cannot fail to bear fruit in good works, the performance of good works is possible even in the absence of faith and love. Thus Paul can say of even the most radical expressions of love, that one can give away all that one has and even sacrifice one's life, and yet "not have love" (1Co 13:3).

There is also the difficulty of ruling out the possibility that such individual and social changes as may be associated with a particular religion have nonetheless been independent of it or effected less because of it than in spite of it. One of the striking things to me about the behavior of human beings in extreme situations is that religious or philosophical affiliation seems to make relatively little difference. During the Nazi time in Germany, for instance, the resistance against Hitler included persons of the most diverse religious and philosophical persuasions, even as the same was true of those who passively supported his regime or actively collaborated with it. But then what force can there be in arguing for the truth of a specific religion from changes occurring in either individuals or societies in its particular context?

The still deeper difficulty, however, is with the underlying assumption of any such argument — namely, that the truth of a specific religion could be logically determined from its effectiveness as a context of salvation or liberation. To make this assumption, so far as I can see, is to fall into a serious logical confusion — as serious, indeed, as if one were to suppose that the truth of ordinary judgments of fact could be determined from their effectiveness in getting themselves sincerely believed. To believe ever so sincerely that a factual judgment is true is to do nothing whatever from which its truth could be determined. If it is true, it is not because it is believed, but because it is worthy of belief, even if no one ever believed it; and whether this can or cannot be said depends entirely upon whether or not it can be validated by the procedures appropriate to verifying judgments of fact. In the same way, one may most sincerely understand oneself as a specific religion calls one to do without providing even the least reason for thinking that the religion is true. If it is true, it is so, not because one in fact so understands oneself, but because one ought so to understand oneself, even if one were to fail to do so; and whether this is or is not the case entirely depends upon whether or not one's self-understanding can be validated by the procedures appropriate to determining religious truth. For this reason, the extent to which a specific religion is effective in securing even the most committed adherents is logically irrelevant to validating its claim to be formally true.

But even if pluralists were to adduce some other, more appropriate kind of evidence, they still could not validly argue that there are many true religions or ways of salvation without also implying some normative conception of religion or salvation. This is true, at any rate, so long as pluralism is something different from a complete relativism for which all religions are equally true. Insofar as it allows that there at least can be false as well as true religions or ways of salvation, it cannot validly judge any religion or way to be true except by employing some norm of truth. But then pluralism itself cannot escape the difficulty that pluralists sometimes seem to suppose is peculiar to inclusivists — namely, the difficulty of taking some one specific religion or philosophy to be formally true, even if other religions may well be substantially true when judged by it. Thus, when pluralists argue, say, for a "theocentric" as against a christocentric norm for judging religions, they make themselves vulnerable to an analogous form of the same argument, to the effect that even God is controversially normative as between theistic and nontheistic religions, or that religion itself may be controversial as between religious and nonreligious ways of understanding human existence in relation to ultimate reality.

It seems clear, then, that there are a number of difficulties with the case for pluralism — enough at least, to create doubts whether it can be a valid answer to our question. Above all, there is the difficulty that, like exclusivism, it is logically an extreme position. This is evident from the fact that it counters exclusivism's extreme claim that there cannot be more than one religion that is formally true, not with the contradictory claim that there can be, but with the contrary claim that there is — that there are many religions that are true in this sense of the word. The difficulty with extreme contraries on any issue, however, is that while both cannot be true, both can be false. Therefore, it is entirely possible that pluralism's claim that there are many true religions is as false as the claim of exclusivism that there cannot be more than one, which, as we have seen, is the real meaning of its contrary answer to our question.

5. Beyond the Usual Options

So far we have considered two of the three answers that are usually given to our question — with either strongly negative results, so far as exclusivism is concerned, or at best skeptical results, as concerns pluralism. Consequently, we might be tempted to conclude that it is to the third option of inclusivism that we should look for a valid answer. After all, inclusivism is significantly different from both of the other options;

and assuming what has just been said about the common difficulty of logical contraries, we might expect it to provide something like a mean position between the other two extremes.

We would be encouraged in this, naturally, by inclusivists, who tend to think of themselves as occupying just such a third, mediating position between the other more extreme positions. But there is a problem in agreeing with them about this, as should be clear from what has already been said — namely, that inclusivism, being as monistic as exclusivism, is, in its way, also an extreme position. Significantly different as it indeed is from exclusivism in asserting that a decision for Christ's salvation is in some way a universal possibility for each and every human being, it is nonetheless essentially similar to exclusivism in its monistic insistence that Christianity alone is the formally true religion. Like exclusivists, inclusivists hold that the only religion that even can be true in this sense is the religion established by God in the unique saving event of Jesus Christ. Therefore, even though they do indeed allow that non-Christians can be saved by Christ anonymously and unknowingly outside of the visible church and that any religion transformed by his salvation can itself be substantially true, they still maintain that his is the only salvation and that it is mediated explicitly and knowingly as such solely by the Christian religion. To this extent, inclusivists are monists, and are therefore no less extreme logically than exclusivists or pluralists in their answer to our question.

Recognizing this, we may well hesitate to conclude that inclusivism is the option we are seeking. And such hesitation will seem the more prudent if we reflect that, in the case of many a disputed question, the usual options for answering it are not the only answers that are logically possible. On the contrary, nothing is more common than disputes that stubbornly persist precisely because the disputants insist upon both themselves choosing and forcing others to choose between only some of the possible options, any one of which is about as good or as bad as any of the others.

That something like this may be true of the question before us here appears to me highly likely. The several parties to the current discussion more and more tend to assume that the only ways open for answering it are the usual options of exclusivism, inclusivism, and pluralism. Even so, there is at least one other way of answering it that is a distinct alternative to all three of these usual ways, although it has not been clearly recognized, much less carefully considered, in the discussion up to now. The reader will have guessed, I am sure, that it is this fourth way that I judge to be the relatively more adequate option open to us. But whether or not I am right in this judgment, we can hardly expect to be clear about the issue raised for theology by the challenge of pluralism to the other monistic options unless we at least take account of all of the main possibilities for answering our question. The purpose of what follows, then, even as of the foregoing, is not to settle this issue by finally arguing for *the* answer to the question, but rather to clarify the issue itself, by at last attending to this neglected possibility for answering the question beyond all the usual options.

The essential difference between both of the monistic options, on the one hand, and the fourth option, on the other, is that they deny what it affirms — namely, that religions other than Christianity can as validly claim to be formally true as it can. If we ask now what underlies and explains this essential difference, the answer can only be a difference in christology. Whereas exclusivism and inclusivism are alike in holding that the event of Jesus Christ is *constitutive* of the possibility of salvation, the fourth option maintains that this event is rather *representative* of this possibility, which is constituted solely and sufficiently by the primordial and everlasting love of God that is the sole primal source and the sole final end of all things.

I trust that the distinction I have employed here between a constitutive and a representative event is already familiar, in substance, if not also under these particular labels. But if an ordinary example of it is needed, I know of none better than that provided by the old story about the conversation between the three baseball umpires. The youngest and least experienced umpire allows, "I call 'em as I see 'em." Whereupon the second umpire, being older and more sure of himself, claims, "I call 'em as they are." But to all this, the oldest and shrewdest umpire responds with complete self-confidence, "They ain't nothin' till I call 'em!" By an event constitutive of the possibility of salvation I mean an event that is like the third umpire's calls, in that the possibility of salvation is nothing until the event occurs. On the contrary, what I mean by an event representative of the possibility of salvation is an event similar to the calls of the second umpire, in that it serves to declare a possibility of salvation that already is as it is — is already constituted as such — prior to the event's occurring to declare it.

Another example of a representative event drawn from the explicitly religious context is a minister's solemnizing the marriage of a woman and a man. Since it is generally understood that a marriage is constituted as such by the woman and man themselves, each pledging troth to the other, the office of the minister is properly to represent or declare their union, in no way to constitute it. This is evident from the formula customarily used by the minister in performing the service: "Forasmuch as so and so have consented together in holy wedlock . . . I pronounce that they are husband and wife together."

To be sure, other acts performed by Christian ministers are commonly thought to have a constitutive, rather than a merely representative, significance even with respect to salvation. This is particularly true of preaching the word and administering the sacraments, where they themselves are understood, as they typically are by exclusivists, to be constitutive of the possibility of salvation. Baptizing a person, for instance, may be viewed as itself effecting her or his transition from a state of sin to a state of grace, so that she or he could be expected to affirm, in the words of a well-known catechism, that baptism was the event "wherein I was made a member of Christ, the child of God, and an inheritor of the kingdom of heaven." But even for Christian inclusivists, any such view of baptism, or of any other means of salvation, is mistaken. Even in their understanding, all acts of the church's ministry and, for that matter, even the church itself are representative of the possibility of salvation rather than constitutive of it — whence their rejection of the claim of exclusivists that there is no salvation outside of the church.

On the other hand, inclusivists, for their part, continue to insist that the event of Jesus Christ itself has a constitutive, not merely a representative, significance for salvation. Although salvation in their view is and always has been possible for every human being regardless of her or his membership in the visible Christian church, had it not been for the unique saving event of Jesus Christ, there would not be or have been any such possibility of salvation. The distinctive move licensed by the fourth option, however, is to apply to the Christ event itself the same logic that inclusivists have already applied to the sacraments and the church. The result is a view according to which the *primal* Christian sacrament is Jesus Christ himself, from whom the church is then distinguished as the *primary* Christian sacrament, all ordinary sacraments or means of salvation being at best *secondary* and constituted by the church rather than constitutive of it.

But even the primal Christian sacrament is properly a *means* of salvation and therefore has a representative, not a constitutive, significance for salvation. Not even the event of Jesus Christ constitutes the love of God by which alone we are saved, but rather represents it; although, being properly the *primal* Christian sacrament, this event is also the *decisive* representation of God's love, and so constitutes the church and everything specifically Christian, including Christian faith itself. As such, Jesus Christ decisively *re*-presents God's love, in that he makes present again and explicitly the possibility of salvation that is always already presented implicitly to each and every human being as soon and as long as she or he is human at all. This possibility is constituted, however, not by any event in history, but solely by an event in eternity — the ever-new event of God's all-encompassing love, which is at once the beginning and the end of every created thing. It is solely because of this divine love, universally present and efficacious in all human lives, that salvation is always and everywhere possible and that any religious praxis can be so transformed as to become the true religion.

On the other hand, the fourth option is also essentially different from pluralism in not claiming that there in fact are many true religions or ways of salvation. Just as asserting the universal *possibility of salvation* does not require one to assert that *salvation itself* is universal, so one can claim with the fourth option that there *can be* many true religions without having to claim with pluralism that there actually *are* such. All that the fourth option claims a priori, in advance of actually encountering specific religions and validating their claims to truth, is that if the Christian religion itself is true, then any and all other religions can also be true in the very same sense, because or insofar as they give expression to substantially the same religious truth.

This fully allows for holding, as Christians, certainly, have good reason to hold, that there is not a little falsehood and distortion in all religious praxis, including that of persons who think and speak of themselves as Christians. At the same time, it warrants a certain optimism about all of the specific religions, even as about human existence and praxis otherwise. Indeed, it gives one every reason to look for signs of the actuality of the pluralism whose possibility is securely grounded in the completely universal reality of God's love, which is savingly present throughout all human existence and is therefore also at work in all religions.

Such, then, is the other, hitherto largely neglected option for answering our question. My judgment, as I have said, is that, of all the options, it is the least problematic and therefore the most likely to offer a valid answer. But whether I am right in this judgment or not, I trust that I have at least made clear that there are, in fact, four possible ways of answering the question, instead of only the three that alone are usually considered. And the importance of this seems clear. If the fourth option is indeed valid, one *can* not be either an exclusivist or an inclusivist and one *need* not be a pluralist, even if one would always have the possibility of becoming such, provided that the case for pluralism were actually to be made. On the other hand, one can affirm instead that because of the utterly universal and all-embracing love of God decisively re-presented through Jesus Christ, there is a universal possibility of salvation for each and every human being and that for the same reason, there is a corresponding possibility of as many true religions as there are religions so transformed by God's love as to be constituted by it and representative of it.

Whether or to what extent any religion, even Christianity, is true is, in my view, always a theological question. But if the Christian claim to truth is valid, and if the same can be said for the fourth option, there is at least one true religion, and because it is true, there can be many.

Part IV

Theology in Conversation

13

The Experience of God

Critical Reflections on Charles Hartshorne's Theory of Analogy

I

Simply in itself, "the experience of God" is ambiguous in that it can be construed both as a subjective and as an objective genitive phrase. If it is construed as the first, it means God's own experience as an experiencing subject, whether the experience be of God's self alone or also of some object or objects other than God. If it is construed as the second, it means someone's experience of God as experienced object, whether the experience be solely God's own or also that of some other subject or subjects. My contention is that this phrase will prove to be an important term in any adequate Christian theology insofar as, on either construction, it expresses a concept indispensable to the foundational assertions of such a theology. And this is so, I contend, precisely when, on both constructions, it is taken in its fullest sense — as meaning that God is both the subject and the object of experience, not only reflexively in relation to self, but also nonreflexively in relation to others. The reasons for this contention can be explained in three steps.

First of all, by "Christian theology" is properly meant either the process or the product of critically reflecting on the Christian witness of faith so as to understand its meaning and to be able to evaluate any and all claims as to its validity. If the constitutive assertion of this witness, however expressed or implied, is specifically christological, in that it is the assertion, in some formulation or other, of the decisive significance of Jesus for human existence, the metaphysical implications of this assertion are specifically theological in that they all either are, or clearly imply, assertions about the strictly ultimate reality that in theistic religious traditions is termed "God." In this sense, the foundational assertions of Christian witness and theology, as distinct from their constitutive assertion, are all assertions about God; and this means that in the very same sense, the concept expressed by "God" must be as indispensable to Christian theology as it is to the witness of faith on which theology is the reflection.

Second, a Christian theology can be adequate in a given situation only insofar as its assertions as formulated, whether expressed or implied, satisfy the specific requirements in the situation for being at once appropriate to Jesus Christ and credible to human existence: *appropriate,* in the sense that they are congruent in meaning with the assertions of the Christian witness as normatively represented in the witness of the apostles; and *credible,* in the sense that they are worthy of being believed by the same standards of critical judgment as properly apply to any other assertions of the same logical type or types. If this rule holds good of all the assertions of Christian theology, it obviously applies to theology's foundational assertions about God. The adequacy of any such assertion depends on satisfying all that is specifically required by appropriateness and credibility alike, given some historical situation with its limitations and opportunities.

Third, in our situation today, the specific requirements of these two criteria are such that no theology can be adequate unless it makes the assertion of the experience of God, by which I mean that it must assert, in some formulation or other, that the strictly ultimate reality termed "God" is the object as well as the subject of experience, and this in relation to others as well as to self.

One part of this assertion is made necessary by what we now take to be specifically required by the criterion of credibility. If in earlier situations the standards of critical judgment that properly applied to foundational theological assertions allowed for appeals to authorities of various kinds to settle the issue of their credibility, for us today all such appeals can have at most a provisional validity. Sooner or later, appeal must be made beyond all mere authorities to the ultimate verdict of our common human experience, which alone can establish the credibility even of theological assertions. This means, then, that God must be asserted to be in some way the object of human experience, else the foundational theological assertions could never be established as worthy of being believed (cf. Gamwell 1990, 3–8).

The other part of the assertion is made just as necessary by what we now see to be the specific requirements of the criterion of appropriateness. One of the most assured results of the application of historical-critical methods of study to the tradition of Christian witness is the soundness of Pascal's famous judgment that the God of the philosophers is not the God of Abraham, Isaac, and Jacob. Provided this judgment is taken as it should be, not as formulating a timeless principle, but as relative to the classical philosophy that Pascal clearly had in mind in making it, it can claim the full support of contemporary historical, including biblical, theology. So far from being the God of classical philosophy, who is in no way related to others and whose sole object of experience is self, the God of Christian scripture as well as of the

Hebrew patriarchs is consistently represented as the supremely relative One, who is related to all others as well as to self by the unique experiences of creation and redemption. And if this is true of scripture, it is no less true of the normative witness of the apostles, of which the Old and New Testaments are the primary source. This is to say, then, that God must be asserted to be in some sense the subject of the experience of others as well as of self, lest the foundational assertions of Christian theology fail to be congruent in meaning with the apostolic witness that is their norm.

And yet, if assertion of the experience of God is thus seen to be necessary to any adequate contemporary theology, it is nevertheless a problematic assertion, and that in the one part as well as the other. This becomes particularly clear when one takes account of certain basic presuppositions that are now widely shared by theologians as well as philosophers.

Partly as a result of the emergence of modern culture generally, especially science and a science-based technology, but also in part because of developments in philosophy associated, above all, with the work of Immanuel Kant, most of us have long since come to think of the several fields of human experience or reflection as much more clearly differentiated than earlier generations supposed them to be. Thus, if we now understand religion and morality, say, as forms of life and experience that are quite different from that of science, the same can also be said, *mutatis mutandis,* of our understanding of philosophy and metaphysics. We recognize that whereas science can claim to be empirical in a straightforward sense of the word, the same is not true of any of these other forms of praxis and culture or modes of thought, whose empirical connections, if any, are either less direct or more difficult to specify. As a matter of fact, for many of us, neither religion as a form of life, nor theology and metaphysics as modes of reflection, are empirical at all in the strict sense in which science can be said to be so. On the contrary, they are as clearly differentiated from science as we take them to be, precisely because they spring from an interest or concern that is more than merely empirical and because the assertions they typically make or imply are not subject to any strictly empirical mode of verification. Consequently, whatever reservations we may have about Paul Tillich's dictum that "God is being-itself, not *a* being," we can only concur in its essential point about the uniqueness of God. We take for granted that for religion as well as for philosophy, the question of God is extraordinary and cannot possibly be adequately answered on the same basis in experience or in the same terms and concepts as any ordinary question.

To the extent that presuppositions such as these are basic to our whole philosophical or theological approach, any talk about the experience of God, however construed, is bound to raise problems. If such talk is construed objectively, as asserting that God is in some way the object of human experience, the fact that "God" must be understood to express a nonempirical concept means that no empirical evidence can possibly be relevant to the question whether the concept applies, and that therefore God must be experienced directly rather than merely indirectly through first experiencing something else. Moreover, if "God" is correctly understood as in some sense referring to reality itself, its referent, if any, is evidently ubiquitous or omnipresent; and this implies that the experience of God is universal as well as direct — something had not only by mystics or the religious, but unavoidably by every human being simply as such — indeed, by any experiencing being whatever, in each and every one of its experiences of anything at all.

To become aware of such implications, however, is to realize at once why asserting the experience of God is, in this part of the assertion, indeed problematic. Even aside from the consideration that prevalent assumptions as to the limits of human experience scarcely allow for any such direct experience of God, the plain fact is that "God" does not appear to express a universally indispensable concept. On the contrary, the sheer existence of non- and even a-theistic religions and philosophies throughout culture and history is prima facie evidence against the claim that the experience of God is a universal human experience.

The other part of the assertion, which construes "the experience of God" subjectively, as asserting God's own experience of others as well as of self, is hardly less problematic. To be sure, there is nothing new about the fact that the clear assertions or implications in scripture that God is really related to the world as Creator and Redeemer, and hence by experiences of love and care, judgment and forgiveness, create difficulties for theological reflection. It was precisely the attempt to cope with such difficulties that led the church fathers to appropriate Stoic and Hellenistic Jewish methods of allegorical interpretation, and the medieval theologians to develop elaborate theories of analogy and non-literal predication. But one may still question, I think, whether prior to the emergence of the modern scientific world-picture and the sharp differentiation of the nonempirical claims of religion and metaphysics from the strictly empirical claims of science and ordinary language, these difficulties could be felt as acutely as most of us feel them today.

At any rate, it was left to Christian theologians of the last two centuries to try expressly, in one way or another, to "overcome theism"; and only in our own time have there been theologies of "radical demythologizing" and of "the death of God," as well as various attempts to salvage religious discourse by interpreting it exhaustively in noncognitive terms. This strongly suggests, I believe, that any assertion that God is the subject of the experience of others is certain to create a peculiar problem for theology today. However necessary such an assertion may be if justice is to be done to normative Christian witness, it is bound to strike most of us as, on the face of it, a category mistake: the application of a merely empirical predicate to a subject that can be adequately conceived, if at all, only as radically nonempirical.

The fact that the assertion of the experience of God is as problematic as I am arguing is directly connected with what I want to say about the work of Charles Hartshorne as a natural, or philosophical, theologian. One way, certainly, of making the claim for the extraordinary significance of Hartshorne's work for Christian theology is to say that he has done more than any other thinker on the scene to clarify, if not to solve, the problems raised by both parts of this assertion.

To be sure, his contribution toward solving the problems of asserting that God is directly experienced by every experiencing subject is less original and is matched or even excelled in important respects by the essentially similar solutions of other revisionary metaphysicians. Basically, his solution takes the form of distinguishing two different levels of human experience, or more or less conscious thinking about experience, on only the deeper of which is there an experience of God that is both direct and universal. Since such unavoidable experience of God need not be consciously thought about at the higher level and may, in fact, even be absent or denied there, the assertion that God is directly experienced by every human being as such is in no way incompatible with the existence of non- or even a-theistic modes of thought. But, of course, this is very much the solution to the same set of problems that is offered by so-called transcendental Thomist thinkers, beginning with Joseph Maréchal and continuing down to Karl Rahner and Bernard Lonergan. In fact, if Hartshorne's solution can be said to surpass theirs in its explicitly psychicalist claim that God is somehow experienced not only by every human being but by every actual entity whatever, theirs can be said to go beyond his in its more fully elaborated metaphysics of knowledge or cognitional theory. Even so, Hartshorne clearly has his own contribution to make toward solving even this first set of problems; and if his own theory of human experience is hardly as fully developed as certain others, its basic axioms are arguably more adequate because better founded in experience itself.

But where his work clearly seems to me to be unsurpassed in every respect is in the contribution he has made toward clarifying the second set of problems raised by asserting the experience of God, which is to say, by the concept of God as also the subject of experience, of others as well as of self. By working out a neoclassical theory of nonliteral religious discourse consistent with his neoclassical theism generally, he has not only overcome the notorious contradictions involved in classical theism's use of analogy and other modes of nonliteral language, but he has also given good reasons for thinking that our distinctively modern reflection about God results from two movements of thought, not simply from one. At the very same time that it has become clear that the theistic question cannot possibly be discussed as a merely empirical question, it has also become clear, on secular philosophical as well as religious grounds, that contingency and relativity can be as readily predicated of strictly ultimate reality as necessity and absoluteness. To this extent, Hartshorne has spoken, as no one else has succeeded in doing, to the peculiar problem posed by the apparent category mistake of any talk about God as the subject of experience. In fact, his contribution in this respect has been so impressive that a number of us who work at the task of Christian theology have long proceeded as though he had, in effect, solved this second set of conceptual problems.

But as impressive as Hartshorne's achievement still seems to me to be in clarifying both sets of problems, I have become increasingly convinced that his attempted solutions to them also involve certain difficulties, some of which I take to be serious. As a matter of fact, unless I am mistaken, he can be said to succeed in solving one of these sets of problems only insofar as he must be said to fail in solving the other.

2

The source of these difficulties, I believe, is his theory of analogy, by which I mean his attempt, in connection with his neoclassical theory of religious language, to establish a third stratum of meaning, or set of concepts and terms, which is distinct both from the set of plainly formal, strictly literal concepts and terms, on the one hand, and from the set of plainly material, merely symbolic or metaphorical concepts and terms, on the other. In attempting thus to establish analogy Hartshorne, of course, follows a precedent long since set by classical metaphysics and theology. Indeed, although he rarely makes use of the terms and distinctions of classical theories of analogy, the formal parallels between his own theory and that formulated by Thomas Aquinas are remarkably close. Still, as I have already indicated, there are also important differences between Hartshorne's neoclassical theory of analogy and any classical theory such as Aquinas's.

For one thing, he is far more explicit in acknowledging that the whole superstructure of nonliteral predication, whether symbolic or analogical, rests on a base of strictly literal metaphysical claims. If Aquinas at least tacitly acknowledges this by making all analogical predications depend upon the clearly literal distinction between Creator and creature, he can also seem not to acknowledge it by flatly declaring that we cannot know of God *quid sit,* but only *an sit* or *quod sit.* In Hartshorne's case, however, the position is consistently taken that "whatever the qualifications, some abstract feature or *ratio* is implied, and this common feature must not be denied if anything is to be left of the analogy" (Hartshorne 1945, 19).

Another, even more important difference between Hartshorne's and any classical theory is not formal but material — namely, his demonstration that the strictly literal claims that must be made about God if there are to be any symbolic or analogical predications at all must be partly positive, not wholly negative, in meaning. It is just this demonstration, indeed, that enables him, as I said before, to overcome the contradictions between literal and nonliteral claims about God in the classical theistic tradition. By conceiving God as eminently relative, he is not only able to conceive God as also eminently nonrelative or absolute, but is further able, without falling into contradiction, to make the symbolic or analogical assertions about God that are essential to theistic religious faith and worship.

There is no question, then, that Hartshorne's theory of analogy, however similar to classical theories, is free from some of their most obvious and intractable difficulties. But these are not the only, or even the most serious, such difficulties; and, as I now propose to show, it is rather less clear that he has succeeded in surmounting certain others as well. I shall begin by trying to clear up some more or less minor difficulties that appear to be more hermeneutical than substantive. Since some resolution of them is necessary to a coherent interpretation of Hartshorne's meaning, there is nothing to do but to work through them before discussing what I take to be the major difficulties of his theory.

3

In an essay entitled "The Idea of God — Literal or Analogical?" Hartshorne concludes an account of his panentheistic concept of God by asking explicitly, "What, in the foregoing account, is literal, and what is metaphorical, or at least, analogical?" To this he replies: "The psychological conceptions, such as love, will, knowledge, are non-literal. For God's love or knowledge differ *in principle,* not merely in degree, from ours. The criterion of these non-literal concepts is precisely that they involve degrees, that they are affairs of more or less, of high and low. They are *qualitative.* Literal concepts are not matters of degree, but of all or none. They express the formal status of an entity. They classify propositions about it as of a certain logical type" (1956, 134). Hartshorne's main point here, presumably, is that nonliteral concepts like "love" or "knowledge" differ from literal concepts in being matters of degree rather than of all of none. But he also appears to deny this when he says that God's love or knowledge differ from ours "*in principle,* not merely in degree."

What gives the appearance of contradiction, however, is the assumption, which Hartshorne's essay says nothing to disabuse, that his one distinction between differing merely in degree and differing in principle corresponds exactly to his other distinction between being a matter of degree and being a matter of all or none. But my guess is that he is here implicitly depending on a distinction he explicitly introduces elsewhere that invalidates this assumption — namely, the threefold distinction between "infinite," "finite," and "absolute" difference (see, e.g., 1957, 80f.). Assuming this distinction, which turns upon his more basic distinction between "all," "some," and "none," he can assert that God's love and knowledge differ in principle from ours without denying, as he appears to do, that the difference is still not absolute and hence expressible only in nonliteral concepts. In other words, what he means to say is that to differ in principle *is* to differ in degree, but it is not to differ "*merely* in degree," because it is an infinite, as distinct from a merely finite, difference.

A second difficulty is connected with the statement, already quoted, that "Literal concepts are not matters of degree, but of all or none." What makes this and parallel statements in other writings problematic is that some of the very concepts that Hartshorne classifies as "literal" are elsewhere implied to be matters of degree rather than of all or none and are even said to be "analogical" when applied to God. Consider, for example, what he says about the polar concepts "absolute" and "relative."

In one place, where he expressly proposes a classification of theological terms, he speaks of "plainly literal terms like relative and absolute" (1970a, 155). Similarly, he tells us in another passage, whose larger context is closely parallel, that although "God is symbolically ruler" and "analogically conscious and loving," God is "literally both absolute (or necessary) in existence and relative (or contingent) in actuality" (1962, 140). Elsewhere, however, in a discussion of "analogical concepts and metaphysical uniqueness," he makes his usual point that the unique status of deity is "a double one" by arguing that "no other being, in any aspect, could be either wholly relative or wholly nonrelative. Thus, while all beings have some measure of 'absoluteness' or independence of relationships and some measure of 'relativity,' God, and only God, is in one aspect of his being strictly or maximally absolute, and in another aspect no less strictly or maximally relative. So both 'relative' and 'nonrelative' are analogical, not univocal, in application to deity" (1948, 32). This argument is all the more striking because Hartshorne immediately goes on to say that the "completely metaphysical" distinction between deity and all else "may be expressed under any category" and because he subsequently speaks of "a strong or eminent, as contrasted to a weak or ordinary, sense" of the terms "relative" and "absolute" (32, 76; cf. 67, 75).

Such passages confirm that Hartshorne does not always say that categorial terms like "absolute" and "relative," "necessary" and "contingent," being matters of all or none rather than of degree, have a literal rather than an analogical meaning. It is true that the contrast he makes in the passage in which he affirms that these terms are "analogical" in application to deity is not with "literal," but rather with "univocal." But this difference is clearly merely verbal. In the sense in which he uses the term "literal" in the other passages in which he affirms the same categorial terms to have a literal rather than either a symbolic or an analogical meaning, it means nothing other than "univocal" (although, as we shall see presently, this is not the only sense in which he uses the term "literal"!). Thus he argues that, whereas an analogical concept like "feeling" applies to the different things to which it is applicable in different senses, rather than in the same sense, the purely formal concept "contingency" has "a single literal meaning applicable to all cases, the meaning of excluding some positive possibilities" (1962, 140). Or again, he can say of the term "relativity" that "to be 'constituted in some way by contingent relations' is simply and literally that, no more, no less, and no other" (1970a, 154). The fact seems to be, then, that Hartshorne means as well as says that the same categorial terms both are and are not literal rather than analogical when applied to God.

Is this to say that his theory is insofar inconsistent? To the best of my knowledge, he nowhere says anything that directly addresses this question. But it seems to me that there is something he could say that would remove the apparent contradiction.

Essential to his whole metaphysical position is the claim that in addition to "the most general or neutral idea of reality," we need to make certain purely formal distinctions between realities or entities of different logical types, thereby clarifying "metaphysical universals valid only within one type" (1970a, 141). Thus "reality is distinguishable categorially or *a priori* into concrete and abstract," and this distinction breaks down further into logical-type distinctions between "events," "individuals," and "aggregates" (or "groups of individuals"), on the one hand, and "qualities" (or "properties") on two different levels of abstractness, ranging from "species" and "genera" to "metaphysical categories," on the other (90, 141, 57, 101). Moreover, there is the "unique form of logical-type distinction" between "God and other things," or more exactly, "God and any other individual being" (144, 140). Although God as an individual is as contingent in actuality, or with respect to the events embodying the divine individuality, as any individual must be, the existence of God as the one universal, all-inclusive individual is categorially different from that of all other particular, partly exclusive individuals in being necessary, rather than contingent (245–260).

According to Hartshorne, all of these distinctions, including the unique distinction between God and all other individuals, are purely formal and therefore literal, in that they are matters, not of degree, but of all or none. An entity either is or is not an event; and the same may be said about its being an individual or an aggregate, a quality at the lower level of abstractness or at the higher, or the extraordinary individual God. Consequently, while there are metaphysical categories explicative of the meaning of each of these logical types, and therefore applicable only to entities falling within them, these categories too are strictly literal in that they apply to every entity within their respective types, not in different senses, but in the same sense.

Now this much Hartshorne himself clearly says or implies many times over. But then there is something else that he very well could say that would render his apparently contradictory statements consistent — namely, that although such terms as "absolute" and "relative," or "necessary" and "contingent," explicate the meaning of more than one logical type, and thus apply to entities within these different logical types in correspondingly different senses rather than in simply the same sense, they nevertheless apply to the different entities within any single type whose meaning they in some sense explicate, not in different senses, but rather in the same sense.

Thus "relative," for example, means in the broadest sense "constituted in some way or degree by relations to the contingent." As such, it applies in some sense to entities of all logical types, except qualities at the highest level of abstractness, otherwise called "metaphysical categories." But the sense in which "relative" applies to an event, say, is systematically different from the sense in which it applies to an ordinary quality at some lower level of abstractness, whether genus or species. While an event is relative in being internally related to other entities of the same logical type, which it requires by a necessity that is "particular and definite," a species or a genus is relative only in that it requires, by a necessity that is "generic or indefinite," one or more intensional classes (of individuals or of other more specific kinds), all of which are only contingently nonempty (1970a, 101f., 103, 109). Consequently, while there is a perfectly definite sense in which any ordinary quality can be said to be less relative and more absolute than any event, it can be said just as definitely that even the highest genus is infinitely more relative and less absolute than any metaphysical category, or than the necessary individuality of God that is the original unity of all such categories.

This means that if terms like "relative" and "absolute" are taken in their broadest meaning, without regard to distinctions of logical type, Hartshorne has sufficient reason for saying that they can be used in systematically different senses and, therefore, are analogical, not univocal, in application to deity. If, on the contrary, they are taken strictly, in any one of the senses they have when applied solely to entities within a single logical type, he is equally justified in holding that they are then used in the same sense and are, therefore, literal, not analogical, even when applicable to God.

So much, then, for this second difficulty. Because I take my resolution of it to be firmly based in Hartshorne's own essential position, I shall proceed henceforth as though it were a proper interpretation of what he means to say, even though, to repeat, I know of no place where he actually says it.

The third difficulty that must be cleared up was already alluded to parenthetically when I remarked earlier that Hartshorne uses the term "literal," also, in more than one sense. In fact, one could say, somewhat schematically, that if the second difficulty arises from his saying that concepts that he classifies as literal are analogical, the third difficulty arises from his saying that concepts that he classifies as analogical are literal. The difference in this case, however, is that in speaking so, he expressly recognizes that he is using "literal" in a different sense, even though he never explains very clearly just wherein this difference lies.

Thus, after a discussion of the "literalness of theism," in which he argues that it is God who loves literally, while it is we who love only metaphorically, he remarks: "If someone should say that I have been using 'literal' and 'metaphorical' in an unusual, nonliteral, and even metaphorical sense, I should reply that I have apprehensions this may perhaps be true. I should be happy to be taught how to put the matter more precisely" (1948, 38). Elsewhere, having argued that analogical concepts are "not purely formal in the same sense as the other categorial terms," he hastens to add, "And yet there is a strange sense in which the analogical concepts apply literally to deity, and analogically to creatures" (1962, 141; cf. 1970a, 155f.).

It would appear that Hartshorne is here depending, in effect, if not in so many words, upon something like the distinction made in the Thomistic theory of analogy between what is meant by an analogical term — the *res significata* — and how the term means — its *modus significandi* (Thomas Aquinas 1964, 56–59, 66–71). By means of this distinction, one can argue that although the primary sense of a term with respect to how it means is the sense it has as applied to a creature, or ordinary individual, the primary sense of the term with respect to what is meant by it is the sense it has as applied to the Creator, or eminent individual. Accordingly, one may hold that even though God is the secondary analogue with respect to how an analogy means, God is nonetheless the primary analogue with respect to what is meant by the analogy.

A close reading of Hartshorne's writings confirms, I believe, that he typically reasons in much the same way, even if it is Karl Barth or Emil Brunner, instead of Aquinas, with whom he acknowledges his agreement in doing so! But if I am right about this, the third difficulty can also be

resolved. When Hartshorne says that there is a sense in which analogical terms apply literally to God and therefore simply *are* literal in this
application, what he means by "literal" is not that such terms apply to
God in the *same* sense in which they apply to any other entity of the
same logical type — this being, as we have seen, what he otherwise takes
"literal" to mean. He means, rather, that with respect at least to what
is meant by such terms, as distinct from how they mean, they apply
to God in the *primary* sense in which they can be applied analogically
both to God and to all other individuals, their application to such other
individuals being in this respect their secondary sense.

4

Yet a fourth difficulty — actually a complex of difficulties — in Hartshorne's theory has to do with his using certain terms that he classifies
as analogical expressly in senses that render any such classification self-
contradictory. I use "analogical" here in the strict sense implied by what
has already been said about the meaning of "literal" — namely, that
terms are "literal" in the strict sense of the word when, within any single logical type, they apply in the same sense, rather than in different
senses, to all the different entities belonging to the type. By contrast,
terms are "analogical" in the strict sense when, even within the logical
types within which alone they are applicable — which is to say, the logical types of individuals, and hence of the eminent individual God as well
as of ordinary individuals — they apply in different senses, rather than
in the same sense, to all the different entities within the same respective
types. Thus Hartshorne holds that the term "feeling," for instance, can
be said to be analogical in this sense because, or insofar as, it applies to
all entities of the logical type of individuals, including the unique individual God, but does so in suitably different senses to all the different
kinds or levels of individuals, with its sense being infinitely different in
its application to God (1962, 140).

    The difficulty, however, is that it is not only, or even primarily, terms
such as "feeling" or "sentience" that Hartshorne typically classifies as
thus analogical when applied to God. On the contrary, because he seeks
to interpret what is said or implied about God in such theistic religious
phenomena as faith and worship, his preferred theological analogies involve terms like "knowledge," "love," and "will"; and he likes to speak
of God, as in a sentence already quoted, as "analogically conscious and
loving" (1970a, 154ff.; 1962, 140; cf. 1965, 301). At one point, he goes
so far as to say that "the word God...stands for an analogy (difficult no doubt) between the thinking animal and the cosmos conceived
as animate" (1970a, 220). Considering his use elsewhere of the phrase,
"thinking animal," one can only suppose that here too it refers to man,

or a human being, in contrast to other kinds of animals who feel but cannot think, or at any rate, cannot think that they think (1970a, 94; 1971, 208).

But if this supposition is correct, any analogy between such a specific kind of animal and God is not merely difficult, but quite impossible. For by Hartshorne's own criterion of the difference between an analogy and a mere symbol — namely, that the first differs from the second in not drawing a comparison between God and one concrete species of entity in contrast to all others — any comparison between God and the thinking animal cannot possibly be an analogy, but only a symbol (1962, 134). Because "thinking," as Hartshorne expressly uses the word, is, in his terms, a merely "local," rather than a "cosmic," variable, if it can be applied to God at all, it has to be applied symbolically rather than analogically (1937, 111–124).

It would be tedious to show that a similar difficulty rises in connection with most, if not all, of the other terms that Hartshorne typically represents as theological analogies. In each case, the source of the difficulty is the same: in the sense that he himself expressly gives the term, it can be applied at most to entities of some specific kind or kinds and is therefore anything but a variable having "an *infinite* range of values" (116). Of course, he is by no means unaware of such difficulties, as is clear from the admission already cited and clearer still from his statement elsewhere that as compared with the traditional problem of evil, "there are other difficulties in theism" that he at least finds "more formidable." Specifically, he allows, "the old problem of analogy: how if at all to conceive an unsurpassable yet individual form of experience, volition, or love, is still with us" (1966b, 212).

But as clear as Hartshorne may be that there is a problem here, he says very little, if anything, by way of solving it. In fact, in discussions of how God might be conceived as conscious or knowing, his comments range all the way from raising the question whether God is really conscious at all, to speaking none too clearly of "super-linguistic consciousness" or of "the One who knows without symbol (or for whom everything whatever serves as symbol)" (1967, 4f.; 1970a, 94; 1970b, 25f.). And just as significant, I think, he nowhere seems to explain, as he clearly has to explain if "conscious" and "knowing" are analogical, how not only the greatest, but even the least, possible individual must in some sense be said to be conscious and to know, as well as to be aware and to feel.

So far as this fourth difficulty is concerned, then, I see no obvious way of clearing it up. If Hartshorne is to uphold his claim that terms such as "thinking" and "knowing," "loving" and "willing," are analogical in meaning when applied to God, he has to give them a sense infinitely different from the specific sense in which he expressly uses them. But in that event, it is no longer clear why he or anyone else should prefer them as theological analogies to such other psychical terms as "feeling" and "experiencing," "sentient" and "aware." For surely the same thing must then happen to them as happens to "consciousness" when, as he himself allows, "the word means no more than 'experience' or 'awareness' in the most noncommittal meaning" (1963, 4). In other words, the dilemma in which Hartshorne appears to be caught is that he can establish the properly analogical status of his favorite theological analogies only by preserving a merely verbal connection with the primary experience and discourse to which he is concerned to do justice: the faith and worship of theistic religion, which speaks of God in the most vivid symbols, not as one who somehow senses and feels, but as one who loves and cares, judges and forgives.

5

As serious as this dilemma may appear, however, it is still relatively minor in comparison with the other difficulties in Hartshorne's theory that we are at last in a position to discuss. Clearly, it is one question whether certain psychical terms can be coherently established as theological analogies rather than frankly accepted as only symbols, while it is yet another and far more serious question whether any such terms at all can be coherently classified as truly analogical rather than merely symbolic. Hartshorne explicitly recognizes this when he speaks of the terms that he distinguishes as analogical in the strict sense as "problematic," in that they are "neither unambiguously literal nor unambiguously non-literal" (1970a, 156). Even so, he attempts to show that there is indeed such a third class of terms by way of what at least appear to be two lines of argument.

At one point, he observes that "besides obviously formal and obviously material ideas about God we have descriptions whose classification depends partly upon one's philosophical beliefs" (1962, 139). As what follows makes clear, the beliefs he alludes to are those of "panpsychism," or, as he now prefers to say, "psychicalism." According to such beliefs, psychical concepts like "awareness," "feeling," "memory," and "sympathy" do not apply merely to some individuals in contrast to others, as obviously material ideas do, but rather are "categorial, universal in scope" (140). And yet, even for psychicalism — and this explains the qualification "partly" — psychical concepts are also different from obviously formal ideas because they are categorial, and hence universally applicable, not to entities of all logical types, but only to "concrete singulars," which is to say, individuals and events, as distinct both from aggregates, which are concrete but not singular, and all levels of qualities, which are merely abstract and not concrete (141). In fact, in a parallel passage, Hartshorne even speaks of psychical terms as merely "almost categorial" because of this difference in their scope of application from "the strictly categorial notions" like "relativity" (1970a, 154).

But such a confusing, if not self-contradictory, way of speaking is uncalled for. Hartshorne himself explains in an earlier chapter in the same book that "strict metaphysical generality can stop short of literally 'everything,'" because "it is enough if a concept applies with complete and *a priori* universality within one logical level" (89). Moreover, as we learned from our earlier discussion, he can occasionally speak even of a purely formal concept like "relativity" as being in a broad sense analogical, because it has systematically different senses as explicative of the meaning of different logical types. But this implies that any psychical concept that is truly analogical must be just as universal in its scope of application as a purely formal term like "relativity," provided only that this term is taken, as it should be, in the sense in which it alone explicates the meaning of "concrete singular," whether event or individual. The only question, then, is whether any psychical concept is truly analogical; and Hartshorne here appears to support his affirmative answer by appealing to the philosophical beliefs peculiar to psychicalism.

But if he really does intend this as an independent line of argument, which he perhaps does not, it is open to the objection that it begs the question. Granted that psychicalism as a metaphysical position does indeed imply that at least some psychical concepts are truly analogical in their application to God, it is just as clear that psychicalism itself can be established as true only if at least some psychical terms are known to express theological analogies.

Of course, one may very well seek to support a psychicalist metaphysics by appealing, as Hartshorne does, to a direct intuition of experience or feeling other than our own, insofar as "we can consciously intuit our physical pleasures and pains as direct participation in feelings enjoyed or suffered by our bodily constituents" (1976, 71). One may then generalize this intuition and, employing the criterion of "active singularity," further argue by analogy that whatever is experienced to act as one, must also feel as one, whether this be an animal or a cell, a molecule or an atom (1970a, 36, 143f.; 1979, 62). But while these arguments might well suffice to establish psychicalism as a speculative scientific cosmology, and thus to show that "psychics," not "physics," is the inclusive empirical science, they remain merely empirical arguments and as such are insufficient to establish psychicalism as a metaphysical position (1977). Nor can it be established, in my judgment, by Hartshorne's additional argument that since nothing positive can conflict with the presence of mind in some form, it cannot even conceivably be shown to be totally absent (1953, 32f.; 1970a, 160f.). While this argument may indeed suffice to show that psychicalism cannot be falsified, it is not sufficient to show that psychicalism is metaphysically true. This it could show only if "mind" were already known to be a concept having infinite scope of application, and this is the very thing in question.

Consequently, one is forced to conclude that if psychicalism is to be established as indeed a matter of philosophical beliefs and hence as true metaphysically, there is nothing to do but to appeal to a direct intuition of the one individual who is in no way merely empirical, but is strictly metaphysical. Only by directly intuiting that psychical concepts apply primarily to the extraordinary individual God, can one possibly know them to be variables with a strictly infinite range of possible values and therefore truly analogical.

Hartshorne evidently recognizes the force of this reasoning because the other line of argument by which he at least appears to support his claim for a distinct class of theological analogies is to appeal to just such a direct experience of God. In fact, this may quite possibly be his only line of argument, the other apparent one not really being intended as such after all. In any event, in a closely parallel discussion of the very same question — of how problematic terms like "know" or "love" as applied to God are to be classified — he in no way appeals to psychicalism, but argues instead that although they are "in each application not literal in the simple sense in which 'relative' can be," they nevertheless "may be literal if or in so far as we have religious intuition" (1970a, 155). Recalling our earlier discussion of the different senses in which Hartshorne uses the word "literal," we can infer that what he means by saying that "know" or "love" may be literal as applied to God is not that they may apply to God in the *same* sense in which they apply to all individuals, but rather that they may apply to God in the *primary* sense in which they are thus applicable, their application to any other individual being secondary. Thus the point of his argument is that such terms may apply primarily to God, or that God may be their primary analogue if, or insofar as, we directly experience God.

This interpretation is confirmed by Hartshorne's development of his case. "This is the question," he argues, "does our concept of 'know' come merely from intra-human experience, analogically extended to what is below and above the human, or does the concept come partly from religious experience, from some dim but direct awareness of deity?" The answer, he believes, is "that we know what 'knowledge' is partly by knowing God, and that though it is true that we form the idea of divine knowledge by analogical extension from our experience of human knowledge, this is not the whole truth, the other side of the matter being that we form our idea of human knowledge by exploiting the intuition...which we have of God" (155).

If Hartshorne's speaking here of "religious experience" may seem to refer to some special kind of experience in contrast to other kinds or to experience generally, this is not his meaning. Although he often uses the term "religion" and its cognates in a way that would require such a construction, what he intends to say here is not that where there is religious experience there is awareness of deity, but rather, conversely, that where there is awareness of deity there is religious experience. Thus he concludes by holding that experience of God is an essential moment in all human experience: "man's awareness of God is no mere contingent extension of his awareness of himself, but is rather an indispensable element of that awareness. . . . [T]he divine-human contrast is the basic principle of all human thought, never wholly submerged, though it may often be driven rather deep into the dimly-lighted regions of experience" (156).

How successful is this line of argument? To answer this question, I first want to make sure of just what the argument has to show if it is to succeed. And for this purpose I shall cite yet another passage in which Hartshorne argues in very much the same way.

"An animal, which cannot say God," he holds, "equally cannot say I. There is no derivation of the first notion from the second, but the two are from the outset in contrast in experience. The animal feels both itself and God . . . and thinks neither; we feel and can think both. We are, indeed, likely to call the divine 'I,' 'Truth' or 'reality'; that is, we think of certain abstract aspects of the inclusive something, and do not quite realize consciously that it must be an inclusive experience, the model of all experiences in its personal unity" (1948, 39f.). The several parallels here I take to be clear: the same insistence that the divine-human contrast is a priori in experience; the same denial of one-sided derivation of the idea of one side of the contrast from the idea of the other; and the same admission that the contrast may nevertheless not be fully realized at the level of conscious thought.

But what is arresting in this passage, in comparison with the others cited earlier, is the distinction Hartshorne explicitly makes between our merely feeling "the inclusive something," only some of the abstract aspects of which are we likely to think about when we speak of it as "truth" or "reality," and our consciously realizing, and thus thinking instead, that this inclusive something has to be "an inclusive experience," which as such is "the model of all experiences." It evidently follows from this distinction that if "the inclusive something" *must* be "an inclusive experience," it can only be this inclusive experience that we are actually experiencing even when we merely feel something all-inclusive that we are likely to speak about only abstractly in calling it "truth" or "reality." But it just as clearly follows that we not only do not need to experience "the inclusive something" *as* "an inclusive experience," but are even likely to think about it consciously without quite realizing that this is what it has to be. It thus becomes an interesting question whether our merely feeling "the inclusive *something* "is already an experience of "an inclusive *experience.*" Perhaps the only thing to say is that in one sense it clearly is, while in another sense it clearly is not.

At any rate, one thing is certain: only an experience of "the inclusive something" *as* "an inclusive experience" and hence the conscious realization that this is all it can be could possibly warrant the claim that it is "the model of all experiences." I conclude, therefore, that if Hartshorne's argument is successful, this can only be because it shows that we have not only a direct intuition of God, but also a direct intuition of God *as* eminently psychical, and hence also think or consciously realize that the inclusive whole of which we experience ourselves to be parts is a universal subject of experience.

But now what does Hartshorne's argument purport to show? The question is pertinent because he seems to say different things. On the one hand, he claims that our concept of "know" comes partly from "some dim but direct awareness of deity," which may often be driven below the level of conscious thought, even if it is never wholly absent; in a word, we have a feeling of God, as distinct from thinking or knowing God (1970a, 155; cf. 1962, 110). On the other hand, he says that "we know what 'knowledge' is partly by knowing God," which is presumably a different and stronger claim, even though he repeats it later in the same sentence by saying only that "we form our idea of human knowledge by exploiting the intuition... which we have of God."

I am satisfied that Hartshorne's apparent vacillation here is real and that there are good reasons for it. But, however this may be, we have only to look at his own account of such matters to learn that having a feeling of God is one thing, while thinking about God, or having knowledge of God, is something quite different.

Thus, in a recent defense of psychicalism, he stresses that "on the highest levels only does it [*sc.,* the psychical] include what we normally mean by 'thought' or 'consciousness.' Lower creatures feel but scarcely know or think, and if we speak of them as conscious,... we stretch the sense of the word. This can be done, but then we need another word to distinguish high-level, thoughtful cognitive experience or feeling from mere experience or feeling" (1977, 95). The distinction Hartshorne insists on making here as applied to our present question can be expressed by saying that whereas mere experience or feeling of God can be not only direct but immediate, high-level thought or cognition of God, being mediated, as it is, by the conscious judgment or interpretation of such feeling, is of necessity mediate. Moreover, since, according to Hartshorne, "human consciousness is essentially linguistic," the mediation involved in any thinking or knowing of God is also a matter of language or verbal formulation (1959, 178).

To recognize this difference, however, is to understand why Hartshorne's argument cannot possibly succeed if it claims no more than that we have a dim but direct awareness of deity. Even if it were indeed the case that each of us in every moment is directly and immediately aware of God, whether any psychical concept is a true analogy would still be undecided. As Hartshorne himself admits, we may very well have an immediate experience of "the inclusive something" without ever consciously thinking of it, or even, it seems, being likely to think of it as "an inclusive experience." And yet without so thinking of it, we could never know it to be "the model of all experiences" and so the primary analogue of at least some of our psychical concepts. Consequently, if Hartshorne's argument is successful, it is only because it makes the other, much stronger claim that each of us in every moment is not only dimly aware of God, but also thinks or knows God as eminently experiencing subject.

This claim, however, is open to the decisive objection that it could not be true unless human culture and history were radically other than we must suppose them to be. If the claim that God must somehow be experienced directly and universally already appears problematic, given the sheer fact of non- and even a-theistic religions and philosophies, how much more problematic must be the claim that God is everywhere consciously known! Clearly, such a claim could be true only on the absurd supposition that every case of professed non- or a-theistic belief must involve conscious bad faith and intent to deceive.

Not surprisingly, Hartshorne has always been careful to avoid so incredible a claim. Although he has ever insisted that God somehow has to be experienced if anything at all is experienced, he has never failed to make clear, as in several statements already quoted, that God need not be consciously known and may even be expressly denied without conscious insincerity. Indeed, it is precisely the clarity with which he has thus distinguished the different levels of our experience of God that has enabled him, as I claimed earlier, to solve the problems raised by asserting "the experience of God" in the objective construction of this phrase. But this, of course, is exactly why I also implied that the success he enjoys in solving this set of problems explains his failure to solve the other set raised by construing this phrase subjectively. One has only to consult what he himself has consistently taught about our experience of God as object to have the very best of reasons for rejecting out of hand any claim that each of us knows and must know God as experiencing subject.

I have no hesitation, therefore, in saying that Hartshorne's attempt to establish analogy is a failure. Either the claim he makes is weak enough to seem credible, in which case it is insufficient; or else he makes a claim strong enough to seem sufficient, in which case it is incredible.

6

Having said this, however, I think it is important to ask whether the reasons for his failure are merely contingent, in the sense that the attempt itself might well have succeeded, or still succeed, but for inadequacies in his argument that could have been, or yet can be, avoided. My own conviction is that the reasons his attempt fails are, rather, necessary, and that the same fate must overtake any other similar attempt. Because this conviction has an important bearing on the conclusion to be drawn from these reflections, I now wish to explain why it seems to me to be correct.

There is a further objection that might be made to Hartshorne's argument. Even if he could establish the stronger claim that there is a universal knowledge of God as eminent subject of experience, he would have no way of ruling out the possibility that this knowledge as such, as distinct from the immediate experience of which it is the conscious mediation, is entirely a matter of, in his terms, "analogical extension," which is to say, the secondary and derivative application to God of concepts that apply primarily and originally to ourselves, and that are not, therefore, true analogies at all, but mere symbols. He in effect recognizes this when he admits that "we form the idea of divine knowledge by analogical extension from our experience of human knowledge" (1970a, 155). Although he goes on to insist that this is not the whole truth, what he takes to be the other side of the matter is that we form our idea of human knowledge, not by exploiting our intuition of God as eminently knowing, but by exploiting our intuition of God — period. Thus, for all he shows to the contrary, the only thing in our concept of human knowledge that derives from our direct intuition of God is the idea of totality or all-inclusiveness, just as he himself allows that we can very well experience "the inclusive something" without experiencing it as "an inclusive experience" (1948, 39f.).

But even more than this, Hartshorne himself argues again and again in such a way as clearly to imply that the primary, or as he can say, "normal," use of all our psychical concepts is their application to ourselves rather than to God. Thus, in one essay, for instance, he first argues against the idea of providence as a power freely determining all the details of existence by asking, "whence do we have this idea of freedom? Surely, we can conceive it because we have some little freedom of our own. . . . [W]e must have some range of possibilities genuinely open to us, or we could not form any conception of God as having an infinite range of possibilities open to him" (1963–64, 20). Employing the same reasoning, he then argues that we must also know ourselves as causes or creators if we are to have any conception of God in these terms, concluding with the general comment that "we cannot simply nullify the normal meaning of a term and still use the term as basis for an analogical extrapolation to deity" (22). I submit that arguments of this kind can have the force that Hartshorne takes them to have only if the whole of our knowledge of God, beyond our unavoidable experience of "the inclusive something," can be derived from such knowledge as we have of ourselves, and hence is merely symbolic rather than truly analogical. If we could know anything else about God except through the mediation of concepts primarily applying to our own intrahuman experience, who could deny that we might very well know God to be free or creative without first knowing this of ourselves?

But if any knowledge of God mediated by psychical concepts would leave open the possibility of its being merely symbolic instead of truly analogical, what could rule out this possibility? The answer, I believe, is that the only thing that could conceivably exclude it is an immediate knowledge of God as the primary analogue of our psychical concepts. But then, of course, the question is whether there can conceivably be any such thing as an immediate *knowledge,* as distinct from an immediate *experience,* of God, any more than of anything else. Certainly, on Hartshorne's presuppositions, as should by now be clear, any knowledge of God, just as of any other thing, is by its very nature mediate insofar as it is mediated by conscious judgment and interpretation, as well as by verbal formulation of what is immediately given in experience. Nor is it otherwise on the presuppositions of philosophers generally, who concur in analyzing the phrase "immediate knowledge" as expressing a self-contradiction and hence as meaningless.

But if this analysis is sound, the reasons for Hartshorne's failure to establish analogies as a class of terms distinct from symbols are by no means merely contingent. Because the only condition on which any such attempt could possibly succeed is itself impossible to meet, he was sooner or later bound to fail, as anyone else must always be who makes the same attempt.

My conclusion from these reflections, then, is that anything like Hartshorne's distinction between analogy and symbol, however clear it may be in itself, can never be known to apply. If any of our psychical concepts really is a true analogy, in that it applies primarily to God and only secondarily to ourselves, at least with respect to what is meant by it, if not with respect to how it means, we, at any rate, neither are, nor ever could be, in the position of knowing it to be such. For all we could possibly know, all our psychical concepts apply to God, not as analogies, but as symbols, in exactly the same way in which at least some of them clearly must apply if we are to do any justice at all to the faith and witness of theistic religion.

7

The implications of this conclusion are many and far-reaching, for my own work as a Christian theologian as well as for what I understand by the related, but nonetheless distinct, tasks of philosophy and metaphysics. Obviously, if theological analogies cannot be established, the same is true of metaphysical analogies generally, whether those of Hartshorne's psychicalism or those of any other categorial metaphysics necessarily involving analogies, such as materialism, or physicalism, and dualism. Consequently, if metaphysics is to be established at all, it is only as a transcendental metaphysics, whose concepts and assertions are all purely formal and literal, rather than analogical, in the sense that they apply to all the different things within any single logical type whose meaning they explicate, not in different senses, but rather in the same sense.

So far as I can see, the foundations for such a transcendental metaphysics — and a neoclassical transcendental metaphysics at that — are firmly laid in Hartshorne's own systematic clarifications of the strictly literal claims that are necessarily implied by any nonliteral claims about God — that is to say, his analyses of the utterly general idea of reality as such, as well as of the several logical-type distinctions discussed above. Nor does the fact that these analyses, as he develops them, are not adequately distinguished from formulations that he takes to be analogical, but that I can accept only as symbolic, in any way interfere with my appreciating both kinds of formulations as having their proper places in any adequate philosophy. For if, on the one side, he has never left any doubt that they are and must be clearly distinguishable, whether or not adequately distinguished, on the other side, I have no more inclination than he does simply to identify philosophy with metaphysics. On the contrary, I fully share his own view that philosophy has "two primary responsibilities," only one of which is properly metaphysical, the other being rather practical or existential (1970a, xiv). It seems entirely fitting that in carrying out its other responsibility for expressing effectively the meaning of ultimate reality for us, as distinct from describing metaphysically the structure of ultimate reality in itself, philosophy should in its own way make use of the same vivid symbols that religion and theology employ to this end. Thus there is very little in Hartshorne's philosophy for which I do not also find a place, even if I feel compelled to distinguish it as indeed philosophy rather than metaphysics in the strict and proper sense of the word.

But this is not the place to pursue further these or any of the other implications of the conclusion for which I have argued. Suffice it to say, simply, that on the alternative view I have proposed, no less than on Hartshorne's own, the assertion of the experience of God that is now necessary to any adequate Christian theology can receive all the clarification and support that a natural or philosophical theology may be reasonably expected to provide. If, on the one hand, this assertion is construed *objectively*, as asserting that God is the eminent object of experience, because the only individual other than ourselves whom we experience directly and universally, it can be shown to be true both literally and necessarily, on the understanding that such immediate experience of God can become knowledge of God, or even experience of God *as* God, only through the mediation of concepts and terms. If, on the other hand, the assertion is construed *subjectively*, as asserting that God is the eminent subject of experience, because the only individual who experiences all things as their primal source and final end, it too can be shown to be true necessarily, although neither literally nor analogically, but only symbolically, on the understanding that it is nonetheless really and not merely apparently true, because its implications can all be interpreted in the concepts and assertions of a transcendental metaphysics, whose application to God, as to anything else, is strictly literal.

Those who are privileged to have Charles Hartshorne as their teacher know that not the least thing they continue to learn from him is a distinctive philosophical procedure. One of the cardinal principles of this procedure he formulates by saying, "If in philosophizing we choose one of two possible views we should always know clearly what the other view is and why we reject it" (1966a, 92). How well I may have managed to follow this principle I should not wish to say. But since I accept it as binding even on a philosophizing theologian, I hope it is at least clear, especially to my esteemed teacher, that I have in my own way tried to be faithful to it.

14

Rudolf Bultmann and the Future of Revisionary Christology

I

For some time now there has been little question about the most disputed aspect of Rudolf Bultmann's contribution to the ongoing task of revisionary christology. Beginning with a famous lecture by Ernst Käsemann in 1953, even Bultmann's own students who otherwise largely shared his theological position proved to have reservations about it at a critical point (Käsemann 1953). They had become convinced that in criticizing the attempts of an earlier revisionary christology to support its claims by appealing to the historical Jesus, Bultmann had assumed the extreme contrary position of supporting his christology by appealing simply to the Christian kerygma. Consequently, they were concerned to show that despite his strictures against such a procedure, an appeal back behind the kerygma to Jesus himself is not only historically possible, but also theologically necessary. Subsequent developments have tended, on the whole, only to consolidate this position of "post-Bultmannian" theology with its call for "a new quest of the historical Jesus" (Robinson 1959). This is no doubt most obvious in the various political and liberation theologies, where criticism of Bultmann's theology in general invariably includes an appeal against him to the historical Jesus as the norm of christology. But from one end of the theological spectrum to the other, and across wide differences of confession as well as of culture and language, it has long since been agreed that Bultmann's attempt to make the kerygma the norm of christology now belongs to the past of revisionary christology rather than to its future.

It is not surprising, then, that more recent revisionary proposals typically include considerable negative criticism of Bultmann's contribution. Even in the case of proposals whose authors in other respects are expressly appreciative of his work and show every sign of being deeply indebted to it, one finds continued objections to his position on the question of the norm of christology. In fact, the whole purpose of such proposals is to try to secure their own position on this question by representing it as the only tenable alternative to his untenable position to the contrary.

If one looks at these proposals more closely, however, it is by no means obvious that they give promise of a future for revisionary christology. On the contrary, the position for which they argue is in all essentials the very position of the earlier revisionary christology that Bultmann sought to overcome; and my judgment is that the difficulties involved in arguing for this position today are sufficiently serious that one has every reason to leave it behind. It is also my judgment that the criticisms of Bultmann that are usually made by way of trying to secure this position as often as not misunderstand his intentions in taking up his very different position on the question. Even if one allows, as I certainly would, that he may not have always expressed his intentions as adequately as he might have, and that there may be ways of refining and developing his position that we today at least ought to consider, still the evidence is clear that the position he intended to hold is about as different from the one he is criticized for holding as it is from that of his critics.

But if these judgments of mine should prove to be sound, the question of Bultmann and the future of revisionary christology would need to be reconsidered. Far from holding the extreme contrary position that he is widely represented as holding, he would turn out to have opened up a third possibility, distinct at once from two equally extreme alternatives: on the one hand, the position of an earlier revisionary christology as well as of his recent critics; and on the other hand, the position of perhaps a small minority of his followers, which these critics mistakenly attribute to him. In that event, one could hardly avoid asking whether it is not the third possibility opened up by Bultmann's own position that most deserves further attention. As something like the common contradictory of both of the extreme contraries that should indeed be left to the past, it might well be the neglected alternative that opens out to the future.

The strategy of the following argument, then, is this: to compel reconsideration of Bultmann's contribution to revisionary christology by establishing the soundness of my two judgments. To this end, I shall discuss in some detail one of the proposals I especially have in mind in speaking of more recent proposals in revisionary christology. Since my criticisms of this proposal will be largely negative with respect both to its own constructive position and to its criticisms of Bultmann's, I want to stress at the outset that I nonetheless value it for its contribution to our common task. Its existentialist interpretation of the Christian witness seems to me unusually clear and forceful, and any number of its discussions of particular questions have helped me to achieve greater clarity about my own theological intentions. This is not least the case at the very point of my greatest differences with it, fully confirming the truth that we are indebted to all from whom we learn — those with whom we are led to disagree as surely as those who elicit our agreement.

2

The proposal to which I refer is that of James P. Mackey in his book *Jesus, the Man and the Myth: A Contemporary Christology* (1979). Trained in both historical theology and philosophy of religion, Mackey approaches the problem of christology as a systematic theologian. Thus his leading question, to which the book as a whole develops his answer, is the one indicated by its title: Why this myth of this man? If Mackey understands this question to ask for a historical explanation and structures the main body of his book accordingly, he also takes it to ask for a systematic justification, in the sense of what he calls "a living logic of faith" (Mackey 1979, 253; cf. 173f.). "What is the logic," he asks, "which connects the developing myth about the man, Jesus, to Jesus' own myth? What is the logic which binds increasing faith in Jesus to the faith which Jesus' own myth embodied? This is *the* christological question, this is the question concerning the very origin of christology as such..." (184).

Mackey's answer is that the logic in question is indeed a logic of faith, in that it is the logic that connects Jesus' own faith in the Fatherhood of God and in God's coming reign with the faith he inspired in others by virtue of his faith. In places, to be sure, Mackey uses the phrase "the faith of Jesus" to mean "the faith which Jesus recommended," or which was embodied in his myth of the reign of God, as distinct from "his own personal faith" (296 n. 50; cf. 96, 163). But he is also explicit in claiming that the faith of Jesus to which any systematic justification of christology must finally appeal is "the personal faith of Jesus himself (the faith which was a quality of Jesus as personal subject, not the faith of which Jesus is object)" (163). By Mackey's account, then, the whole development of christology, from "the earliest comprehensive myth" of the resurrection to "the full-grown myth" of the Nicene definition, is justified as well as explained by Jesus' own personal faith. "Jesus, because of the life he lived and enabled others to live, because of the grace he knew and allowed others to know, because of the faith he had and inspired others to have, because of the spirit he breathed into a dying world, in his verbal myth, his prayer, his table-fellowship, his practical ministry...Jesus, because of all this, proved significant, to put the matter mildly, in humanity's struggle for life over death; and people who prove significant in this way are the material of which myths are made, for which myths are needed" (189f.). Moreover, "it is the faith of Jesus which is still determinative of how we acknowledge him. It is that distinctive faith of his which, when we catch it from him, allows us to come into contact with the God he called Father, and which then demands that we acknowledge his role between us and God in all the ways in which the orthodox tradition did this" (247).

With this understanding of how even a contemporary christology must justify its claims, Mackey naturally argues for the theological necessity of a quest of the historical Jesus. "The distinctive faith of Jesus, the distinctive spirit of Jesus, is history.... If, then, as would-be followers of Jesus, we would seek the presence of the living God, we are directed, without alternative, to that human history in which it is both hidden and revealed" (242; cf. 3). But if a quest of Jesus is theologically necessary, it is also historically possible. As a matter of fact, Mackey argues that the quest of the historical Jesus "has never finally proved either to be misconceived in its nature or to have failed in its results" (248).

He recognizes, to be sure, that there is no possibility, given the nature of our sources, of reconstructing anything like a full account of the life of Jesus from infancy to death: "In fact, before what is known as his public ministry,... little or nothing can be said with historical certainty about Jesus of Nazareth" (122). Furthermore, "even of the few public years, not many purely factual data can be discovered," and "of [Jesus'] more particular deeds and words... it is difficult now to be certain of the authenticity, much less the more specific occasions of time and place and other circumstances" (123). But while Mackey thus allows that the old quest of the historical Jesus is indeed impossible, he nevertheless insists that "the faith of Jesus, radical as it is, is not outside the human historian's range" (279). Provided one agrees that "the only life of the historical Jesus worth recovering is the life that he literally poured into his public mission of inaugurating the kingdom of God," the fact that his public ministry is all of his personal life that his followers cared to remember and record is no problem (175). What they provided is "more than enough" for us to recover "the cause for which he lived and died," and thus to experience his own personal faith (123; cf. 50). Nor is the fact that all our sources are faith documents intended primarily to arouse the same faith in others any obstacle to such recovery. For "if Jesus' very life was an attempt to inspire faith of a particular kind in others, then, quite clearly, provided they got right the particular kind of faith he tried to inspire, no documents could be truer to his memory than faith documents" (122).

As for present disenchantment with the quest, Mackey believes that much of it is due, "not to the kind of inadequacies which a professional historian might find in the source material — for in this case... the source material is adequate to our purpose; the disenchantment is due, rather, to the persistence of questers in bringing to this material their own varying expectations and each seeing a different expectation fulfilled" (12). But if this suffices to explain the past difficulties of the quest, one may be guardedly optimistic about its future prospects. "The problem is not, as some think, that the quest has gone on too long or gone too far; the problem is that it has not yet been pursued with that combination of unqualified enthusiasm and unprejudiced professionalism which it deserves" (256).

Throughout this argument for the quest of the historical Jesus, Mackey is keenly aware of the alternative position of Bultmann. And yet, unlike many English-speaking theologians, he rightly recognizes that Bultmann's most serious challenge to his argument is not directed against the historical possibility of the quest. Bultmann is indeed "both heir and defiant defender of a long century of growing skepticism about the ability of the New Testament text to tell us anything at all certain about the historical Jesus" (164). But "we are not entitled to conclude that he is totally skeptical about the prospect of discovering the historical Jesus. His particular challenge to the historical quest...is based on considerations concerning Christian faith, not on distrust of the historical sources" (252; cf. 250, 255).

To be exact, Bultmann challenges the quest at the very point where Mackey speaks of "the logic by which the myth about Jesus developed from Jesus' own myth of the reign of God" (253). Just where Mackey tries to see "the connections of a living logic of faith,...Bultmann insists on an unbridgeable gap" (253). "The fact that Jesus is our Lord precisely because he, the historical Jesus, inserts into our history the challenge and the possibility of new faith and new life, by his preaching which is continued in various forms, by the prayer he introduces to our lives, by the ritual he invites us still to celebrate and the service to which he inspires us — this Bultmann is not prepared to admit" (253). On the contrary, "in Bultmann's system the specific content of Christian faith,...the lesson we learn from the cross, comes to us from the risen Lord presented in the preaching and not from the historical Jesus. The man in whose action God acts, in whose destiny God is at work, in whose word God speaks, is the Son of God, not the historical Jesus" (252). Moreover, according to Mackey, Bultmann expressly holds, in a warning issued to Ernst Fuchs, that "the kerygma does not permit any inquiry into the personal faith of the preacher (that is, Jesus)" (164). Precisely because the faith demanded by the Christian kerygma is not the faith of Jesus in the coming reign of God, but faith in Jesus himself as God's decisive act of salvation, we shall never understand, and we certainly can never justify, the kerygma's demand by historical inquiry into Jesus' own personal faith.

To this contention of Bultmann's, however, Mackey makes a twofold reply. In the first place, "if we range outside the context in which the word 'faith' itself is specifically used, to others which use an equivalent phrase, we shall see that the New Testament writers frequently and insistently present Jesus as a man of faith, and we shall then have all the warrant we could expect for doing so ourselves" (166). In the second place, "the conception of the historical Jesus as himself a man of faith can help rather than hinder our understanding of the conviction, expressed in the myth of Jesus, that in him we do indeed encounter the one, true God..." (165).

In fact, there is one reason that makes it more than plausible to look to Jesus' own personal faith both to explain and to justify the faith expressed in the myth about him. "This kind of faith, it seems, can only be spread by contagion. Only carriers can truly give it to others" (169; cf. 196). In the end, Mackey argues, we can be brought to that experience of all life and existence as grace which is Christian faith only through the grace of another human person through whom we find ourselves forgiven, accepted, and served and in this way enabled and inspired to forgive, accept, and serve others. "And there is really no possibility of dissimulation here." For "power-seeking in service, like condescension in giving, or cowardly envy in forgiving, is too easily perceptible, if sometimes, unfortunately perceived too late, and no good comes of it, no sense of life and existence as grace, no faith or love, no hope" (170).

Consequently, if we have in fact come to Christian faith, and if it really is to Jesus, finally, that we somehow owe our having done so, we must conclude to his own personal faith as its only sufficient ground. "So Jesus cherished all life and existence, and especially other people, as God's precious gift, and so, without ulterior motive, he accepted all and served their needs, and so enabled and inspired them to discover the treasure hidden in their lives.... The only alternative here is to see the human personality of Jesus as a purely passive mask for the dramatic speeches of divinity. And that neither the scriptures nor the great tradition allows us to do" (170f.).

There is no question that Mackey has Bultmann in mind, even if not exclusively, in what he thus characterizes as "the only alternative" to his position. In his view, either faith has its source and origin, under God, in the faith of the historical Jesus, or else it does not really arise out of history at all. Thus he speaks of Bultmann's thesis that "history and faith can find no common ground in research into the origins of Christianity" as "this new (and old) idea that faith, at least in its source, is entirely above and beyond history, and that documents presenting faith are not therefore amenable to source-research of the normal rational kind" (44f.). In the same vein, he can ask a series of rhetorical questions about the origin of Christian faith and proclamation, only to observe: "Clearly Bultmann does not want such questions asked or answered" (255). But more even than this, Mackey claims that those who, like Bultmann, "force a dichotomy between faith and history are really the last of a long line of human beings who have given up on history" (256). Indeed, Bultmann's theory of Christian faith devalues "the world of our historical experience" in the same way, even if not quite as much, as do "literal theories of special divine revelatory interventions, on the one hand, or absolute theories of fallen nature, on the other" (256).

So far as Mackey is concerned, then, the issue between his position and Bultmann's is clear: either "our world and its history is itself the source of our faith in God" or else its source must be found in "some proclamation into the origin of which we may not even inquire" (256).

3

In turning now to criticism of Mackey's proposal, I wish to begin with his constructive position. Students of revisionary christology since Friedrich Schleiermacher will readily agree, I believe, that the essentials of this position are hardly new (see Faut 1904). And students of Bultmann's early work will be equally quick to recognize that it was an earlier version of essentially the same position over against which Bultmann defined his own in his critical discussion with Wilhelm Herrmann and Emanuel Hirsch as well as with Johannes Weiss (Bultmann 1954, 85–113, 245–267; cf. also Grass 1963; 1973, 93–99). Still, the very fact that Mackey develops his position explicitly as an alternative to Bultmann's makes clear that it is not simply the same as that of an earlier revisionary christology. Even if all the essentials of its claims are familiar enough, the arguments required to establish these claims today involve difficulties of their own, which are nonetheless serious for being in some respects new.

This is particularly true of the claim that the personal faith of Jesus himself is not outside the range of the human historian. For all that Mackey says about the sources being adequate — indeed, providing "more than enough" to allow us to recover Jesus' faith — it is significant that he nowhere offers the least evidence or argument against one of the most secure conclusions of historical-critical study of these sources — namely, that even the earliest of them are secondary and have the character of engaged witnesses of faith rather than disinterested historical reports. Of course, this is a literary-critical conclusion about the character of the traditions redacted in the gospels, not a historical-critical judgment about what can or cannot be known by controlled inferences from the traditions to the history lying behind them. But if it thus leaves room to use the sources for a historical inquiry into Jesus' faith, it also renders any such inquiry peculiarly problematic. Because all the sources are at best secondary, and are witness, not reportage, any inference from them about Jesus himself can be controlled, if at all, only by yet another inference of exactly the same kind.

In other words, one can never make an operational distinction between Jesus as he really was and Jesus as he is represented in the earliest of these sources. Because the only evidence one has for the first is strictly identical with whatever evidence one has for the second, any distinction one may make between them must either remain merely theoretical or else beg the question. But if this means, in general, that one can never talk historically about what Jesus said and did, as distinct from what he was heard to have said and seen to have done by those whose witness to him provides our only sources, it just as surely means that one can never talk historically about Jesus' own personal faith, as distinct from such faith as he may have been understood to have had by these same earliest witnesses.

To be sure, one might conceivably try to infer Jesus' faith indirectly from material authentically reporting his words and deeds. But not only would one then still be faced with the problem of distinguishing Jesus' own words and deeds from the sayings and actions attributed to him in the earliest witness, but one would confront the further difficulty of backing up the warrants required to license one's inference sufficiently to make them acceptable historical warrants.

Just how serious this difficulty is, is clear from the warrant Mackey invokes in asserting that there is really no possibility of dissimulating faith. Not only does he quite fail to provide any evidence or argument for this assertion, but it is incredible, on the face of it, if one keeps in mind that what is meant by "faith" here is not particular words or deeds or even some more fundamental trait of observable behavior, but rather the utterly personal act of accepting one's own existence and all existence as grace. Clearly, any such act can be experienced by another even in principle only through its putative expressions; and of these one must always be able to say what Paul says of even the most radical expressions of love: even "if I give away all my possessions, and if I hand over my body to be burned," the possibility remains that I "do not have love" (1Co 13:3). In short, there really is a possibility of dissimulation here, and Mackey's warrant is so far from being an acceptable license for historical inferences as to give every appearance of special pleading. But this means that, for all he shows to the contrary, the faith of Jesus *is* outside the human historian's range, and, since this is true in principle as well as in fact, no christology that supposedly gives expression to this faith as its historical source, his own included, can even possibly be either explained or justified.

The same conclusion about the character of our sources, as well as of the New Testament writings generally, suffices to undermine the argument for another of Mackey's claims — to the effect, namely, that the New Testament writers provide all the warrant we could expect for presenting Jesus as himself a man of faith. Mackey actually offers two arguments for this claim: first, that there are contexts in the New Testament, such as the Epistle to the Hebrews, where Jesus is implicitly presented as believing in God by describing him in equivalent terms as hearing and obeying God's word or will; and second, that in a passage like Galatians 2:16, the original Greek usually translated so as to refer to the faith of which Jesus is the object could be read as easily and even more literally as referring to the personal faith of Jesus himself (163). The difficulty with both of these arguments, however, is that they ignore the conclusion overwhelmingly confirmed by historical-critical study that all the New Testament writings are, first and last, documents of faith and witness. Thus, even if Mackey were to succeed in showing that their authors present Jesus, as he claims, "frequently and insistently" as a man of faith, the question would remain whether this in any way warrants his own talk of Jesus' faith as the one historical source of Christian faith and witness. It is one thing to bear witness to Jesus as the Christ because one experiences him to be a man of faith; it is another and very different thing to bear witness to Jesus as a man of faith because one believes him to be the Christ.

This difference becomes all the more significant if one takes seriously the rule already laid down that the personal faith of one human being can never be experienced by another except through its putative expressions, from which it can never be certainly inferred. Assuming that the earliest witnesses' experience of Jesus could not have been an exception to this rule, one can only conclude that anything they may have said or implied about Jesus' faith had a very different import from that which Mackey's arguments presume it to have had. Far from explaining or justifying their christological assertion by appealing to its historical source, their talk about Jesus' faith could only have been one among a number of other ways of formulating this very assertion. And this conclusion becomes irresistible when one considers the obviously idealized way in which the New Testament writings actually speak of Jesus' faithfulness to his vocation and submission to God's will (Mt 4:1–11 par.; Mk 14:32–42), his godly fear and obedience (Heb 5:7ff.), his exemplary endurance of suffering (1Pe 2:21ff.), or his sinlessness (Heb 4:15; 7:16ff.). All such talk undoubtedly has the literary character of legend, being in every way comparable with the accounts of Jesus' miraculous conception and birth or of his equally miraculous appearances after death. But insofar as this is itself christology, rather than an attempted historical explanation or justification thereof, it provides no warrant whatever for Mackey's attempt to explain and justify christology historically by presenting Jesus as himself a person of faith.

This brings us to the other claim that Mackey makes in replying to Bultmann's contention that we can never understand, much less justify, the demand of the Christian kerygma by inquiring historically into Jesus' own personal faith. On the contrary, Mackey claims, the conception of Jesus as himself a person of faith can help, rather than hinder, our understanding of the belief expressed in the myth about Jesus that in him we meet the one, true God. Here again, the difficulties involved in trying to establish Mackey's claim are serious.

Consider, first of all, his use of the old premise that Christian faith, or — since they are really one and the same — the distinctive faith of Jesus, can only be conveyed by contagion, in that one must catch it from a carrier who already has it. Obviously, if this premise were true without exception, one could establish the fact of Jesus' faith only by immediately raising the question about the carrier from whom he, in turn, had to have caught it. But then if one were to allow this question by allowing that such a carrier could indeed be identified, Jesus would be relativized to simply one more in the intervening chain of carriers, and one would have to withdraw any claim that his faith is the unique source of the faith that others have caught from him. If, on the other hand, one were to try to uphold the claim for the uniqueness of Jesus' faith, one would have to disallow the question about its own source, thereby implying the falsity of the premise save insofar as it admitted of at least this one notable exception. But if it were to admit of this one exception, it could presumably admit of any number of others, in which event Jesus' faith would not be the unique source of faith after all.

There is little question that Mackey's argument avoids the first horn of this dilemma. He at no point allows the question about the carrier of faith by whom Jesus himself was infected, and he clearly intends Jesus to be an exception to his premise, although, admittedly, he does not so formulate it as to allow for this exception. Thus, in arguing that "we can only sense ourselves and our world valued and cherished by God when we feel ourselves valued and cherished by others," he expressly distinguishes Jesus from "the rest of us" by insisting that "it is very likely that his power to value [others] went far beyond anyone's ability to value him" (170). Elsewhere this still qualified claim for Jesus' exceptional status gives way to such unqualified claims as that he "fully realized and actualized" the possibility of faith and that "he was no sinner" (238, 243; cf. 232). But it is just such unqualified claims — which, incidentally, no quest of the historical Jesus could ever possibly verify — that reveal the difficulty of Mackey's argument; for if they enable him to avoid the second horn of the dilemma as well, by defeating the presumption that there could be any number of exceptions to the premise besides Jesus, they themselves are completely groundless claims, for all that he says to support them. This is so, at any rate, unless one allows that they are perhaps tacitly supported by the very mythical belief that the conception of Jesus as himself a person of faith is supposed to help us understand.

It is evident that this conception can be of no help whatever in understanding that belief unless it is the conception of Jesus' faith as a unique personal faith. But, as I have shown, one cannot derive such a conception either from a quest of the historical Jesus or from the kind of talk about Jesus' faith that may be found in the New Testament. If, on the contrary, any claims for the uniqueness of Jesus' faith are simply one more or less adequate way of formulating the belief that he is the Christ, or that he is of decisive significance for human existence, the difficulty of Mackey's argument is serious indeed. Far from helping our understanding of the belief expressed in the myth about Jesus, the conception of Jesus as a man of faith must itself be helped by this very belief before it can be even so much as relevant to such understanding.

If this conception does not help our understanding, however, what about the other part of Mackey's claim that it does not hinder our understanding? To make good on this part of his claim he would have to show, as distinct from merely assuming, that being the unique man of faith that he takes Jesus to have been is the sufficient condition for truly asserting the belief about Jesus expressed in the myth about him. He would have to show this, I say, because if this were not the case, if the belief about Jesus were grounded in anything other or more than his unique personal faith, then to appeal, as Mackey does, simply to the conception of Jesus as having such faith in order to understand the belief would indeed hinder our understanding of it — namely, by confusing at best a partial explanation or justification with a complete one. As it happens, however, Mackey does not even begin to show that this most fundamental assumption of his position is well-founded.

The sufficient proof of this is that he nowhere considers, much less succeeds in meeting, the objections that have long been urged against the same assumption when it has been made by others proposing an essentially similar position. Thus, not only does he ignore Bultmann's repeated arguments against this assumption, but he does not even take account of the parallel arguments more recently advanced by at least one English-speaking theologian with whose work he otherwise seems to be familiar (see Hick 1958; 1966).

According to these counterarguments, however, not even a Jesus whose faith was as unique as Mackey takes it to have been would be sufficient to explain or justify the belief expressed in the myth about him. At most, such a Jesus would be merely one more human being among others, on the same level as ourselves, even if first and foremost among us; whereas the whole point of the myth is that Jesus is infinitely more than a mere man, on the same level as God, even if also distinct from God as the one through whom God is decisively encountered. If this is undoubtedly the point of what Mackey calls "the full-grown myth" of Jesus' deity as formulated at Nicaea, it is not any less the point even of the original myth of Jesus' resurrection and of the titles attributed to him in the earliest witness. For while this earliest form of the myth was indeed cast in terms drawn from Jewish religious tradition, and thus represented Jesus as in every way human, in no way divine, its point nonetheless was to place him on *God's* side of the relation between God and human beings generally, not on the side of human beings who more or less fully believe in God. As he whom God has made Messiah by raising him from the dead, Jesus is not merely a believer in God, not even the "original and originative" believer, but is rather the one through whom God has spoken and acted in a final decisive way to re-present the possibility of faith to all who would believe.

If such counterarguments are sound, however, and this really is the point of the myth about Jesus, this last difficulty of Mackey's argument is certainly not the least. By failing to show that the unique faith of the historical Jesus is the sufficient condition of making this essential point, he is open to the decisive objection of proposing a christology that at best makes another and very different point, and hence hinders rather than helps our understanding of what any christology is supposed to be all about.

4

But if Mackey's position is clearly untenable, is the only alternative, as he claims, the position he criticizes as Bultmann's? Must we locate the source of our faith in God, not in the Jesus of history, but in some proclamation into whose origin we may not even inquire? No, this is not our only alternative, because, as I now propose to show, Bultmann's real position is sufficiently different from the one Mackey attributes to him to be a third distinct possibility.

Two points may be made immediately about Mackey's criticisms. In the first place, to suggest, as he does, that Bultmann forbids inquiry into the origin of the Christian proclamation or regards documents of faith as not amenable to normal, rational source-research is not to describe Bultmann's position, but to caricature it. Bultmann not only nowhere tries to keep questions about the origin of faith and proclamation from being asked or answered, but again and again asks and answers them himself — as he does, for instance, even in his criticism of the new questers, when he argues for a strict historical continuity between Jesus' own proclamation and the early church's message about Christ (Bultmann 1960b, 11f., 15f.). Likewise, one of the most characteristic themes of his theology is the "paradox" or "scandal" of the eschatological event, which lies precisely in the fact that the very phenomena that Christian faith proclaims as eschatological — Jesus himself, the apostles who proclaim him, and the church constituted by their proclamation — are all genuinely historical phenomena "that are subject to historical, sociological, and psychological examination" exactly like any other (1951, 48; cf. 1984b, 41f.).

But if this means that Bultmann in no way exempts documents of faith from the same source-research that applies to all historical documents, it also means that he is unequivocal about the genuinely historical source of our faith insofar as it derives from the apostolic proclamation that constitutes the church. Therefore, Mackey is misleading, in the second place, when he represents Bultmann as forcing a dichotomy between faith and history and thus devaluing the world of our historical experience. Even if Bultmann were to maintain as simply as Mackey claims he does that the source of Christian faith is the kerygma, his unambiguous assertion of the historicity of the kerygma itself, both as the church's present proclamation and as the normative proclamation of the apostles, would falsify Mackey's claim that he asserts the essential independence of Christian faith and history.

The truth, however, is that Bultmann does not maintain in any such simple or unqualified way that the kerygma is the source of Christian faith. As a matter of fact, in his view, in contrast to the one for which Mackey criticizes him, any such tenet is evidently subject to two important qualifications.

The first of these becomes apparent in a highly instructive discussion of how the meaning of the cross as the salvation event comes to be understood. If Mackey's criticism were to the point, one would naturally expect Bultmann simply to deny that there was ever any need to understand the historical Jesus in order to understand the significance of his cross. In fact, however, he precludes any such simple denial by explicitly distinguishing between our own situation today and that of the first proclaimers. If there is indeed no need for us first to understand the historical Jesus in order to understand the point of the cross, this is because we are already confronted with the Christian kerygma in which its point is explicitly proclaimed. It was otherwise, however, with those first proclaimers to whom we owe this very kerygma, since their only recourse was the historical Jesus. "They experienced the cross of the one with whom they had been bound in the living present. Out of this personal bond, in which the cross was an event in their own lives, it became a question for them and disclosed its point" (1951, 43f.; cf. 1984b, 36).

Interestingly enough, Bultmann explicitly refers here to "the historical Jesus" (*den historischen Jesus*), even if in other, closely parallel passages he expresses himself more carefully — for instance, by speaking simply of "facts of the past" that become "historical phenomena" (*geschichtliche Phänomene*) only by acquiring a meaning for a subject who exists in history and participates in it and is therefore "bound up with them in historical life" (1952a, 229; cf. 1984b, 84). Either way, however, his point is clear: it was through the first proclaimers' own immediate experience of the Jesus of history as a "fact of the past" that his cross first came to be understood as having decisive significance. And this interpretation is fully confirmed by what Bultmann says elsewhere on the same point: "The decision to accept Jesus' having been sent that his 'disciples' had once made by 'following' him had to be made anew and radically in consequence of his crucifixion. The cross, so to say, raised once again the question of decision; for as little as it could call into question the *what* of his proclamation, so much it could and did make questionable the *that* of his proclamation — his legitimation, the claim that he was God's messenger bringing the final decisive word. The church had to overcome the scandal of the cross and did so with the faith of Easter" (1965a, 47).

Of course, this first qualification that Bultmann makes of any claim that faith has its source simply in the kerygma is, in a way, self-evident. After all, the kerygma is a historical emergent whose source could only be found beyond itself in the immediate experience and faith of those to whom we owe it. But if Bultmann leaves no doubt that the experience and faith that are thematized in the kerygma are those of Good Friday and Easter, he is equally clear that neither the question of decision raised by the cross nor the answer given to this question by faith in the resurrection was completely new and unprecedented. In fact, he explicitly affirms in the passage just quoted that the cross raised *"once again"* the same question of decision that had already been raised by Jesus' proclamation, and that the decision that had to be made anew and radically in consequence of his crucifixion was the same decision the disciples had already made *"once"* by following him during his lifetime. In other words, in Bultmann's view, not only did the disciples' experience of the cross depend upon their prior experience of Jesus' life to disclose its meaning, but even the faith to which they came at Easter only renewed and radicalized the faith to which they had already come in accepting Jesus as sent by God.

It is only natural, then, that Bultmann's many discussions of the origin of christology typically point, first of all, not to the disciples' experience of Jesus' death and resurrection, but to their prior experience of his proclamation. More exactly, it is their experience of the *that* of Jesus' proclamation that Bultmann represents as christologically decisive. Thus, according to one typical account, Jesus appeared as a prophet and teacher proclaiming the imminent coming of God's reign and the radical demand of God's will. Although he presented no teaching about his own person, his summons to decision for or against his proclamation as God's own word in the last hour definitely implied a christology. This christology became explicit in the early community to the extent that it confessed that God had made Jesus Messiah and that it was as such that he would soon come. "This shows," Bultmann observes, "that the community understood Jesus' word — and this means, not its timeless content of ideas, but his having spoken it and their having been addressed by it — as the decisive act of God. But this is also to say that their transmission of Jesus' proclamation could not consist in a simple reproduction of his ideas. Instead, the proclaimer had to become the one proclaimed. Precisely the *that* of his proclamation is decisive" (1954, 204f.).

Elsewhere Bultmann offers much the same account, only to formulate his distinction between the *that* and the *what* of Jesus' proclamation by also distinguishing between Jesus' "person" and his "personality":

> Whether Jesus knew himself to be the Messiah or not is indifferent. If he did, it would only mean that he became conscious of the decisive character of his work in terms of a contemporary Jewish idea. But, of course, his summons to decision implies a christology, although neither as metaphysical speculation about a heavenly being nor as a character sketch of his personality as having a messianic consciousness. Rather, it is a christology that is proclamation or personal address. Therefore, if the early community designates Jesus as the Messiah, it expresses in its way that it has understood him. . . . The proclaimer had to become the one proclaimed because the decisive thing about his proclamation is its *that,* not his personality, but his person, its being here and now, its event, its commission, its personal address. In designating him the Messiah, the early community understands him as the decisive event, the act of God, that inaugurates the new world. (1954, 265f.)

The significance of this passage, I submit, is to make clear that and why any distinction Bultmann makes between the Christian kerygma and the historical Jesus has nothing like the axiomatic status in his position that Mackey represents it as having. No doubt when Bultmann refers to our situation today, he uses this distinction to argue that our faith does indeed arise in response to the kerygma rather than the historical Jesus. But when he discusses the origin of christology in the experience of the first proclaimers, this distinction proves to be derived — namely, from the original distinction that he formulates either by distinguishing between the *that* and the *what* of Jesus' proclamation or by distinguishing between Jesus' person and his personality. Certainly, so far as these first Christians were concerned, the source of Christian faith was no more the kerygma than it was the historical Jesus, in the sense of the personality of Jesus endowed with messianic consciousness, the *what* of whose proclamation was nothing other than radicalized Jewish prophetism. Rather, the source of the Christian faith in which the kerygma itself had its origin was the person of Jesus, the *that* of whose proclamation was already understood to be the decisive act of God by those who made the decision to follow him. Thus Bultmann can say that "the real content of the Easter faith that God has made the prophet and teacher Jesus of Nazareth the Messiah" is "that Jesus' having come

was itself the decisive event through which God has summoned his con-
gregation, that this event itself was already eschatological occurrence"
(1965a, 45; cf. also 1926, 197f., where Bultmann argues that the earliest community confessed Jesus to be the Messiah "on the authority of
his words.").

But even if Bultmann thus holds that the faith of the first proclaimers
had its source in their immediate experience of the person of Jesus, has
it not already become clear that he gives a very different account of
the source of our faith today? Is not Mackey justified in his criticism
at least to the extent that, so far as we are concerned, Bultmann allows
the kerygma alone to be the source of our faith?

I should not wish to deny that there is a certain amount of evidence
to which one could appeal in support of Mackey's criticism. As I have
indicated, Bultmann distinguishes our situation today from that of the
first proclaimers insofar as our faith arises in response to the kerygma
rather than the historical Jesus. Moreover, there are even passages in
which he expressly affirms that Jesus Christ can be encountered only in
the kerygma and nowhere else. But whatever one is finally to make of
this affirmation, one can hardly expect to understand it correctly except
by interpreting these passages in the light of others things that Bultmann
expressly says — in which case one will have to take account of his
consistent teaching that even for us today there can be an existentialist interpretation of, and hence an existential encounter with, Jesus' own
proclamation and that this proclamation at least implied Jesus' claim to
be the Christ.

More important, however, is the fact that Bultmann's own understanding of the kerygma in no way allows it to be taken simply in itself
independently of the Jesus to whom it bears witness. On the contrary, it
remains entirely dependent for its authority on Jesus himself, and as the
proclamation of his decisive significance for human existence, the experience it mediates is precisely an experience of him. Consequently, when
Bultmann takes the position that it is the kerygma rather than the historical Jesus that is the norm of christology, he is not denying, but rather
affirming, that the primal source of Christian faith even for us today is
nothing other than Jesus himself.

This becomes clear from his repeated statements that it is precisely
Jesus as a genuinely historical event by which the present proclamation of the kerygma is authorized or legitimated. Significantly, Mackey
not only completely ignores such statements, but by focusing on another statement of Bultmann's in isolation from them, gives his reader to
understand that Bultmann simply contrasts legitimating with faith, "so
that one rules out the other..." (Mackey 1979, 304 n. 19). Bultmann
does indeed contrast legitimating and faith as mutually exclusive in
the sense that the kerygma's existential-historical assertion that Jesus is

the Christ logically could not be legitimated by any empirical-historical assertion about the historical Jesus. But to rule out legitimating the kerygma in this sense is not to rule out legitimating it altogether; and there is another sense in which Bultmann repeatedly states that the kerygma by its very nature can and must be legitimated.

Thus, in arguing at one point that New Testament theology performs a necessary theological task, Bultmann reasons as follows: "Since the kerygma today acquires its legitimation from the Christ event of the past, present preaching and systematic theology with it have need of a critical control that secures its identity with the apostolic preaching — namely, New Testament theology" (1979, 17f.; cf. 1984b, 62). If this statement confirms how seriously Mackey misunderstands Bultmann in criticizing him for making faith completely independent of historical inquiry, it also makes clear how different Bultmann's theological norm is from Mackey's. What must be secured if present preaching is to be legitimate, Bultmann holds, is its identity with "the apostolic preaching," not its identity with the preaching or faith of the historical Jesus. But it is no less clear from this statement that even the apostolic preaching is the *primary norm* of the kerygma today, not the *primal source* from which it acquires its legitimation insofar as it is identical in substance with the apostolic preaching. The only primal source of its legitimation, Bultmann affirms, is "the Christ event of the past," by which all preaching, including the uniquely normative preaching of the apostles, is authorized or legitimated.

What Bultmann refers to here as "the Christ event of the past" is clearly one and the same with what we have seen him speak of elsewhere as "the *that* of Jesus' proclamation," or "Jesus' person, its being here and now, its event, its commission, its personal address." Thus, in interpreting Johannine theology, he can say that Jesus is there represented as himself the word of Christian proclamation because "this word in which judgment and forgiveness, death and life, become event is established, authorized, and legitimated by the event Jesus" (1954, 292). And he interprets Paul's teaching that the new age becomes a reality in the kerygma and in the faith that works by love as affirming that this all happens precisely "*through the historical Jesus* [*den historischen Jesus*]. But not through the 'personality,' whether understood as a character or as a 'figure' embodying certain ideas, so that the new age would be a new epoch in the history of culture. Christ is accessible only through the kerygma, and the new age is to be seen only in faith." Even so, Bultmann insists, when Paul speaks of the obedience and love of Christ, referring thereby to the pre-existent one rather than to any attributes of the historical Jesus (*des historischen Jesus*), he intends nothing other than the service performed for us by "Jesus, the historical person" (*Jesus, die geschichtliche Person*). For "the 'obedience' of Christ is the fact of his historical person in its service to us, and his 'love' is God's saving act in him..." (1954, 212f.).

Rightly understood, the present proclamation of the kerygma is not some other source of faith to be taken in itself independently of the Jesus of history, but rather the very means by which he himself can be experienced here and now as faith's only primal source. Accordingly, Bultmann can say that the word of God is "not the mysterious word of some oracle but sober proclamation of the person and destiny of Jesus of Nazareth in their significance as history of salvation" (1951, 48; cf. 1984b, 41). Earlier in the same context he explains more fully what he means by this by speaking of "genuine historical understanding" (*echt geschichtliches Verständnis*) of Jesus' crucifixion:

> It is precisely not to mythological but to historical [*geschicht-lichem*] understanding that the historical [*historische*] event dis-closes itself as the salvation event, insofar as genuine historical understanding understands a historical event in its significance. Ba-sically, the mythological talk seeks to do nothing other than to express the significance of the historical event. In the significance that belongs to it, the historical [*historische*] event of the cross has created a new historical [*geschichtliche*] situation; the proclama-tion of the cross as the salvation event asks its hearers whether they are willing to appropriate this meaning, whether they are willing to be crucified with Christ. (1951, 43; cf. 1984b, 35f.)

In other words, the present proclamation originates in the kind of immediate experience of Jesus that Bultmann calls "genuine historical understanding" of his significance; and in proclaiming him to be the salvation event, it seeks to do nothing other than to express this very significance, thereby mediating to the hearer the same kind of experi-ence of Jesus himself. With good reason, then, Bultmann can accept the statement often made as a criticism of his view that it is in the kerygma that Jesus is risen. Rightly understood, this statement does indeed pre-suppose that the kerygma itself is eschatological occurrence, but what it affirms is "that Jesus is really present in the kerygma, that it is *his* word that encounters the hearer in the kerygma" (1960b, 27).

The evidence is thus doubly clear that Bultmann's theology is any-thing but the kind of "kerygma-theology" that Mackey, like so many others, attributes to him. Not only does he clearly point to the apos-tles' immediate experience of Jesus' person as the primal source of their original and originating faith and preaching, but he is also clear in in-sisting that even our own faith today, in response to the proclamation normed by their preaching, has its only primal source in the same kind of experience of Jesus himself. Of course, our experience of Jesus, being mediated by theirs, can only be a mediate, not an immediate, experience, for exactly the same reasons that would apply to our experience of any other fact of the past that we could not possibly experience at all except through the experience of others. But provided that the proclamation to which we respond is indeed normed by the apostles' preaching, which itself arose out of their immediate experience of Jesus' person, the primal source of our experience no less than of theirs is not the kerygma, but precisely and only the Jesus of history.

To recognize this, however, is to understand why the real issue between a position like Mackey's and Bultmann's very different position is not at all as Mackey represents it. It is not at all the issue of *whether* the Jesus of history is the source of our Christian faith in God; it is entirely the issue of *what* Jesus of history is rightly said to be the source of our faith. Is it, as Mackey contends, the Jesus of history whom we first come to know only more or less probably by historical inquiry back behind the preaching of the apostles as well as of all other Christians who follow after them? Or is it, rather, as Bultmann holds, the Jesus of history whom we already know most certainly through the same apostolic preaching as well as all later Christian preaching insofar as it is authorized by that of the apostles? Either way, we clearly have to do with the Jesus of history as a fact of the past, even if in the one way exactly as in the other, our experience of him today is and must be a mediated experience.

Nevertheless, there remains the issue — and it is a rock-bottom, fundamental issue — between a position like Mackey's, for which the apostolic preaching that mediates our experience is forced to function as the primary source from which the Jesus of history must still be reconstructed, and a position such as Bultmann's, for which this same earliest preaching is allowed to function as the primary authority through which the Jesus of history is even now to be encountered. In the one case, we have to do with the Jesus of history in his being in himself then and there in the past; while in the other case, we have to do with the Jesus of history in his meaning for us here and now in the present.

Of course, to show, as I have tried to do, that this is the real issue that Bultmann poses for most other proposals in revisionary christology, both earlier and more recent, is not to answer the question whether his way of resolving this issue really leads to the future. Perhaps when it is freed from misunderstandings and seen for what it is, it will prove to be as untenable a position as Mackey's, or, at any rate, less adequate than some other alternative that is open to us. But if Mackey's criticisms are at all representative — and if they fail in being so, surely it is only in being more, rather than less, understanding of Bultmann's intentions than most others — the grave weakness of the larger discussion of Bultmann's position up to now is that this further question of its adequacy has hardly been fairly raised, much less finally answered.

No one who knew Rudolf Bultmann could doubt that he was serenely confident about the future of his contribution, believing as he did with Paul that we cannot do anything against the truth, but only for it (1966, 42). But in fairness both to him and to the future of revisionary christology, those of us who now bear responsibility for this future simply must reconsider the question of their relationship. Certainly, he would have asked for nothing more; and anyone who owes him as much as I do can settle for nothing less.

– 15 –

Women and the Canon

Some Thoughts on the Significance of Rudolf Bultmann for Theology Today

I

One of the most basic and characteristic insights of Rudolf Bultmann is that facts of the past acquire their significance as historical events only in relation to the present. "[H]istorical phenomena are not facts that can be neutrally observed but rather disclose themselves in their meaning only to one who approaches them alive with questions." Consequently, "they are always understandable only now in that they speak anew to every present situation, out of the claim of the now, out of the problem that is given with the now" (Bultmann 1960a, 148; cf. 1984b, 150). Bultmann gives no reason whatever to doubt that the facts of the past are to some extent open to the objectifying view of the historian, and that any valid interpretation of them is therefore the interpretation of something given and hence far from a creature of fantasy (see 1965b, 131f.; cf. 1984b, 158f.). But he is insistent that:

> [a]s historical phenomena they do not exist at all without a histor-
> ical subject who understands them. For facts of the past become
> historical phenomena only when they become meaningful for a
> subject who exists in history and participates in it. They become
> historical phenomena only when they speak, and this they do only
> for the subject who understands them. This is not to say, of course,
> that the subject simply attaches a meaning to them by arbitrary
> preference; it is to say, rather, that they acquire a meaning for any-
> one who is bound together with them in historical life. Thus, in a
> certain sense, it belongs to a historical phenomenon that it should
> have its own future in which it alone shows itself for what it is.
> (1952a, 229; cf. 1984b, 84)

If I propose now to share some thoughts on the significance of Bultmann himself for theology today, it is in the sense and under the conditions that he so effectively clarifies in elaborating this basic insight. This means, above all, that it is from the standpoint of our own partic-ipation today in the same theological task that claimed him that I shall speak to the question of his significance, keeping in mind the implication that the future in which his theological work will thereby disclose its significance is the future for which we now bear responsibility (1960a, 113; cf. 1984b, 137).

By promising to offer only some thoughts on Bultmann's significance, however, I have tried to indicate the limits of my project. Aside from the fact that he well understood that "what a historical event means always becomes clear only in the future" and therefore "can show itself definitively only when history has come to an end," I have no intention of offering anything like a comprehensive account of his significance even for theology today (1960a, 148; cf. 1984b, 151). So far as I am concerned, there is practically no part of the present theological task for which his work does not constantly prove to be of fundamental significance. In fact, I find that it is precisely at the point of our most difficult and intractable theological problems — such as, for example, at last coming to terms with the full scope and depth of global cultural and religious plurality — that his contribution invariably turns out to be the most significant. However, for the purposes of the present discussion, I have deliberately restricted my attention to but one of the points where, in my judgment, the significance of his work for Christian theology today is profound. Of course, in thus focusing my attention on the issue of "women and the canon," I have also hoped to do something appropriate in honor of my friend, Antje Bultmann Lemke.* But I could not hope to honor her any more than to discuss the significance of her father's work except by doing my best to deal with one of the most important issues with which Christian theology would now be required to deal whether or not the three of us were involved at all.

2

Before turning to this issue, I want to state summarily what I take to be the facts of the past that any discussion of Bultmann's significance for theology today, including my discussion here, must somehow take into account.

The first and most important such fact is that Bultmann was, above all, a Christian theologian. To be sure, his special field of competence as a theologian was the New Testament, and it is quite possible that he is the most influential scholar in this field in the twentieth century. His first major work, *The History of the Synoptic Tradition* (1921), established him as one of the cofounders of form criticism of the synoptic gospels and, together with his book *Jesus* (1926) has been decisive

---

*This essay was originally contributed to the Rudolf Bultmann Symposium honoring Antje Bultmann Lemke on the occasion of her retirement from Syracuse University in 1986.

for the ongoing quest of the historical Jesus, as well as for subsequent critical study of the tradition redacted in the gospels. Hardly less significant for research in the field are his studies of the Fourth Gospel, epitomized by the commentary that is perhaps his masterwork, *The Gospel of John* (1941), and his interpretation of the theology of Paul, especially in his other major work, *Theology of the New Testament* (1948–53; 5th ed., 1965). In any number of other respects as well, from the general problem of biblical hermeneutics to the special question of Gnosticism and the New Testament, his work and the critical discussion of it continue to be determinative for serious study of the New Testament.

Even so, it is not only or primarily as a New Testament scholar that Bultmann is significant for theology today. In his own mind, certainly, he was, first and last, a Christian theologian who did all of his historical work in service of the church and its witness; and it is in this capacity that he has since come to be widely regarded as one of the two or three Protestant theologians of this century whose impact on theology promises to be lasting. The warrants for this promise in his case are many, but two features of his thought in particular are basic to its significance.

The first is that he was distinctive among his contemporaries in clearly distinguishing and resourcefully addressing both of the essential tasks of Christian theology. Thus, as much as he agreed with Karl Barth that theology's first task is to interpret the Christian witness appropriately in accordance with the normative witness to Jesus Christ attested by scripture, he differed from Barth in insisting that theology also has the task of interpreting this witness understandably, in terms that women and men today can understand and find credible. On the other hand, if his efforts to carry out this second, apologetic task brought him into close proximity to Paul Tillich, his deep concern with the first, dogmatic task gave his thought a very different character from the more speculative, unhistorical cast of Tillich's kind of philosophical theology.

The other equally basic feature of Bultmann's thought was his thoroughgoing interpretation of the Christian witness, as of religion generally, in existentialist terms. In this respect, there is no question of the formative influence on his theology of the existentialist philosophy of the early Martin Heidegger, who was his close colleague in Marburg from 1923 to 1928. But if Heidegger undoubtedly provided the conceptuality or terminology for Bultmann's existentialist theology, he had already learned from the Lutheran pietism out of which he came, and above all, from his revered teacher, Wilhelm Herrmann, that faith can be understood only as an existential phenomenon. Consequently, while he never doubted for a minute that faith does indeed have to do with the strictly ultimate reality called "God," he was convinced that faith always has to do with this reality, not in its being in itself, but in its meaning for us, and hence as authorizing our own authentic self-understanding.

The first of the four volumes of Bultmann's collected essays, *Faith and Understanding* (1933; 2d ed., 1954), shows that the theology defined by these two basic features had already taken shape during the 1920s. But it is also clear from the three later volumes (1952, 1960, 1965) as well as from his other writings during the so-called demythologizing debate, all of which appeared in the series, *Kerygma and Myth* (1948–1955), that the same theology found its classic expression in 1941 in the programmatic essay that provoked this famous debate, "New Testament and Mythology: The Problem of Demythologizing the New Testament Proclamation." If Bultmann was insistent in this essay that theology has no alternative but to demythologize the New Testament without remainder, he was also clear that the demand for demythologizing is not merely apologetic, but is also, as he later formulated it, "a demand of faith itself" (1952b, 207; cf. 1984b, 121). And when he explained what he meant by demythologizing positively, as a hermeneutical procedure for interpreting rather than for eliminating myth, it proved to be nothing more than thoroughgoing existentialist interpretation now applied to the mythological formulations of the New Testament.

3

With this much by way of recalling the facts whose significance for us today I wish to discuss, I now turn to the issue of women and the canon. More exactly, I want to consider the way in which this issue is raised in the work of Elisabeth Schüssler Fiorenza, especially her book of essays, *Bread Not Stone: The Challenge of Feminist Biblical Interpretation* (1984). In my opinion, Schüssler Fiorenza's way of raising this issue commands attention both because she too is, above all, a Christian theologian with special competence in New Testament, and because she is equally concerned with preserving a historical-critical approach to interpreting the Bible and with going beyond historical criticism to deal with the problem of biblical hermeneutics. Moreover, her proposal for resolving the issue is presented as — and in my opinion, actually is — a distinct alternative to the resolutions proposed both by other feminist theologians and by postbiblical feminists.

To understand Schüssler Fiorenza's proposal, one must begin where she begins — namely, with the experience of women, or of Christian women, in their "struggle for self-identity, survival, and liberation in a patriarchal society and church" (Schüssler Fiorenza 1984, x). In the course of this struggle, "Christian women have found that the Bible has been used as a weapon against [them] but at the same time it has been

a resource for courage, hope, and commitment in this struggle. Therefore, it cannot be the task of feminist interpretation to defend the Bible
against its feminist critics but to understand and interpret it in such a
way that its oppressive and liberating power is clearly recognized" (x).
To this end, Schüssler Fiorenza seeks to develop what she calls "a feminist biblical hermeneutics, that is, a theory, method, or perspective for
understanding and interpretation" (x). In the nature of the case, such a
hermeneutics cannot but be critical, since it cannot accept the Bible simply as divine revelation. "[B]iblical texts are not the words of God but
the words of *men*," in the gender specific sense of male human beings
whose whole outlook on the world was profoundly androcentric; and
"the Bible still functions today as a religious justification and ideological
legitimization of patriarchy" (xf.). For these reasons, feminist biblical
hermeneutics "seeks to develop a critical dialectical mode of biblical interpretation that can do justice to women's experiences of the Bible as
a thoroughly patriarchal book written in androcentric language as well
as to women's experience of the Bible as a source of empowerment and
vision in [their] struggles for liberation" (xiii).

Elsewhere, Schüssler Fiorenza represents her hermeneutics as the solution to "a foundational theological problem," which she expresses in
first person terms as follows: "Is being a woman and being a Christian
a primary contradiction that must be resolved in favor of one to the
exclusion of the other? Or can both be kept in creative tension so that
my being a Christian supports my struggle for liberation as a woman,
and my being a feminist enhances and deepens my commitment to live
as a Christian?" (53). Because feminist theology, in Schüssler Fiorenza's
view, is a Christian theology, and as such "is bound to its charter documents in Scripture, it must formulate this problem with reference to
the Bible and biblical revelation" (53). But then, when the problem
is so formulated, it demands for its solution the critical feminist biblical hermeneutics for which she argues, since any other hermeneutics
leaves unresolved the contradiction between being a woman committed
to feminism and being a Christian theologian bound to the witness of
the Bible.

Any criticism, however, requires some norm or criterion; therefore,
Schüssler Fiorenza rightly recognizes that "we cannot avoid the question
of the 'canon,' or the criterion that allows us to reject oppressive traditions and to detect liberating traditions within biblical texts and history"
(58). By "canon" here she means something other than "the collection
of biblical writings acknowledged by Christians as Sacred Scriptures,"
for which, like theologians generally, she otherwise uses the term (12).
She means instead the norm or criterion by which even the canon of
scripture itself must be judged, so that a feminist critical evaluation of
the biblical writings will be able both to "uncover and denounce bib-

lical traditions and theologies that perpetuate violence, alienation, and oppression" and to "delineate those biblical traditions that bring forward the liberating experiences and visions of the people of God" (60). But when "the question of the 'canon' " is raised in this sense, Schüssler Fiorenza is clear that the usual answer, according to which there is "a critical principle of revelation" in the form of "a normative biblical tradition" or a "canon within the canon," cannot be accepted by a critical feminist hermeneutics (12f., 59). "[T]he canon and norm for evaluating biblical traditions and their subsequent interpretations cannot be derived from the Bible...but can only be formulated within the struggle for the liberation of women and all oppressed people. The canon and evaluative norm cannot be 'universal,' but must be specific and derived from a particular experience of oppression and liberation....The personally and politically reflected experience of oppression must become the criterion of 'appropriateness' for biblical interpretation" (60).

Thus, in Schüssler Fiorenza's view, "[a] feminist theological interpretation of the Bible...has as its canon the liberation of women from oppressive sexist structures, institutions, and internalized values" (60). It formulates "a criterion or canon that limits inspired truth and revelation to matters pertaining to the salvation, freedom, and liberation of all, especially women. But it derives this canon, *not* from the biblical writings, but from the contemporary struggle of women against racism, sexism, and poverty as oppressive systems of patriarchy and from its systematic explorations in feminist theory....Its vision of liberation and salvation is informed by the biblical prototype but is not derived from it. It places biblical texts under the authority of feminist experience insofar as it maintains that revelation is ongoing and takes place 'for the sake of our salvation' " (14).

In other passages, Schüssler Fiorenza qualifies this appeal to the primary authority of "feminist experience" in general by speaking more specifically of "the theological authority of the church of women" as "an authority that seeks to assess the oppressive or liberating dynamics in all biblical texts" (13). "The spiritual authority of women-church," she holds, "rests on the experience of God's sustaining grace and liberating presence in the midst of our struggles for justice, freedom, and wholeness of all. It rests not simply on the 'experience of women' but on the experience of women struggling for liberation from patriarchal oppression" (xvi). Likewise, she can sometimes qualify her appeal simply to "the contemporary struggle of women" as the source of the canon by appealing more comprehensively to "women of the past and present whose life and struggles are touched by the role of the Bible in Western culture" (15). "The *locus* of divine revelation and grace is therefore not simply the Bible or the tradition of a patriarchal church but the 'church of women' in the past and in the present" (xv).

But however qualified, Schüssler Fiorenza's answer to the question of the canon involves nothing less than "a paradigm shift," which she herself describes as "a shift from an apologetic focus on biblical authority to a feminist articulation of contemporary women's experience and struggle against patriarchal oppression in biblical religion" (1f.). In this, of course, her proposal for resolving the issue of women and the canon bears a definite resemblance to the more extreme resolution of postbiblical feminists, who, having concluded that biblical religion cannot be retrieved for the feminist cause, simply abandon the Bible as any kind of resource in their struggle for liberation (84f.). But if Schüssler Fiorenza agrees with such feminists to the extent of locating the primary source of authority even for judging the Bible in the experience of women, or women-church, in their ongoing struggle for liberation, she also disagrees with them in understanding herself as a Christian theologian who as such remains bound to the church's charter documents in the biblical writings. In this respect, her proposal more closely resembles the less extreme resolution of other feminist theologians who, in one way or another, are also bound to the Bible because they continue to look to it, as well as to their own experience and struggle as women, as a source of authority.

But here too, Schüssler Fiorenza's resolution involves difference as well as similarity. Although she refuses to abandon the Bible and seeks instead to reclaim biblical religion as the heritage of feminists, she is emphatic that "such a reclaiming...can only take place through a critical process of feminist assessment and evaluation" and that "[in] this process...the Bible no longer functions as authoritative source but as a *resource* for women's struggle for liberation" (xiif., 14). Thus she not only agrees, but also disagrees, with feminist theologians who still attempt to derive "a critical universal principle or normative tradition" from the Bible itself (12f.). Insofar as such attempts avoid making an untenable distinction between "form and content, linguistic expression and revelatory truth," they are in danger of choosing one particular text or tradition as normative, thereby advocating "a reductionist method of theological critique" that relinquishes "the historical richness of biblical experience" (13). Furthermore, these attempts are like the extreme contrary positions of "Christian apologists," on the one hand, and "postbiblical feminists," on the other, in still moving within the old paradigm with its apologetic focus on biblical authority. Even they "assume that the Bible has authority independently of the community to which it belongs" (9, 13). For Schüssler Fiorenza, on the contrary, such authority as the Bible possesses depends entirely on the community of women or of women-church who make it their own — namely, by a process of critical interpretation for which their own experience of struggling to be free provides the canon.

4

Even this extended analysis and interpretation of Schüssler Fiorenza's argument cannot do justice to her detailed development of it. But I trust I have gone into it sufficiently to give a fair account of the way in which she raises the issue of women and the canon. In any event, I now want to take the next step in my own argument by explaining why Bultmann's theology seems to me to be of the utmost significance for any attempt to deal with this important issue by coming to terms with her proposal for resolving it.

I begin with the obvious point that there is a close analogy between the problem that Schüssler Fiorenza is concerned to solve with her critical feminist biblical hermeneutics and the problem to which Bultmann proposed a solution in "New Testament and Mythology," whose subtitle, it may be recalled, is "The Problem of Demythologizing the New Testament Proclamation" (1951, 15; cf. 1984b, 1). In saying that there is an analogy between these two problems, however, I want to signal my recognition that they are not only similar in important respects, but also different, and that the differences between them are by no means unimportant. One of my students remarked once that while she can at least sometimes leave the problem of demythologizing on her desk, she is never free of the problem of depatriarchalizing. If her remark may be justly faulted for minimizing the first problem, I see no reason to think that it exaggerates the second.

But whatever their differences, the basic similarity between the two problems appears at once when one compares Schüssler Fiorenza's question whether she can be both a woman and a Christian with the question Bultmann raised in face of the conflict between myth and modernity: "Can there be a demythologizing interpretation that discloses the truth of the kerygma as kerygma for those who do not think mythologically?" (1951, 26; cf. 1984b, 14). And the similarity at this point only becomes the more striking when one recalls that Bultmann's own biblical hermeneutics, his own theory, method, or perspective of radical demythologizing and existentialist interpretation, was developed, finally, to support his affirmative answer to this question.

To recognize the close analogy between their basic problems, however, is to be struck all the more forcefully by the profoundly different ways in which the two theologians proceed to solve them. Whereas Schüssler Fiorenza looks for the solution to her problem in the same experience of women struggling for liberation that leads to the problem in the first place, given the thoroughly patriarchal shape of the biblical writings, Bultmann, by contrast, looks away from the experience of modern women and men for whom the mythological formulations of the

New Testament have now become problematic as incapable in principle
of yielding any solution to the problem.

This is not to say, naturally, that Bultmann is in any way casual or in-
different about modern experience or inclined to minimize the problem
to which it leads, given the thoroughly mythological form of the New
Testament proclamation. On the contrary, he is notorious for concluding that "[i]f the New Testament proclamation is to retain its validity,
there is nothing to do but to demythologize it" (1951, 22; cf. 1984b, 9).
But no sooner has he drawn this conclusion than he appeals to his reader
to give him credit for accepting the condition on which he draws it. "Of
course," he adds, "we cannot set out on this path [sc., of demythologiz-
ing] on the basis of a postulate that the New Testament proclamation
must under all circumstances be made viable in the present. On the contrary, we simply have to ask whether it really is nothing but mythology
or whether the very attempt to understand it in terms of its real intention does not lead to the elimination of myth" (1951, 22; cf. 1984b, 9).
In other words, as insistent as Bultmann is that modern human experience creates a problem for theology that it cannot evade or minimize, he
is equally insistent that theology can find the solution to this problem,
not by uncritically assuming the normativeness of modern experience,
but only by inquiring openly and without prejudice whether the New
Testament proclamation itself really is anything more than mythology.

This explains, of course, why Bultmann goes on to argue that both
the nature of myth in general and its use in the New Testament in
particular allow, even require, demythologizing, at least in the form of
existentialist interpretation. It also explains why he sees an important
difference between his own attempt at demythologizing and the earlier
attempts of liberal theologians. For even if his demand that the New
Testament mythology be interpreted instead of simply eliminated does
not mean that elimination of particular mythologumena is precluded, it
does mean, as he says, that "the criterion for any such elimination must
not be derived from the modern world view but from the understanding
of existence of the New Testament itself" (1951, 24; cf. 1984b, 12).

Above all, Bultmann's way of proceeding to a solution to the problem of demythologizing explains the justification he finally offers for his
whole procedure:

> If the task of demythologizing was originally called for by the con-
> flict between the mythological world picture of the Bible and the
> world picture formed by scientific thinking, it soon became evident
> that demythologizing is a demand of faith itself. . . . In point of fact,
> radical demythologizing is the parallel to the Pauline-Lutheran
> doctrine of justification through faith alone without the works of
> the law. Or, rather, it is the consistent application of this doc-

trine to the field of knowledge. Like the doctrine of justification, it destroys every false security and every false demand for security, whether it is grounded on our good action or on our certain knowledge. (1952b, 207; cf. 1984b, 122)

But now it is precisely this kind of a justification that Schüssler Fiorenza not only does not, but also cannot, offer for her hermeneutical procedure. Far from appealing to the demand of faith itself or to the New Testament's own understanding of existence to justify her feminist biblical hermeneutics, she is content to argue as Bultmann would have argued if he had taken the modern scientific world picture and self-understanding as themselves the criterion for a demythologizing interpretation of the New Testament. In fact, it is evident that she sets out on the path of depatriarchalizing the Bible on the basis of the postulate that biblical religion must under all circumstances be made viable in the present, which means in her terms that it must be reclaimed as the heritage of women in their struggle against sexist oppression.

But to realize this, in my judgment, is to understand at once why her whole procedure simply will not do. It will not do because it in effect rejects the condition on which this, like any other form of the apologetic task of theology, can alone be undertaken — namely, that any proposal for executing the task must serve equally well to carry out theology's first and equally essential *dogmatic* task. This means that if a feminist interpretation of the Bible is justified, it is so, not only or primarily because the experience and struggle of women demand it, but also and first of all because it is a demand of faith itself. And it means, similarly, that if such an interpretation certainly does not preclude the elimination of particular patriarchal texts and traditions, the criterion for such elimination is nevertheless not the world view of contemporary feminism, but the New Testament's own understanding of human existence.

Such, at any rate, is the clear implication of Bultmann's theology for the problem that Schüssler Fiorenza is now concerned to solve. And the fact that it clearly implies this alternative solution seems to me to be evidence enough of its significance for theology today. Moreover, as I have suggested, its significance in this respect is wholly positive, since the solution it implies is at least in principle adequate, whereas hers, by contrast, is in principle inadequate as a theological solution to the problem.

This is in no way to question that she is as concerned as Bultmann was, or as I am, to be a Christian theologian, and that she therefore insists on remaining bound to the biblical writings that are the church's charter. But I quite fail to see what it can mean to remain bound to the Bible if the canon of one's theological judgments is in no way derived from it or from what it, in turn, takes to be normative, but is derived entirely from one's own experience as a woman or even as a Christian woman. For whether one's experience is, in fact, *Christian* experience is always the question, and unless it is, one is in no different position in principle from that of postbiblical feminists for whom the experience and struggle of women provide the only norm of critical judgment.

In short, the significance of Bultmann's theology for us today is to make clear over against Schüssler Fiorenza what any proposal must succeed in doing if it is to be an adequate resolution of the issue of women and the canon: it must establish that the canon for determining what is appropriately Christian as little belongs to the community of women as it does to any other human community, and therefore possesses an authority that no more depends on the experience and struggle of women than on the experience and struggle of any other group or individual.

If it were possible to do so, I should like to pursue the question of the canon to consider whether or to what extent an adequate answer to it today would need to be different in fact, even if not in principle, from Bultmann's. So far as I am aware, he never explicitly questioned the classical Protestant answer to this question in its essential claim that the canon for all Christian witness and theology is scripture or the New Testament. On the other hand, it is clear even from some of the passages already cited that what he typically appeals to as canon or criterion is not simply scripture or the New Testament, but rather "the New Testament proclamation" or "the understanding of existence of the New Testament itself." Moreover, a close reading of his writings discloses the unique role he assigns to those whom he variously speaks of as "the first disciples," "the first witnesses," or "the first proclaimers," and thus the unique authority he acknowledges in "the kerygma of the earliest community" or "the apostolic preaching" (1951, 47, 43; 1979, 18; 1952b, 206; 1940; 1965a, 2; cf. 1984b, 40, 36, 62, 121). As a matter of fact, in at least one passage where he explicitly claims scripture as "the sole authority for theology," he makes clear that the basis for this claim is not any established dogma concerning scriptural authority, but simply the fact that it is in scripture that the Christian proclamation is encountered for the first time (1984a, 168f.).

But I cannot further pursue this question here. Even if one concludes, as I do, that Bultmann's reasoning in the last passage clearly points to the witness of the earliest community rather than to scripture or the New Testament as the sole primary authority for witness and theology, one's issue with his theology, such as it may be, is still but an issue of fact, in no way an issue of principle. The crucial point remains that an adequate feminist theology as much as any other must not only be credible in terms of the experience of women or of women-church, but also appropriate when judged by normative Christian witness.

5

Crucial as it is, however, this is not the only point to be made in resolving the issue of women and the canon. As insistent as Bultmann was that any theology must be accountable to the normative witness of the New Testament, he was also clear that the most important question to be asked about this, just as about any other norm, is how it is to be interpreted if it is to function properly as norm. He was well aware, of course, that any answer to this question must itself be judged for its appropriateness by reference to the same normative witness. This is why, in justification of his own answer to it in terms of the hermeneutical procedure of existentialist interpretation, he finally appealed, as we have seen, to "faith itself," or to "the New Testament proclamation" to which faith is the response. But allowing for the fact that the justification of any hermeneutical procedure must be similarly circular, I now want to argue that the existentialist interpretation that is the other basic feature of his thought is also of the utmost importance for any adequate resolution of the issue of women and the canon.

The essential point of my argument is easily made. The implication of contending, as Bultmann did, that the appropriate way to interpret the canon is in existentialist terms is that the question to which it is addressed precisely as canon is the existential question somehow asked by each and every person about her or his authentic self-understanding. It follows from this, in turn, that the authority of the canon as such is limited solely to its decisive authority in answering this existential question. Thus, in his own way, Bultmann took account of the point that had been made by Protestant orthodoxy when it insisted that the perfection of scripture is not global and unrestricted, but is rather a *perfectio respectu finis* — a perfection with respect to the one end of human salvation. Analogously, the authority of the New Testament, or of the apostolic preaching, in Bultmann's view is its authority with respect to the one end of attaining authentic human existence.

This implies, among other things, that the authority of the canon does not extend to the various assumptions naturally made by those to whom we owe it when they formulated the preaching of the apostles or explicated the self-understanding arising from the apostolic preaching. On the contrary, all such assumptions, together with the conceptualities and terminologies in which they were formulated, remain subject to criticism by reference to the word and faith for whose expression in some particular situation they were merely the assumptions.

But a still more important implication of Bultmann's view is that even the consequences that are drawn in the canon for belief and action depend for their authority entirely upon the self-understanding of faith. To the extent that they are indeed necessarily implied by the existential understanding evoked by the New Testament proclamation, they too are normative for witness and theology. But insofar as they are due simply to assumptions made in the situations in and for which this self-understanding was explicated, they no longer have any binding authority beyond such contribution as they may possibly make to working out the implications of faith for belief and action in other more or less different situations.

In this connection, Bultmann was wont to emphasize the inherent incompleteness of theological thinking, which can never be overcome by later generations gradually supplying what is wanting in the witness and theology of earlier ones. Theology cannot but be incomplete, he argued, because the understanding of faith itself is inexhaustible, just as in life generally the consequences of understanding myself on the basis of someone's love for me or of some responsibility entrusted to me are of necessity always incomplete. Thus it is only to be expected that the consequences drawn in the New Testament for life in society and in the state should be incomplete, since the possibilities and problems of such life that have emerged in the course of subsequent history could not possibly have been known to the New Testament authors. Likewise, science and technology have posed new tasks for the understanding of faith that persons living at the time of the New Testament could not even have thought of (1965a, 586).

I submit that a closely analogous point is to be made about the situation in which we find ourselves today with respect to what we know about women and men and what have now emerged as the problems and possibilities of their life together in society and the church. But if I am right about this, there is evidently still more to be said about the significance of Bultmann's work for theology today. If we are to come to terms with our situation so as to face up to its problems and to realize its possibilities, nothing is more necessary than a way of interpreting the canon that frees us in principle from the assumptions and consequences of patriarchalism that are involved both in its metaphysical beliefs and in its teachings about moral action. Clearly, existentialist interpretation is calculated to secure us such freedom; for, as I have pointed out, it so limits the authority of the canon that even the consequences drawn there for belief and action are binding on us today only to the extent to which they are necessarily implied by the self-understanding of faith in our situation here and now, rather than following simply from assumptions that were made in another and importantly different situation.

The question I would ask, however, is whether there is any procedure other than existentialist interpretation that so completely frees us to resolve the issue of women and the canon. Because I am strongly inclined to think there is not, I am attracted to the conclusion that, in this respect even more than in the first, the significance of Bultmann's theology for ours today is incomparable.

In saying this, I cannot but remark a considerable irony. Nothing more securely belongs to the conventional wisdom of recent theology than the assumption that Bultmann's existentialist theology must be left behind if one is to develop any kind of adequate political theology or theology of liberation, including the feminist theology of liberation that Schüssler Fiorenza seeks to develop. Thus, for all of her obvious agreements with Bultmann in wanting to preserve a historical-critical approach to the Bible even while going beyond it to deal with the problem of hermeneutics, she expressly dissociates herself from "his method of demythologization" and "his neo-orthodox existentialist position" (Schüssler Fiorenza 1984, 154 n. 22). Not surprisingly, her understanding of how the biblical writings have to be interpreted to have any authority is fundamentally different — not only because her canon for criticizing them is the experience and struggle of women, but also because of her way of conceiving the salvation for the sake of which the writings exist. Although she is like Bultmann in limiting the Bible's authority to matters pertaining to salvation, she insists that salvation "should not be understood just as salvation of the soul, but in the biblical sense of total human salvation and wholeness. It cannot be limited to the liberation from sin, but must be understood to mean also liberation from social and political oppression" (40).

Consistent with this understanding, she thinks of the Bible, not as the proclamation that authorizes the self-understanding of faith, but rather as "the model for Christian life and community" and, more exactly, as "a historical prototype open to its own critical transformation" (14, xvii). The irony in this, however, is that it is precisely this way of thinking of the Bible as a "model" of, or "prototype" for, our own belief and action that makes it the warrant for "patriarchal oppression" as well as, of course, a "resource" for "emancipatory praxis," provided it is critically assessed and evaluated by the canon of women's experience (xvii).

Contrariwise, Bultmann's way of thinking of the New Testament completely undercuts any utilization of it to legitimate patriarchal oppression, even while acknowledging it, or the apostolic preaching lying behind it, as itself the canon. At the same time, his existentialist interpretation completely obviates the need for the kind of anachronism typical of other theologies of liberation, which can accept the Bible as canonical only by taking it to teach an emancipatory praxis that they have in fact read into it out of their own very different situation.

My point in remarking this irony, however, is in no way to suggest that Bultmann's theology as he left it is entirely adequate, or that theologies of liberation in general and Schüssler Fiorenza's in particular have no contribution to make to contemporary theology. My conviction, on the contrary, for which I have argued at length elsewhere, is that existentialist interpretation needs to be developed so as to include specifically political interpretation, and that in so developing it, we have much to learn from Schüssler Fiorenza and other feminist and liberation theologians beyond anything that Bultmann can explicitly teach us (see Ogden 1992b, 89–96, 157–165; 1992c, 134–150). But having said this, I remain impressed by the thought that it is precisely Bultmann's procedure of existentialist interpretation that not only requires, but also allows for, such further development. And with this thought I rest my case for the significance of his contribution for theology today.

Fundamentum Fidei

Critical Reflections on Willi Marxsen's Contribution to Systematic Theology

I

In orthodox Lutheran dogmatics, "dogma" was typically used broadly enough to include all doctrines of faith and of the Christian religion, "the false or heretical" as well as "the true or divine" (Hirsch 1951, 296; cf. Schmid 1983, 76). Therefore, considerable attention was given to distinguishing "foundational articles of faith" (*articuli fidei fundamentales*); and in this connection the crucial question was as to "the foundation of faith" (*fundamentum fidei*), by reference to which such foundational articles can alone be identified. To this question a classic answer was given by Nikolaus Hunnius on the basis of a threefold analysis of the concept, "the foundation of faith" (Hirsch 1951, 296f.).

There is, first of all, "the essential or substantial foundation of faith" (*fundamentum fidei essentiale aut substantiale*). By this is meant "that reality or being [*res sive ens*] which is the first cause of faith in the human heart, in which it places its trust, in that it is from the goodness of this being that it expects its essential blessedness. And this foundation is God, who promises saving grace and in his time will give it, and Christ, who by his merit brings it about that such grace can be poured out upon human beings to the cancellation of sins and the restoration of righteousness" (297). Secondly, there is "the organic or ministerial foundation of faith" (*fundamentum fidei organicum seu ministeriale*), which is "the word of God, insofar, namely, as this word is the seed from which Christians are born (Lk 8:11), or, more correctly, reborn (1Pe 1:23). This same word is also called the foundation of faith insofar as it is the means of generating faith and bringing about blessedness" (297). In the present age of the church, however, in which the word is preached to us, not by God immediately or even through living prophets and apostles, but through such human beings as can err and deceive, this foundation can only be scripture, "to which God has willed to call us back as the first principle of saving knowledge and the rule (Gal 6:16; Phil 3:16)" (297). There remains, thirdly, "the dogmatic or doctrinal foundation of faith" (*fundamentum fidei dogmaticum seu doctrinale*), which is "that part of heavenly doctrine that, when presented to human beings, alone generates justifying and saving faith in them, and without the presentation of which saving faith cannot be generated." As such, "the true foundation of faith is one,... one chain consisting of many links or members that are bound together and make up one complex unity." Although it contains "many special dogmas," they are all so coordinated as to make up "a single foundation" (297f.).

The details of this analysis need not concern us, since it obviously belongs to another theological situation that is, in important ways, very different from ours. But I am myself convinced that the question as to the foundation of Christian faith to which it served to give an answer is as crucial a question for systematic theology today as ever, and that its threefold analysis of this foundation is still quite helpful in understanding the different facets of the question. I also happen to believe that, rather as with Wilhelm Herrmann and Rudolf Bultmann before him, Willi Marxsen's important contribution to systematic theological reflection can be appropriately interpreted and evaluated as in effect a revisionary answer to essentially the same threefold question.

Of course, to justify either of these convictions fully would require a more extended discussion than I can possibly conduct here. But recognizing this, I nonetheless want to argue for them to the extent of, first, interpreting Marxsen's systematic theological contribution as an answer to the question of the foundation of faith; and then, second, offering some critical reflections on his answer by way of evaluating his contribution.

In so proceeding, however, I make no claim that it is the only, or even the most fruitful, way of appropriating his work. Aside from the fact that it focuses, not on the exegete, but on "the exegete as theologian," it is clearly only one way, however appropriate, of coming to terms with his systematic theological contribution, which I have decided to follow, finally, because of my own preoccupations as a systematic theologian. This needs to be borne in mind particularly when considering my critical reflections. Far from claiming that they do justice to all aspects of Marxsen's work, I freely admit that they too are relative to my own continuing concern with the question about the foundation of Christian faith. But beyond this, what I myself am most sensible of in offering my criticisms is not only my extensive agreement with Marxsen at the level of our basic theological intentions, but also my profound indebtedness to him even where we disagree. In all of my own efforts to answer the question, there is perhaps no one from whom I have learned more, or for whom I have more reason to be grateful.

2

In order to interpret Marxsen's work as a revisionary analysis of the threefold foundation of faith, I need to make two preliminary points.

The first has to do with his understanding of the faith whose foundation he seeks to clarify. It is here, above all, that his revisionary theology is significantly different from orthodox dogmatics. For while he certainly agrees that faith, in its way, is a knowing of the truth, he also maintains that faith is primarily the personal trust whereby one grounds one's existence in a reality beyond oneself (Marxsen 1968a, 120ff.; 1975, 122–129). Moreover, in rejecting orthodoxy's typical "intellectualizing of faith," he is insistent that faith by its very nature involves acting, and hence must be lived and enacted concretely in one's actual praxis. Precisely because faith is a matter of the heart and not simply of the head, it has to be expressed somehow by the whole of one's life; and only where something is done as well as known is faith really present (1978, 58–80, 107–129). Thus, in his more recent contributions to a systematic christology, Marxsen argues against both the "left" and the "right" for an understanding of faith as doubly determined: on the one hand, "christologically," insofar as it first involves entrusting oneself "passively" to the breaking in of God's rule through Jesus; and on the other hand, "practically," insofar as it then involves enacting God's rule "actively" in one's own life and praxis toward others (see esp. 1978, 11–35, 36–57).

The other preliminary point pertains to Marxsen's understanding of the proper role or task of Christian theology and, specifically, of systematic theology or dogmatics. Fundamental to his understanding is the notion that Christian faith itself requires a certain kind of thinking or critical reflection. Although being precisely faith, it can itself be neither acquired nor verified by any kind of critical reflection, it nonetheless has need of such reflection if its claim to be truly Christian is to be responsibly controlled and answered for. To this extent, critical reflection performs the essential service to faith of seeing to it that any witness through which it expresses itself is and remains an expression of Christian faith rather than of something else. But it is this very service that is, in a special way, the task of Christian theology. Theology is simply a special form of the critical reflection that answers for Christian faith's being precisely and only that — its difference from such reflection generally being due simply to the expert knowledge and skill that properly belong to it as theology (1975, 122–129).

Thus, in Marxsen's view, theology is rightly defined as "the servant of faith," analogously to the scholastic definition of philosophy as *ancilla theologiae* (1968a, 12, 156ff.). If this definition applies, presumably, to all of the theological disciplines, at least insofar as they are distinguishable moments in a single complex process of critically reflecting on

Christian witness, it peculiarly applies to systematic theology or dogmatics, which is the heart and center of this process (1969, 140–146; cf. also 129–137). In fact, Marxsen can speak of exegesis as "only an auxiliary theological discipline," and I know of nothing that he says about practical theology that would preclude his thinking about it in a somewhat similar way (1986, 319). In any case, what he calls "the real theological work" of answering for the claim of faith to be truly Christian is the responsibility of systematic theology or dogmatics, which alone can provide "the control of exegesis" (*genitivus objectivus!*) necessary to establishing this claim (1969, 104–114, 198–213; cf. 1985, 58f.).

In certain contexts, Marxsen understandably represents this work primarily in negative terms — as a matter of removing the "barriers" or the "false scandals" created by traditional witness that so often stand in the way of encountering "the *real* scandal" of Christian faith (1968a, 12, 156ff.). But while he thus recognizes that the effect of theological reflection may indeed be negative in taking away "false supports" of faith, he sees "the servant task of theology," when rightly performed, as thoroughly positive. Although theology can relieve no one of the risk involved in the decision of faith, it can so clarify what is and is not implied by this decision that anyone willing to assume its risk can confidently and conscientiously make it — as a decision of *Christian* faith rather than of some other faith.

Given this understanding of the proper task of theology, it is not surprising that the crucial question for Marxsen, even as for orthodoxy, is as to the foundation of faith. He too typically speaks of Christian witness broadly enough to include all the forms through which faith has found expression, the false or heretical as well as the true or orthodox. But then he also has to pay particular attention to how true witness is to be distinguished from false; and in this connection, he too is compelled to ask about the "foundation," or "foundations," of faith, or, as he sometimes says, "the ground of faith" (see, e.g., 1969, 104–114, 246–264).

The reason for this is that in his view also, true witness of faith can only be either formally or substantially the foundational witness through which faith first found expression. Either true witness simply is this first witness, or else it is some appropriate interpretation and reformulation of this witness, so that the claim of the witness can still be understood and responded to even by persons living and thinking in another more or less different historical situation. Marxsen also maintains, however, that even this first and formally foundational witness has a foundation beyond itself — not, of course, in any earlier witness, but in the twofold reality of God's becoming event for us through Jesus Christ, in which all Christian faith and witness, including the first, are essentially founded. On the other hand, he too recognizes that not everything even in the first witness belongs to the foundation of faith as such, but that even within it distinction must be made between what is and is not foundational. Understanding theology as he does, then, he is faced in his own way today with orthodoxy's question of the foundation of faith as *the* theological question.

This is not to say, naturally, that there are not also important differences between Marxsen's answer to this question and orthodoxy's. On the contrary, the differences between the two answers are great enough that one might well say that they actually answer different questions, which are at most analogous or possibly functionally equivalent. But however one best takes account of the differences, they are clearly such that Marxsen's analysis of the foundation of faith is not orthodox, but revisionary. If we ask about the reasons for this, the summary answer is that his analysis is fully informed, as orthodoxy's neither was nor could have been, by modern historical consciousness and by the historical-critical study of the tradition of Christian witness that is of a piece with such consciousness.

This is evident, for example, in his keen awareness of the difference between what a Christian witness means and what it says, or, as he can also put it, its "abiding substance" and its "variable formulations" (1969, 113, 183). Since this difference applies to the first and formally foundational witness just as much as to any other, it demands to be taken into account in testing whether any later witness is true Christian witness. In a somewhat similar way, Marxsen insists that the assertions of faith that comprise Christian witness always have to be interpreted in the same direction in which they themselves have arisen, lest what in fact is last be mistaken as first. Thus, while statements about Jesus' miraculous birth or saving death may precede accounts of his resurrection in both scripture and the creeds, they can be correctly understood only on the basis of the faith of Easter, rather than the other way around (169f.).

Marxsen also takes account of the continuing historical-critical study of scripture and of the entire tradition of Christian witness of which the New Testament is simply a part. This means, among other things, that he can no longer understand the New Testament canon itself to be the first and formally foundational Christian witness. The very fact that the writings included in it make use of sources, oral and/or written, earlier than themselves undercuts any claim that they are the first and foundational witness by which the claim of all later Christian witness has to be tested.

In short, given Marxsen's thoroughly historical approach to theological reflection, what is and is not foundational for Christian faith has become a new and much more difficult question. He expressly confirms this when, having criticized the orthodox doctrine of the verbal inspiration of scripture, he allows that "we are no longer as certain of our foundations as an earlier (happier?) time could be" (1969, 111).

Even so, and even though his answer to the question is perforce revisionary, the structure of the question itself, and consequently of his answer to it, is helpfully illumined by the threefold analysis of orthodox theology.

Thus he may be said to hold, first of all, that "the essential or substantial foundation of faith" is the twofold reality of God as the One who becomes event through Jesus, and of Jesus as the one through whom God becomes event. If the christocentrism of Marxsen's theology could never have been questioned, its profound theocentrism has become increasingly obvious over against theologies on the "left" for which faith tends to be reduced to "continuing 'the cause of Jesus,'" understood as a program of social activism. Against any such "Jesusistic" reduction, Marxsen has been emphatic that "the cause of Jesus" was and is God's becoming event, and that "Jesus is not to be had without his God" (1978, 34).

But if in all this Marxsen's answer seems eminently orthodox, there is nevertheless a fundamental difference. Even though faith, as he sees it, is essentially founded in God and in Jesus Christ as both real beyond ourselves, he insists that this *extra nos* of faith is knowable as such only *pro nobis,* through faith itself (1968a, 146ff.). In other words, he holds that the truth that faith in its way knows about the twofold reality in which it is founded is an "existential truth," and that the assertions in which it formulates this truth can be understood, accordingly, only as "existential assertions" (1968b, 134–143).

This means, for one thing, that Marxsen clearly distinguishes in the case of each such assertion between the substance of the assertion itself, and the concepts and terms in which it is formulated, which always belong to the particular historical situation out of which some believer or believers made it. But it also means, more importantly, that he clearly distinguishes all such assertions from any kind of "objectifying" assertions, whether historical, scientific, or metaphysical. As properly existential assertions, they all have to do with the meaning of God and Jesus for us, not with the structure of their reality in itself.

A second basic difference in Marxsen's answer appears in his account of "the organic or ministerial foundation of faith." Although he fully agrees with orthodoxy that Christian faith in God and Christ is, in a sense, also founded in the word of God, and that for any postapostolic age of the church this word is formally accessible only through the first and foundational witness of the apostles, he rejects the orthodox identification of this witness with the canon of scripture or of the New Testament. He does so, as we have seen, because the methods and results of historical-critical study of the New Testament writings have shown that the apostolic witness, in the strict sense of the first and formally foundational Christian witness, could not possibly be the canonical, but only a *pre*-canonical, witness (1969, 104–114, 198–213). Relative to this "canon *before* the canon," which, admittedly, can be made available only by reconstruction from the earlier New Testament writings and their sources, the canon as such is not properly "scripture" but "tradition," simply "a certain stage in the relatively early Christian 'history of dogma' " (109).

To this extent, of course, Marxsen's account is similar to other revisionary accounts that have relativized the authority of scripture or of the New Testament by appealing to some still earlier witness as foundational. But while his account bears certain resemblances both to Bultmann's appeal to the early Christian kerygma, and especially to the continuing appeal of others to the historical Jesus, its own appeal is distinctively different, insofar as it is made to what Marxsen calls the "Jesus-kerygma." By this he means neither the post-Easter "Christ-kerygma" of the church, nor the kerygma of Jesus himself, but rather the pre-Easter witness to Jesus on the part of his first disciples, which makes up the earliest stratum of tradition that can now be reconstructed from the synoptic gospels. It is here, in these earliest Jesus-traditions, Marxsen argues, that we find the first and formally foundational Christian witness; so it is here and nowhere else that we have both the real first principle from which all other faith and witness derive and the real rule or norm by which their claim to be substantially Christian must always be tested (1969, 139–159, 246–264).

The third and final basic difference between Marxsen's revisionary answer and that of orthodoxy is evident in what, for him, amounts to "the dogmatic or doctrinal foundation of faith." According to the orthodox analysis, the need to distinguish this third sense of the concept is twofold: on the one hand, scripture teaches not only the doctrines of faith or "dogmas" in which faith can alone be founded, but also moral doctrines as well as certain things about history; on the other hand, even among the dogmas of faith, properly so-called, there is a certain order, since faith can exist without believing some of them, while it cannot exist without believing others. By "the dogmatic or doctrinal foundation of faith," then, is meant all of the dogmas without which faith would be impossible; and in the orthodox account, this includes all of the doctrines concerning the person and work of Jesus Christ and the triune God already explicitly taught in scripture even if definitively formulated against heresy only in the later teaching of the church councils. For Marxsen, by contrast, even these supposedly irreducible doctrines of faith are nothing of the kind. Not only are they at most implicit in the foundational witness of the apostles expressed in the Jesus-kerygma, but they are simply alternative ways of formulating the point of this witness that are completely interchangeable (1968b, 128–132).

Thus we already noted how Marxsen insists on interpreting the doctrines concerning Jesus' miraculous birth and saving death as interchangeable formulations of the Easter faith of the disciples. But even the Easter faith itself is, in a way, reducible, in his view. For while the disciples' experience of Jesus at Easter was indeed constitutive of their continuing to bear witness to him even after his death, the faith formulated in their belief in his resurrection was already implicit in their faith and witness during his lifetime (1968b, 96, 106; 1969, 154f.). In fact, the whole point of this belief was to reaffirm in face of his crucifixion what they had already affirmed through their Jesus-kerygma — namely, his decisive significance as the one through whom God becomes event. Therefore, Marxsen reasons, "the post-Easter faith (in the risen one) has no other contents than the pre-Easter faith to which Jesus called his hearers" (1968a, 128).

The point of this reduction, of course, is in no way to deny the validity of the doctrine of Jesus' resurrection or of any of the other doctrines through which faith in his decisive significance has also found expression. On the contrary, Marxsen unhesitatingly allows any doctrine to be valid that appropriately expresses the same faith, including not only the orthodox dogmas of the trinity of God and of the divine-human person of Jesus Christ, but even the adoptionist christology also attested in the New Testament and, for that matter, the Mariological dogmas of the Roman Catholic Church (1968b, 123–132; 1969, 169). His claim, however, is that none of these many doctrines, as valid as it may be, is really foundational for Christian faith. It is at most a particular interpretation or formulation, interchangeable with every other, of what alone is thus foundational — namely, the twofold assertion, in some concepts and terms or other, that Jesus is the one through whom God becomes event, and that God is the One who becomes event through Jesus. This, in Marxsen's account, is the one "truth of faith" of which all the many "truths of faith" are simply alternative interpretations or formulations (1968b, 134–143). Consequently, where this truth is believed, even if only implicitly, justifying and saving faith is present and real. On the other hand, where it is not believed, at least by implication, Christian faith as such is not really present.

3

Assuming that this is an accurate, if certainly limited, interpretation of Marxsen's contribution, I now want to offer some critical reflections on it. Although the reflections themselves are critical, their aim is constructive, insofar as, arising out of my own continuing concern with the question of faith's foundation, they seek a deepened understanding of the question by appropriating Marxsen's way of answering it. Here, especially, however, I must ask for the reader's understanding of the severe limits of my argument. Far from settling any of the basic issues, I can do little more than suggest an agenda for continuing discussion.

My first reflection is on Marxsen's understanding of the proper role or task of systematic theology. That Christian faith itself requires a certain kind of reflection, and that theology — in the usual sense of professional, or even academic, theology — is simply the expert form of such reflection, seems clear enough. Moreover, I too should say that the service to faith distinctive of dogmatics is to test the claim expressed or implied by any witness to be truly Christian. But I see no good reason to suppose that this is the only service to faith that systematic theology exists to perform. On the contrary, the critical reflection that faith requires seems to me to include answering for yet another claim equally essential to faith itself and hence also expressed or implied by any Christian witness — namely, the claim to be true, in the sense of being genuinely credible or worthy of belief, not only by Christians, but by any and all human beings whatsoever. Therefore, as I see it, systematic theology properly performs the service to faith of also conducting a more or less expert test of faith's own essential claim to universal truth.

One may suggest, naturally, that conducting this second test is the proper business of apologetics rather than of dogmatics, which is rightly restricted to testing faith's other claim to be truly Christian. But however we assign the different tasks of systematic theology, my point is that conducting the second test belongs as essentially to them as conducting the first, and for exactly the same reason: because of the claims to validity expressed or implied by Christian faith and witness themselves.

As for Marxsen's contention that faith itself can be neither acquired nor verified by critical reflection, I find no need to dispute it. For faith in the proper sense of personal trust and loyalty is one thing, while the assertions that faith makes or implies are another. Therefore, to contend, as I do, that assertions of faith must be somehow verified if faith's own claim to truth is a valid claim does not require me to hold that faith itself can be verified. I must indeed speak of a justification *through* faith, but I regard any talk of a justification *of* faith as a category mistake — unless what is meant by it is simply such *indirect* justification of faith by verifying its assertions as is in fact possible — and necessary, in my view.

But would not any verifying of faith's assertions in effect relieve women and men of the risk of faith? Here again, I find it imperative to distinguish clearly between the assertions that faith makes or implies and faith itself. Rightly understood, the risk proper to faith is a matter of the heart rather than of the head, of personal trust and loyalty rather than of intellectual belief. Therefore, it is as little the risk of believing assertions that one has no reason to hold true, as it is the risk of accepting a witness that one has no reason to think Christian. By the same token, theology's critically validating faith's assertions as true would no more relieve anyone of the risk of faith than would its critically validating a particular witness as truly Christian. In this case, exactly as in the other, all that theology could do would be to clarify the decision of faith — in such a way, namely, that all who are willing to risk making it can do so with confidence and in good conscience, knowing that it is a decision in keeping with the truth, rather than contrary to it.

This brings me to a second and closely related reflection on Marxsen's treatment of "the essential or substantial foundation of faith." I readily concur in his judgment that this foundation can only be the twofold reality of God as the One who becomes event through Jesus, and of Jesus as the one through whom God becomes event. But as much as I also agree with him that the truth that faith knows about this reality is an existential truth, and that the assertions in which it formulates this truth are existential assertions, I am frankly troubled by what he apparently takes this to imply. His inference from it seems to be that the truth of faith and its assertions are not only distinct from any kind of objectifying truth and assertions, but are also logically independent therefrom — and that this is equally so whether the other kind of truth and assertions be historical, scientific, or metaphysical. But if this inference were correct without important qualification, I fail to see how Marxsen could consistently uphold the *extra nos* of faith, as beyond any question he intends to do, and as I can only insist has to be done.

What I judge to be right in his inference is that the truth and assertions of faith, being properly existential, are indeed logically independent of both properly historical and properly scientific kinds of truth and assertions. Thus, in my view, the truth or falsity of faith's assertions about the twofold reality in which it is essentially founded in no way depends or even can depend upon the truth or falsity of any historical or scientific assertion. But this cannot be said, in my judgment, about any metaphysical assertion, at any rate, not if metaphysics is properly understood as fundamentally different logically from both history and science.

Provided metaphysics is understood as it should be — as critical reflection on our at least implicit understanding as human beings of ultimate reality, in the sense of the necessary conditions of the possibility of our own existence and of all existence — it is clear that any properly existential assertion, including any assertion of Christian faith, both implies and, to an extent, is implied by the truth of certain properly metaphysical assertions. It implies the truth of some such assertions simply because it is existential and as such has to do with the ultimate reality of our own existence and of all that our existence necessarily presupposes. Consequently, even though it itself asserts something about the meaning of this reality for us, not about the structure of this reality in itself, it nevertheless implies certain assertions about this structure that have to be true metaphysically if it is itself to be true existentially.

Thus when faith asserts the possibility of existing here and now in personal trust in God and in loyalty to God's cause, it necessarily implies not only that anyone to whom it asserts this is the kind of being that can understand its assertion and responsibly make the decision for which it calls, but also, and crucially, that the strictly ultimate reality called "God" is in itself such as to be the foundation for this kind of personal trust and loyalty. Unless God is ultimately real and is the kind of reality that we can both trust and loyally serve, faith's assertion of the meaning of God for us could only be false. On the other hand, if metaphysical assertions to this effect are indeed true, then faith's existential assertions are also true, or at least can be true.

Because this is so, however, I can accept Marxsen's existentialist treatment of the essential foundation of faith only by urging the indicated qualification. The alternative, as I see it, would be to follow him in rejecting a misguided objectivism only to back into yet another way of falsely separating the *extra nos* and the *pro nobis* — namely, the kind of subjectivism, common enough on the contemporary scene, for which the utterances of faith are not properly assertions about reality at all, but only ways of expressing such things as our own intentions to act, *bliks,* or historical perspectives. Everything I know about Marxsen confirms that we are united in our opposition to any such subjectivism. I have some hope, therefore, that he might be patient of this reflection and reconsider what seems to me to be his position on the basic issue of faith and metaphysics.

Yet a third point that provokes critical reflection is the consistency with which Marxsen develops his account of "the organic or ministerial foundation of faith." One of the strengths of his account, certainly, is that it reflects a serious attempt to identify all of the relevant alternatives and to do justice, as far as possible, to the legitimate motives in each of them. Thus, while his account differs, as we have seen, not only from orthodoxy's but also from other typical revisionary accounts, it nonetheless has resemblances to all of them that tend to soften the differences. This is especially true of the type of account expressed or implied by theologians who have continued to insist that a quest of the historical Jesus, new if not old, is theologically necessary. In fact, the differences here sometimes become so blurred that Marxsen is confusing, if not confused, about the account he wishes to give.

What is distinctive about his account, insofar as he consistently develops it, is his appeal to the Jesus-kerygma as the first, and therefore formally foundational, Christian witness. But if this appeal is sound, any insistence on the theological necessity of appealing to the historical Jesus clearly must be resisted. For of a piece with such insistence, if only implicitly, is a contrary account according to which it is Jesus himself or his own kerygma, instead of the disciples' kerygma about him, that is the real principle and rule of Christian faith and witness.

Clear as this is, however, Marxsen is so far from having resisted the insistence that an appeal to the historical Jesus is necessary as to have joined in it (see, e.g., 1969, 139–159, 160–170, 246–264). In doing so, to be sure, he has also tried to do justice to the legitimate concerns of Bultmann by voicing a form critical reservation about the sources for such an appeal and by stressing that the decision called for by the Christian kerygma can never be obviated by historical research (256f.). But in all his contributions to the debate between Bultmann and the "post-Bultmannians," he has characteristically argued against Bultmann for the necessity of appealing to the historical Jesus. In keeping with this, he has even acknowledged the difficulty that would arise theologically if it could be established historically that Jesus himself did not want the same faith from persons that the Jesus-kerygma calls them to have. In that event, he argues, one would either have to surrender this faith altogether as error or else, believing the Jesus-kerygma to be true, have to make it "the real locus of revelation," despite its own claim to be related rather to Jesus himself as this locus (112).

But in all this, I am convinced that Marxsen is at radical cross purposes with his own appeal to the Jesus-kerygma as formally foundational. If this appeal is valid, then the fact — if it were a fact — that Jesus himself did not call for the faith for which the Jesus-kerygma calls would be theologically irrelevant, whatever its historical significance. Conversely, if establishing this fact historically could give rise to the theological difficulty that Marxsen acknowledges, then it is not the Jesus-kerygma, but Jesus or Jesus' own kerygma, that is really foundational; and Marxsen's appeal to the first is as invalid in principle as orthodoxy's appeal to the canon of scripture or any appeal Bultmann may have made to the Christ-kerygma.

I underscore "in principle" here, because there are significant differences in fact between Marxsen's application of what he calls the "apostolic principle" to the Jesus-kerygma and these other applications of the same principle to scripture or the New Testament and the Christ-kerygma respectively (1969, 134f.). Indeed, I strongly incline to think that Marxsen's single most important contribution to systematic theology is the case he has so resourcefully tried to make for his application of this principle over against both of these other ways of applying it. But if I am at all right in thinking this, it can only be because his account, no less than theirs, is an application precisely of this "apostolic principle" and as such must be as opposed as theirs are to any account expressing or implying the contrary principle that it is the historical Jesus, rather than the apostles, who is formally foundational for Christian faith and witness.

For someone like myself, then, who takes Marxsen to have made his case, it is Bultmann, rather than the "post-Bultmannians," who was right in principle about the need for a new quest. Whatever the deficiencies in fact in Bultmann's position — and about the conventional account of these I also have questions (see above, pp. 210–229) — he was only consistent with his own application of the "apostolic principle" in resisting any insistence that theology must appeal to the historical Jesus. He clearly saw, as I believe we too must see, that the deeper reason for resisting this insistence is not that the sources for a quest of Jesus make it difficult if not impossible, or that it risks confusing the *certitudo* of faith with the *securitas* of historical research, but simply that any such quest is theologically unnecessary.

This leads directly to a fourth and final reflection on what, in Marxsen's analysis, amounts to "the dogmatic or doctrinal foundation of faith." I put the matter in this way because, given his revisionary understanding of faith as primarily a personal trust that must be lived and enacted, it is much less clear than in orthodoxy that faith has, or even can have, a dogmatic foundation in the proper sense. Even so, he certainly recognizes the functional equivalent of such a foundation in what, as we noted earlier, he distinguishes as the one "truth of faith" that is somehow interpreted or formulated in the many "truths of faith." Among the several ways in which he formulates this truth is the one I have generally followed heretofore in speaking of his twofold assertion that Jesus is the one through whom God becomes event, and that God is the One who becomes event through Jesus.

Another way of formulating it, however, is equally prominent in his writings. In it the key concept is "faith" rather than "event," and the assertion is formulated accordingly by saying that Jesus is the one who brings or calls us to faith in God, and that God is the One to faith in whom Jesus brings or calls us. But in the places where Marxsen formulates it in this way, he commonly speaks also of "the faith of Jesus," meaning thereby, not the faith in God to which Jesus brings or calls us and of which we are therefore the subjects, but rather the faith in God of which he himself was the subject, in that he lived and enacted it in his own life and witness (1975, 9–27, 28–45, 46–63; 1978, 11–35, 36–57, 58–80). What is more, Marxsen can speak of Jesus' own personal faith in God as though it were necessarily implied by any assertion of the one truth of faith. Thus in response to the question, "To what extent is Jesus the Son of God?" he can answer simply, "Jesus believed God" (1978, 32).

But with this kind of an answer, as with his talk of Jesus' own personal faith altogether, Marxsen comes into sharp conflict with some of his own most basic principles. I have in mind principles that are fundamental to an argument like the one he develops in *The Resurrection of Jesus of Nazareth* (1968). One such principle is that historical-critical research such as is required to establish facts of the past is not in a position either to support faith and its assertions or to endanger them. On the other hand, he also argues from the principle that the truth of faith's assertions does not provide grounds for asserting facts of the past that historical-critical research is not in a position to establish (1968a, 156, 121f.; cf. 1964, 10ff.). But if he were correct in answering that Jesus is the Son of God to the extent that he himself believed God, these basic principles would have to be abandoned. For that Jesus believed God could only be a fact of the past. At the same time, the answer implies that this fact is both the necessary and the sufficient condition for the truth of faith's assertion that Jesus is the Son of God. But then, if it is a fact of the past that historical-critical research is in a position to establish, such research would also be in a position either to support faith and its assertion that Jesus is the Son of God or to endanger them. If, on the contrary, it is a fact of the past that historical-critical research is not in a position to establish, there would still be grounds for asserting it, provided that the assertion of faith is true that Jesus is the Son of God.

Nor are these the only basic principles with which Marxsen's talk of the faith of Jesus is clearly in conflict. Aside from his form critical reservation, which obviously renders any such talk peculiarly problematic, he himself lays down the general rule that "no one is in a position to control another faith.... One can never establish *whether* someone believes, not even if he claims to do so." He adds, to be sure, that "one very well can know the *expressions* of another faith insofar as witnesses to them are available" (1968a, 125). But this addition is clearly in danger of *petitio principii;* for whether such *expressions* of faith as the available witnesses permit us to know are, in fact, expressions *of faith* remains precisely the question. In any case, any expressions of Jesus' faith, like his faith itself, could only be facts of the past; and to argue even that they are a condition of the truth of faith's assertions about him would once again be to argue against Marxsen's own principles of argument.

It is not easy to understand, therefore, why he should allow for so arguing. Like his inconsistent appeal to the historical Jesus with which it is evidently of a piece, it seems to belong to another contrary theological position with which his own tends to get confused. At any rate, his own most basic principles, which I judge to be well founded, preclude any such argument. They require one to argue, on the contrary, that neither Jesus' faith, nor its expressions, is in any way implied by any assertion of the truth of faith. For Jesus is the Son of God, or any of the other things that faith appropriately asserts him to be, not to the extent that he believed God, but solely to the extent that decisively through him, as we encounter him through the Christian witness, we ourselves and others through us are or can be brought to faith in God.

Works Cited

Alston, William P.
1994   "Divine Action: Shadow or Substance." In *The God Who Acts: Philosophical and Theological Explorations,* ed. Thomas F. Tracy. University Park, Pa.: Pennsylvania State University Press: 41–62.

American Association of University Professors (AAUP)
1988   "The 'Limitations' Clause in the 1940 Statement of Principles" (Report of a subcommittee of Committee A on Academic Freedom and Tenure). *Academe* 74/5:52–57.

Apel, Karl-Otto
1973   *Transformation der Philosophie.* Frankfurt: Suhrkamp Verlag.
1979   "Types of Social Science in the Light of Human Cognitive Interests." In *Philosophical Disputes in the Social Sciences,* ed. S. C. Brown. Brighton: Harvester Press: 3–50.

Augustine
1953   *Earlier Writings,* ed. and trans. John H. S. Burleigh. Philadelphia: Westminster Press.

Bernstein, Richard J.
1971   *Praxis and Action: Contemporary Philosophies of Human Activity.* Philadelphia: University of Pennsylvania Press.

Betz, Hans Dieter
1979   *Galatians: A Commentary on Paul's Letter to the Churches in Galatia.* Philadelphia: Fortress Press.

Brümmer, Vincent
1982   *Theology and Philosophical Inquiry: An Introduction.* Philadelphia: Westminster Press.

Bultmann, Rudolf
1921   *Die Geschichte der synoptischen Tradition.* Göttingen: Vandenhoeck & Ruprecht.
1926   *Jesus.* Berlin: Deutsche Bibliothek.
1940   Review of Emanuel Hirsch, *Die Auferstehungsgeschichten und der christliche Glaube. Theologische Literaturzeitung* 65:242–246.
1941   *Das Evangelium des Johannes.* Göttingen: Vandenhoeck & Ruprecht.
1949   *Das Urchristentum im Rahmen der antiken Religionen.* Zürich: Artemis Verlag.
1951   "*Neues Testament und Mythologie. Das Problem der Entmythologisierung der neutestamentlichen Verkündigung.*" In *Kerygma und Mythos* 1, ed. H. W. Bartsch. 2d ed. Hamburg: Herbert Reich Evangelischer Verlag: 15–48.
1952a   *Glauben und Verstehen* 2. Tübingen: J. C. B. Mohr.

1952b   "Zum Problem der Entmythologisierung." In Kerygma und Mythos 2, ed. H. W. Bartsch. Hamburg: Herbert Reich Evangelischer Verlag: 179–208.
1954   Glauben und Verstehen 1. 2d ed. Tübingen: J. C. B. Mohr.
1960a   Glauben und Verstehen 3. Tübingen: J. C. B. Mohr.
1960b   Das Verhältnis der urchristlichen Christusbotschaft zum historischen Jesus. Heidelberg: Carl Winter Universitätsverlag.
1965a   Theologie des Neuen Testaments. 5th ed. Tübingen: J. C. B. Mohr.
1965b   Glauben und Verstehen 4. Tübingen: J. C. B. Mohr.
1966   "Ist Jesus auferstanden wie Goethe?" Der Spiegel, 25 July:42–45.
1979   "Theologie als Wissenschaft." In Protokoll der Tagung "Alter Marburger" 2.-5. Januar 1979 in Hofgeismar. Berlin: Zentrale Universitätsdruckerei: 1–23.
1984a   Theologische Enzyklopädie. Tübingen: J. C. B. Mohr.
1984b   New Testament and Mythology and Other Basic Writings, ed. and trans. Schubert M. Ogden. Philadelphia: Fortress Press.

Chadwick, Henry
1983   "The Chalcedonian Definition." In Actes du Concile de Chalcédoine, Sessions III–VI: La Definition de la foi, trans. A. J. Festugière. Geneva: Patrick Cramer: 7–16.

Christian, William A.
1964   Meaning and Truth in Religion. Princeton: Princeton University Press.

Coakley, Sarah and Pailin, David A. (eds.)
1993   The Making and Remaking of Christian Doctrine: Essays in Honour of Maurice Wiles. Oxford: Clarendon Press.

Ebeling, Gerhard
1964   Wort Gottes und Tradition. Studien zu einer Hermeneutik der Konfessionen. Göttingen: Vandenhoeck & Ruprecht.

Farley, Edward
1983   Theologia: The Fragmentation and Unity of Theological Education. Philadelphia: Fortress Press.

Faut, S.
1904   Die Christologie seit Schleiermacher. Ihre Geschichte und ihre Begründung. Tübingen: J. C. B. Mohr.

Flew, R. Newton and Davies, Rupert E. (eds.)
1950   The Catholicity of Protestantism. London: Lutterworth Press.

Furnish, Victor Paul
1977   "The Ministry of Reconciliation." Currents in Theology and Mission 4, 4:204–218.
1981   "Theology and Ministry in the Pauline Letters." In A Biblical Basis for Ministry, ed. E. E. Shelp and Ronald H. Sunderland. Philadelphia: Westminster Press: 101–144, 234–236.
1984   II Corinthians. Garden City, N.Y.: Doubleday.

Gamwell, Franklin I.
1990   The Divine Good: Modern Moral Theory and the Necessity of God. San Francisco: HarperSanFrancisco.

Geertz, Clifford
1973   *The Interpretation of Cultures: Selected Essays.* New York: Basic
         Books.

Gerrish, B. A.
1982   *The Old Protestantism and the New: Essays on the Reformation
         Heritage.* Chicago: University of Chicago Press.

Grass, Hans
1963   *"Die Christologie der neueren Systematischen Theologie: 19. Jahr-
         hundert und Gegenwart."* In *Jesus Christus. Das Christusverständ-
         nis im Wandel der Zeiten.* Marburg: Elwert Verlag: 109–121.
1973   *Christliche Glaubenslehre* 1. Stuttgart: W. Kohlhammer Verlag.

Griffin, David Ray and Hough, Joseph C., Jr. (eds.)
1991   *Theology and the University: Essays in Honor of John B. Cobb, Jr.*
         Albany: State University of New York Press.

Habermas, Jürgen
1968   *Technik und Wissenschaft als "Ideologie."* Frankfurt: Suhrkamp
         Verlag.
1973   *Erkenntnis und Interesse. Mit einem neuen Nachwort.* Frankfurt:
         Suhrkamp Verlag.
1976   *"Was heisst Universalpragmatik?"* In *Sprachpragmatik und Philoso-
         phie,* ed. K.-O. Apel. Frankfurt: Suhrkamp Verlag: 174–272.

Hartshorne, Charles
1937   *Beyond Humanism: Essays in the New Philosophy of Nature.*
         Chicago: Willett, Clark.
1945   "Analogy." In *An Encyclopedia of Religion,* ed. Vergilius Ferm. New
         York: Philosophical Library: 19f.
1948   *The Divine Relativity: A Social Conception of God.* New Haven:
         Yale University Press.
1953   *Reality as Social Process: Studies in Metaphysics and Religion.*
         Glencoe, Ill.: Free Press.
1956   "The Idea of God — Literal or Analogical?" *Christian Scholar*
         39:131–136.
1957   "Whitehead and Berdyaev: Is There Tragedy in God?" *Journal of
         Religion* 37:71–84.
1959   "A Philosopher's Assessment of Christianity." In *Religion and Cul-
         ture: Essays in Honor of Paul Tillich,* ed. Walter Leibrecht. New
         York: Harper & Brothers: 167–180.
1962   *The Logic of Perfection and Others Essays in Neoclassical Meta-
         physics.* LaSalle, Ill.: Open Court.
1963   "Sensation in Psychology and Philosophy." *Southern Journal of
         Philosophy* 1, 2:3–14.
1963–64 "Man's Fragmentariness." *Wesleyan Studies in Religion* 56, 6:17–
         28
1965   *Anselm's Discovery: A Re-examination of the Ontological Proof for
         God's Existence.* LaSalle, Ill.: Open Court.
1966a   "Criteria for Ideas of God." In *Insight and Vision: Essays in Philos-
         ophy in Honor of Radoslav Tsanoff,* ed. Konstantin Kolenda. San
         Antonio: Principia Press of Trinity University: 85–95.

1966b   "A New Look at the Problem of Evil." In *Current Philosophical Issues: Essays in Honor of Curt John Ducasse,* ed. Frederick C. Dommeyer. Springfield, Ill.: Charles C. Thomas: 202–212.

1967   *A Natural Theology for Our Time.* LaSalle, Ill.: Open Court.

1970a   *Creative Synthesis and Philosophic Method.* LaSalle, Ill.: Open Court.

1970b   "Equality, Freedom, and the Insufficiency of Empiricism." *Southwestern Journal of Philosophy* 1, 3:20–27.

1970c   "Two Forms of Idolatry." *International Journal for Philosophy of Religion* 1, 1:3–15.

1971   "Can Man Transcend His Animality?" *Monist* 55:208–217.

1976   "Why Psychicalism? Comments on Keeling's and Shepherd's Criticisms." *Process Studies* 6:67–72.

1977   "Physics and Psychics: The Place of Mind in Nature." In *Mind and Nature: Essays on the Interface of Science and Philosophy,* ed. John B. Cobb, Jr. and David Ray Griffin. Washington, D.C.: University Press of America: 89–96.

1979   "God and Nature." *Anticipation* 25:58–64.

Hick, John
1958   "The Christology of D. M. Baillie." *Scottish Journal of Theology* 11:1–12.

1966   "Christology at the Crossroads." In *Prospect for Theology: Essays in Honor of H. H. Farmer,* ed. F. G. Healy. London: James Nisbet: 137–166, 233f.

1984   "The Foundation of Christianity: Jesus or the Apostolic Message?" *Journal of Religion* 64:363–369.

Hick, John and Knitter, Paul F. (eds.)
1987   *The Myth of Christian Uniqueness: Toward a Pluralistic Theology of Religions.* Maryknoll, N.Y.: Orbis Books.

Hirsch, Emanuel
1951   *Hilfsbuch zum Studium der Dogmatik.* Berlin: Walter de Gruyter.

Hough, Joseph C., Jr. and Cobb, John B., Jr.
1985   *Christian Identity and Theological Education.* Chico, Calif.: Scholars Press.

James, William
1911   *Some Problems of Philosophy: A Beginning of an Introduction to Philosophy.* New York: Longmans, Green.

Käsemann, Ernst
1953   "*Das Problem des historischen Jesus.*" Zeitschrift für Theologie und Kirche 51:125–153.

Küng, Hans and Tracy, David (eds.)
1989   *Paradigm Change in Theology: A Symposium for the Future,* trans. Margaret Kohl. New York: Crossroad.

Landmann, Michael
1961   *Der Mensch als Schöpfer und Geschöpf der Kultur. Geschichts- und Sozialanthropologie.* Munich/Basel: Ernst Reinhardt Verlag.

1964   *Philosophische Anthropologie. Menschliche Selbstdeutung in Geschichte und Gegenwart.* 2d ed. Berlin: Walter de Gruyter.

Mackey, James P.
1979   *Jesus, the Man and the Myth: A Contemporary Christology.* New York: Paulist Press.

Marxsen, Willi
1964   *Die Auferstehung Jesu als historisches und theologisches Problem.* Gütersloh: Gütersloher Verlagshaus Gerd Mohn.
1968a   *Die Auferstehung Jesu von Nazareth.* Gütersloh: Gütersloher Verlagshaus Gerd Mohn.
1968b   *Das Neue Testament als Buch der Kirche.* Gütersloh: Gütersloher Verlagshaus Gerd Mohn.
1969   *Der Exeget als Theologe. Vorträge zum Neuen Testament.* 2d ed. Gütersloh: Gütersloher Verlagshaus Gerd Mohn.
1975   *Die Sache Jesu geht weiter.* Gütersloh: Gütersloher Verlagshaus Gerd Mohn.
1978   *Christologie — praktisch.* Gütersloh: Gütersloher Verlagshaus Gerd Mohn.
1985   *"Historisch-kritische Exegese?"* In *Kirchliche Dienst und theologische Ausbildung: Festschrift für Dr. Heinrich Reiss.* Bielefeld: Luther-Verlag: 53–62.
1986   *"Der Streit um die Bergpredigt — ein exegetisches Problem."* In *Studien zum Text und zur Ethik des Neuen Testaments: Festschrift zum 80. Geburtstag von Heinrich Greeven,* ed. Wolfgang Schrage. Berlin: Walter de Gruyter: 315–324.

Morgan, Robert with Barton, John
1988   *Biblical Interpretation.* Oxford: Oxford University Press.

Niebuhr, H. Richard
1960   *Radical Monotheism and Western Culture.* New York: Harper & Brothers.

Norris, Richard A., Jr.
1966   "Toward a Contemporary Interpretation of the Chalcedonian Definition." In *Lux in Lumine: Essays to Honor W. Norman Pittenger,* ed. Richard A. Norris, Jr. New York: Seabury Press: 62–79, 177f.

Norris, Richard A., Jr. (ed.)
1980   *The Christological Controversy.* Philadelphia: Fortress Press.

Oakeshot, Michael
1975   *On Human Conduct.* Oxford: Oxford University Press.

Ogden, Schubert M.
1975   "The Criterion of Metaphysical Truth and the Senses of 'Metaphysics.'" *Process Studies* 5:47f.
1989   *Faith and Freedom: Toward a Theology of Liberation.* 2d ed. Nashville: Abingdon Press.
1992a   *Is There Only One True Religion or Are There Many?* Dallas: Southern Methodist University Press.
1992b   *The Point of Christology.* 2d ed. Dallas: Southern Methodist University Press.
1992c   *On Theology.* 2d ed. Dallas: Southern Methodist University Press.

Outler, Albert C.
1957   *The Christian Tradition and the Unity We Seek.* New York: Oxford University Press.

Pattillo, Manning M., Jr. and Mackenzie, Donald M.
1965   *Eight Hundred Colleges Face the Future.* St. Louis: Danforth Foundation.

Robinson, James M.
1959   *A New Quest of the Historical Jesus.* London: SCM Press.

Ruether, Rosemary Radford
1985   "Theology as Critique of and Emancipation from Sexism." In *The Vocation of the Theologian,* ed. Theodore W. Jennings, Jr. Philadelphia: Fortress Press: 25–36.

Schleiermacher, Friedrich
1960   *Der christliche Glaube nach den Grundsätzen der Evangelischen Kirche im Zusammenhang dargestellt,* ed. Martin Redeker. 7th ed. Berlin: Walter de Gruyter.

Schmid, Heinrich
1983   *Die Dogmatik der evangelisch-lutherischen Kirche dargestellt und aus den Quellen belegt,* ed. H. G. Pöhlmann. 10th ed. Gütersloh: Gütersloher Verlagshaus Gerd Mohn.

Schüssler Fiorenza, Elisabeth
1984   *Bread Not Stone: The Challenge of Feminist Biblical Interpretation.* Boston: Beacon Press.

Streng, Frederick J.
1985   *Understanding Religious Life.* 3d ed. Belmont, Calif.: Wadsworth.

Thomas Aquinas
1964   *Summa Theologiae 3: Knowing and Naming God* (Ia. 12–13), ed. Herbert McCabe, O.P. New York: McGraw-Hill.

Watson, Philip S.
1959   "Luther and Sanctification." *Concordia Theological Monthly* 30: 243–259.

Wiles, Maurice
1967   *The Making of Christian Doctrine: A Study in the Principles of Early Doctrinal Development.* Cambridge: Cambridge University Press.
1974   *The Remaking of Christian Doctrine.* London: SCM Press.
1986   *God's Action in the World.* London: SCM Press.

Wolterstorff, Nicholas
1969   "On God Speaking." *The Reformed Journal* 19, 6:7–11.
1983   *Until Justice and Peace Embrace.* Grand Rapids, Mich.: Eerdmans.

Wood, Charles M.
1985   *Vision and Discernment: An Orientation in Theological Study.* Atlanta: Scholars Press.
1994   *An Invitation to Theological Study.* Valley Forge, Pa.: Trinity Press International.

Index